THE LIFE

EXPERTISE

CULTURES AND
TECHNOLOGIES
OF KNOWLEDGE

EDITED BY DOMINIC BOYER

*A list of titles in this series is available
at www.cornellpress.cornell.edu.*

THE LIFE INFORMATIC

Newsmaking in the Digital Era

DOMINIC BOYER

CORNELL UNIVERSITY PRESS
ITHACA AND LONDON

First published 2013 by Cornell University Press
First printing, Cornell Paperbacks, 2013

Printed in the United States of America

Library of Congress Cataloging-in-Publication Data

Boyer, Dominic.
   The life informatic : newsmaking in the digital era / Dominic Boyer.
      p. cm.
   Includes bibliographical references.
   ISBN 978-0-8014-5188-1 (cloth : alk. paper) — ISBN 978-0-8014-7858-1 (pbk. : alk. paper)
   1. Electronic news gathering.   2. Journalism—Data processing.
3. Journalism—Computer network resources.   4. Journalism—Technological innovations.   5. Online journalism.   6. Digital media.   I. Title.
   PN4784.E53B69 2013
   070.4'30285—dc23

                                                                    2012033795

Cornell University Press strives to use environmentally responsible suppliers and materials to the fullest extent possible in the publishing of its books. Such materials include vegetable-based, low-VOC inks and acid-free papers that are recycled, totally chlorine-free, or partly composed of nonwood fibers. For further information visit our website at www.cornellpress.cornell.edu.

Cloth printing   10 9 8 7 6 5 4 3 2 1
Paperback printing   10 9 8 7 6 5 4 3 2 1

For Olivia and Brijzha, two originals in an age of imitation

Contents

Acknowledgments

A book is an authorial labor of love but also a bundle of relations, gifts, and debts. My words are necessarily briefer than the individuals and organizations mentioned here deserve. This project was funded principally by a Humboldt Foundation Research Grant from 2008 to 2010, and I want thank the staff and officers of Humboldt not only for supporting my research over the past fifteen years but also for epitomizing the best, most selfless spirit of *Kultur* and *Wissenschaft*. My German field research was further sponsored and supported by the Institut für Kulturanthropologie and Europäische Ethnologie at the Goethe Universität Frankfurt. Prof. Dr. Gisela Welz, one of the leading lights of anthropology in Germany, was the most generous and brilliant of hosts. I cannot thank her and her colleagues enough for their goodwill and intellectual engagement and for making my time in Frankfurt and Berlin so rewarding and enjoyable. The field research would also very obviously not have been possible without the generosity of the staffs of the Associated Press German Service, T-Online News, and mdr info. I want to thank them and their parent organizations for their willingness to participate in this research project. Although so many kindnesses were shown me in each of these locations, let me just thank a few individuals for going above and beyond the call of duty: Frank Biehl, Jana Hahn, Mike Heerdegen-Simonsen, Johannes Kaufmann, Dietz Schwiesau, Michael Stüber, Marc Vesshoff, Peter Zschunke. Lastly, I would also like to thank the following organizations for participating in the background research for this study: derwesten.de, dpa, Hessischer Rundfunk, *Frankfurter Neue Presse*, National Public Radio, Newseum, the Online News Association, RBB-Inforadio, *Der Spiegel*, Südwestrundfunk, *Wall Street Journal*, washingtonpost.com, and WBEZ-Chicago.

A book, especially an anthropological book, is traveling knowledge. When I set out on this adventure, I was employed by Cornell University and when I returned it was to Rice University. I want to thank colleagues, staff, and administrators at both institutions for their patience, support, and understanding of a life in transition. The writing phase of the project would not have been nearly as much fun had it not taken place in the wonderful, vibrant intellectual community of Rice Anthropology. There exists no better, more risk-taking and rigorous place, in my opinion, to do reflexive anthropology. My senior colleagues, James Faubion and Nia Georges, have been terrific inspirations close at hand while George Marcus has supported and enlivened this work from afar. And, special thanks to Jeff Fleisher and Susan McIntosh for attuning me to the history of cybernetics in archaeology. Rice Anthropology's unique culture of graduate mentoring and faculty-student collaboration has incubated many of the ideas in these pages. For their contributions and commitment to this project and to our intellectual community, thanks to Camille Barnett, Lina Dib, Ereich Empey, Nessette Falu, Mike Griffiths, Seda Karslioglu, Marcel LaFlamme, Jessica Lockrem, Ian Lowrie, Liz Marks, Val Olson, Rachael Petersen, Maria Vidart, Than Vlachos, Jing Wang, and Ethan Wilensky-Lanford (and, of course, to all our friends at Poison Girl and Double Trouble).

Books are materializations of conversations and intuitions, but above all inspirations. This project took shape over several years of talking and thinking digital media. I owe thanks to many interlocutors: Debbora Battaglia, Stefan Beck, Pablo Boczkowski, Tom Boellstorff, Don Brenneis, Charles Briggs, Gabriella Coleman, Steve Coleman, Alex Dent, Alfred Eichhorn, Patrick Eisenlohr, Tarek Elhaik, Jess Falcone, Mike Fischer, Faye Ginsburg, Andreas Glaeser, Ulf Hannerz, Ariana Hernandez, Michael Herzfeld, Charles Hirschkind, Doug Holmes, Graham Jones, Chris Kelty, Kira Kosnick, Paul Liffmann, Joseph Masco, William Mazzarella, James Meador, Anand Pandian, Mark Allen Peterson, Beth Povinelli, Paul Rabinow, Deepa Reddy, Seth Sanders, Hoon Song, Kaushik Sunder Rajan, Helena Wulff, Alexei Yurchak, Kate Zaloom and Barbie Zelizer. Your words and writings have all enriched me and you will find mutant appropriations of them somewhere herein. Two anonymous reviewers for Cornell University Press were all that an author could hope for: smart, supportive, and challenging. Peter Potter, the editor in chief at Cornell University Press, has been a close collaborator on this book and on the Expertise project as a whole. He has taught me as much as anyone about the possibilities and challenges of academic publishing in the digital era.

Finally, a book is also a phase of life. Thanks to my family, especially to my mother, father, and sisters for rock solid support *während der Verwandlung*. To my daughters for unconditional love. To the love of my life, Cymene Howe, for This joy that transects every orbit. I thank her also for being a superbly generous colleague and collaborator. Having read and commented on every page of this book at least twice, it has become hers as well as mine.

PROLOGUE

This Text Informatic

This book is an ethnography of the practices and understandings of digital information in contemporary news journalism. It is also a work of digital information in its own right. One of the most striking realizations for me in doing fieldwork with news journalists was how much of their practice was intimately familiar to another office-based, digitally enabled professional like an anthropologist. Although anthropologists happily consider themselves as fieldworkers at heart, the truth is that we spend most of our time as screenworkers, even in "the field." Like my journalistic research partners, my average workday unfolds in front of a personal computer, often with a word-processing program open on my desktop. Like them, I check e-mail frequently (compulsively some sources say) for the purposes of professional correspondence and coordination. Although for somewhat different reasons than they do, I use online news sources frequently throughout the day and have alerts set up to inform me of events relevant to my research and interests. I, too, utilize electronic archives and search engines. My cell phone is, needless to say, also always at hand. In the course of this average workday, therefore, I find myself frequently shifting back and forth between producing texts and managing a variety of information channels, some of which demand that I respond to them on a fast-time basis.

I hasten to add that the differences between the information practices of news journalism and anthropology are also many. One of the more striking differences is that the normal production cycle of anthropological research and writing is much longer and more flexible than that of news journalism. Because we largely set our own timetables for writing, I rarely feel as though I am working on the clock; my deadlines are measured in weeks and months rather than hours and minutes, a fact that my journalist friends seem to both envy and pity.

My point is simply that contemporary news journalism and contemporary anthropology share a "life informatic"; in the digital era they have both become "information professions." Like so many anthropological research encounters with professionals and their "cultures of expertise," one finds oneself studying practices that are, at least to some extent, shared within organizational environments that are far from unfamiliar.[1]

Being entangled in one's objects of reflection represents, to my mind, no necessary barrier to effective ethnography. Indeed, as a long tradition of critical reflexive scholarship has pointed out, the expectation of a radical gap between ethnographer and research subject has been fantasy-laden in its own right, whether in the name of scientific objectivity, literary exoticization, or political advocacy.[2] In this case, I think entanglement creates a reflexive anthropological opportunity. The overlapping information practices and ecologies of anthropology and news journalism generate what news journalists might call an "echo chamber"[3] in which shared experiences and concerns amplify, permitting us to hear more clearly how anthropological research practice is transforming in the digital era. This could potentially become a very long and complicated discussion but in the interest of provocative brevity, I will limit myself to three reflections.

Anthropological Writing and Reading in the Era of Digital Communication

I assume that many readers of this book have heard something about the current "crisis" facing contemporary broadcast journalism and especially newspaper journalism.[4] In short, the "business model" of the postwar period is in deep trouble: sales and advertising revenues are plummeting as viewers and readers abandon traditional media for the Internet and social media. As advertisers migrate to the digital aftermarket of search engines and social media, the expensive business of original news production is becoming increasingly difficult to finance. To many observers the eventual diminishment, even death, of newspapers and broadcasters seems inevitable and for some, desirable.[5]

One hears much the same story line (minus the fleeing advertisers) applied more and more to academic print publishing as well.[6] Digital information technology, so the story goes, has catalyzed new reading practices, which are in turn making the scholarly monograph an increasingly redundant form. On the one hand, it is said that there is a rising demand for interactivity and multimediality in academic communication; on the other, there is a demand for more mobile, flexible texts—texts that can be located and read from a laptop, tablet, or other mobile data device. Books do fall short on both these fronts and so there are genuine concerns about the print monograph's future viability as a medium of professional communication. However, if one wishes to speak of a crisis in academic publishing it is just as important to highlight a global neoliberal reform trend in higher education since the 1980s that has sought, for example, to reinvent university presses as market-oriented, for-profit publishing units. At the same time as many universities are cutting or reducing subsidies to their presses, administrators are making it clear that they expect presses to continue publishing the specialized print monographs that remain essential to the credentialing of the professoriate.

Publishing insiders such as Lindsay Waters have proclaimed this an unsustainable paradox with crippling implications for academic presses.[7] But what are the alternatives? Digital monographs (e-books) have been slow to catch on as replacements for academic books, even as short-form scholarship (journal articles) is transitioning rapidly to digital formats. Even if digital monographs became widely accepted this would not entirely solve presses' financial concerns because the reality is that review, editorial, and layout/design, which constitute the majority of the production costs of monograph publishing, remain largely constant in the move to a digital standard.[8] The logical response has been to create efficiencies in the publishing process (through outsourcing labor, or reducing text length, or both) in an effort to reduce costs, while simultaneously seeking out ways to increase sales volume. It is not surprising therefore that presses and acquisitions editors (including myself for the Expertise series) now express a preference for shorter, more tightly argued books that are accessible to a wider audience that includes multiple academic readerships and perhaps even nonacademic readers. All of this makes writing an academic book these days a process exquisitely overdetermined by factors that transcend the more traditional scholarly concerns of originality, substance, and quality.

But the pressures of academic publishing are not simply those of the market; they also involve basic considerations of scholarly communicability in the era of digital media. Just as for news journalists, anthropologists must process a level of information that vastly exceeds that of two decades ago, when I began my own professionalization process. E-mail is a commonly identified culprit in terms of heightened expectations for fast-time availability and communicability. And, the growing popularity of social media and mobile entertainment should not be underestimated for its demands of time and energy. But another obvious source of our growing information "overload" is the seemingly ever-expanding world of academic publishing, now often referred to as "scholarly communication." Driven by the combination of professional desires for recognition and credentials, and the commercial publishing industry's desire to widen its revenue stream, the academic journal business is expanding, meaning more journals, more articles, more "content" to produce and to process. The situation is particularly acute in the so-called STM (scientific, technical, and medical) fields where commercial publishers, with operating profit margins close to 40 percent,[9] charge thousands of dollars for annual journal subscriptions. In the United Kingdom, for example, 65 percent of the money spent on content acquisition at academic libraries now goes to journals,[10] which means less money for buying books, e-books, and every-thing else. Given that academic authorial and review labor is most often nonmone-tized, this is a particularly lucrative business model for commercial publishers and one that we can expect them to pursue aggressively in the future, even as it increasingly overwhelms us with content and exhausts us with expectations. One of my most cher-ished and erudite colleagues lamented to me over a beer one evening, "No one has the time to read anymore," which of course means also the time to read books and journal articles, especially those unrelated to one's immediate teaching and research interests. And, by extension, one could say that no one has the time to write books anymore, at least long and complex ones of possibly marginal interest to publishers and a dis-tracted overtaxed audience.

For all of these reasons, I found myself thinking about *The Life Informatic* from the beginning as a short, accessible, and above all "teachable" book, at least in comparison to my previous work. I have deliberately streamlined my presentation and, wherever possible, confined references to endnotes. In view of digital searchability, there is no print index to this book. But "accessibility" means to me not only efficiency of argu-ment and clarity of language but above all trying to recognize the aforementioned pressures facing academic readers today. It is no longer safe to assume that the average reader has the time or energy to read every word of a book, so I have organized *The Life Informatic* in a modular fashion that can be absorbed in pieces. The prologue and epilogue, for example, work together as more meta-level reflexive brackets to the core project, focusing on the impact of digital media and information in anthropology and the human sciences. The remainder of the book offers a more focused anthropologi-cal study of office-based news journalism today. The ethnographic studies in chapters 1 through 3 are also meant to be relatively self-contained units; the ethnography and analysis in each chapter is presented in such a way that the reader is not expected to have read all the other chapters. Whether or not these experiments to enhance modularity and accessibility are successful is for the reader rather than the author to decide. But as I was writing this book, I found myself confronting questions about the future of anthropological communication that are hauntingly similar to those cur-rently circulating in the news industry as the postwar paradigm of journalism unrav-els without a new formation clearly in sight. What, for example, are the long-term effects for anthropological knowledge of "downsizing" ethnographic richness and theoretical elaboration in the interests of producing more streamlined, argument-driven, and teachable texts? In the world of journal publishing especially, how much longer do we want to be beholden to commercial interests who profit from our volun-tary labor without compensation?[11] What institutional partners can we find to help extend nonprofit and open access models of scholarly communication?

Anthropological Research in the Era of Digital Information

When I began the research for this project in 2008 I made a conscious effort to see if it had become truly possible in the age of digital information to produce a work of anthropological ethnography without setting foot in a research library. This would have been an unthinkable experiment in the late 1990s when I was writing the first draft of my previous monograph. With full disclosure, I slipped up many times, mostly in an effort to find print editions of books that were otherwise unavailable. But, I was surprised at the extent to which electronic journal databases, the proliferation of electronic versions of larger texts, and other online information resources made it possible to do the vast majority of the contextual and comparative research for this project via screenwork. As noted above, anthropology justly prizes fieldwork as its core research practice.[12] But there are a great many other kinds of information practice that converge in the making of anthropological ethnography, few of which receive the attention that fieldwork has.[13] Perhaps the most important of these is the lateral research that anthropologists perform in order to historicize and contextualize their field research. This research normally bears fruit in the form of in-text quotations and citations and is thus essential to the socialization and temporalization of our texts as "timely interventions" in a field of knowledge.

Like contemporary news journalists, anthropologists have come increasingly to rely on online information sources and functionalities to perform such contextual and archival research. The implication of this, for both journalists and anthropologists, is that we increasingly rely on a similar source matrix and on parallel research and writing strategies. In just the past ten years, for example, search engines have emerged as indispensable tools for anthropological research just as they have in news journalism, tools that are used to locate relevant information sources, to fact check, to synchronize oneself with current events. Although at first something of a joke for the professoriate, blogs and wikis have also become, in a period of just a few years, essential tools of research and teaching, often vying with print resources for veracity and reliability and greatly exceeding them in terms of convenience. And despite our common valorization of original authorship, both anthropologists and journalists make frequent use of copy/paste features of browsers and word-processing software to highlight relevant information and to aid in text composition. Finally, anthropologists tend to access online news media as avidly (if perhaps not quite as continuously) as news journalists do. Alongside e-mail and social media, I would argue that such information practices have made a kind of 24/7 mobile research continuum a social reality in a way that is quite distinct from bygone generations of anthropological field, office, and library work. This book, for example, has been researched, composed, and edited on my laptop as I have traveled across North America, Latin America, and Europe attending conferences, visiting family, giving lectures, and doing fieldwork. This is possible because laptops, tablets, and smartphones have unprecedented capacities for mobile information organization and storage: All of my field research materials as well as a great many other supporting documents are archived digitally. What I could not bring with me, I could often access via Wi-Fi. Much as reporters now carry their libraries and writing instruments everywhere with them, it seems as though the distinction between field research and other kinds of research is weakening for anthropologists. I will not comment here on whether purely online research can produce the same intimacy and quality of knowledge that we typically attribute to long-term monosited or multisited offline fieldwork because the experiences of both online and field research vary so dramatically.[14] But I will say that if anthropological research has long shared a common field orientation with certain forms of journalistic practice, particularly the work of foreign correspondents,[15] then we might recognize that the office and mobile information practices of news journalism and anthropology are becoming increasingly aligned as well.

Which also means that common dilemmas likely await us. For example, a rising concern in news journalism is the industry's reliance upon a shrinking pool of original news sources. When a multiplicity of news organizations republishes common source material, it can produce the illusion of authority through consensus even in those cases, like hoaxes, where the shared sources prove to be unreliable. Anthropologists should be concerned about this informational phenomenon as well. After all, our awareness of events transpiring in distant places very often depends upon news reporting and a great many ideas for anthropological research projects can be retraced to news stories. But the effects of this dependency are underexamined. In this book, for example, both my journalist interlocutors and I struggled with the narrative of "crisis" in contemporary news media. While none of us was fully convinced that "crisis" is the only, let alone the best, way of describing what is happening with the news, we all felt compelled to participate in this discourse to some extent, because the constant echoing of the crisis narrative in both academic and industry accounts has made it something of a baseline intuition in our epistemic environments.

Anthropological Knowledge in the Era of Digital Reason

One of the more provocative claims I make in this book is that anthropology is, and has been for some time, awash in digital thinking. By this, I mean two things. First, anthropologists are familiar with various well-publicized and well-circulated notions of "the digital era," such as the ideas that digital media inevitably undermine existing organizations (especially centralizations) of power, that digital media compress perceptions of space and time, and that digital media are in the process of revolutionizing our senses of community and individuality.[16] Even if my field research has made me skeptical of some of these claims, I argue not that such ideas are right or wrong but rather that we must try to understand them as part of an informatic ideology in which practical intuitions derived from experiences with digital information and communication are converted into truths about the digital era and its influence.

Second, I mean that the analytical practices of anthropology and the human sciences have been deeply, quietly influenced since the middle of the twentieth century by models of knowledge and communication that are intimately linked to the industrialization of electronic computation. In the epilogue, I detail how the information theory developed by Claude Shannon and others in the 1940s emerged from wartime research on cryptography and gunnery systems, and from the industrialization of data transfer and storage. But information theory's conversion of communication and feedback into mathematical and engineering problems also naturalized a particular formalist ideology of knowledge in which relevant signal (e.g., "information") can be sharpened via a binary (e.g., "digital") coding method that erases the (supposedly) irrelevant noise of the continuous signal spectrum. As information theory was absorbed into human scientific concept work in the 1950s and 1960s (notably in the form of structuralism) this epistemological formalism endured, redefining knowledge in terms of binary information and challenging more "analog" models of knowledge that viewed epistemic form as part of a continuum of thinking and understanding. Similarly, I discuss how the applied information theory of cybernetics influenced anthropological conceptions of culture, power, and social systematicity.

Digital thinking never exercised an absolute hegemony over anthropological knowledge by any means, but it has been strongly "informative" of key areas of anthropological thought such as culture theory in ways that have been remarkably silent. So why do we hear the echoes here and now? My argument is that the intersecting and overlapping digital information practices, understandings, and environments of news journalism and anthropology generate a critical density of digital experience that, in turn, elicits recognition of the presence of what I term an "informatic unconscious" within anthropological knowledge. In this project, the digital thinking of the anthropologist and the digital thinking of the informant amplify each other to the extent that a typical division of labor between anthropology and its research partners (where the former offers the theory and the latter, the data) is disabled. As I discovered in my earlier research on dialectical knowledge as well,[17] this is a case where the ethnographic "data" already prefigures to some extent the language of analysis. So rather than simply rearticulating that language of analysis in a different way (in the hopes of producing a more "sophisticated" and naturalized version of the same), I believe we are confronted with the challenge of explaining where the doubled form of knowledge (in this case, digital thinking) comes from in the first place. That reflexive investigation is one of my underlying objectives in this work.

Our Lives Informatic

But I will defer that objective until the epilogue. A deeper investigation of news journalism in the digital era beckons. I close here with an explanation of this book's title. Long before the dawn of electronic computation, the English word "information," drawing upon the Latin root *informare*, meant the formal aspect of knowledge, especially in the context of instruction. Formalism has therefore accompanied the word "information" from the very beginning. My title also invokes the German word *Informatik*, coined by the German cybernetic pioneer and scholar of machine intelligence Karl Steinbuch to denote not just epistemological formalism but rather the automation of information processing and thought itself.[18] The term "informatic" signals the convergence of automaticity, intelligence, and knowledge in the context of electronic computation and digital information. The ethnographic studies in this book describe the experiences of professional journalists who work closely, as virtually all journalists do today, with computerized digital news information technologies. They are keenly aware of this "informatic" dimension of their news practice and often feel that their information technologies exert a strong degree of influence over the organization and flow of their work.

And, yet, news journalists also feel as though they remain intellectuals and craftspersons who resist automaticity and infuse their work with "life" by exercising their professional judgment on news value and form and by acts of original authorship and editing—in short, by "making news." My titular juxtaposition of "life" and "informatic" is meant to highlight the seemingly paradoxical condition of feeling at once automated and agentive. This is the affective and conceptual terrain of my ethnography. In the case studies that follow, we find journalists constantly oscillating between praxiological (e.g., practice-centered) and mediological (e.g., medium-centered) reflections on their practice and on the news. My argument is that neither kind of reflection is more valid than the other. [19] Recognizing the phenomenological adequacy, indeed necessity, of their continuous oscillation tells us, however, a great deal about the experience of news journalism today and of how news journalists make sense of that experience.

We might recognize this necessity in how we come to terms with our own academic information professions as well. Is it not possible in the era of digital media to feel that we are mobile, powerful agents of analysis and representation? Consider all the dazzling instruments of information now under our control. And, yet, upon a moment's reflection, how vulnerable and contingent our epistemic labors prove to be.

We are awash in too much information, screen-bound with no time to read and no one reading us. But, wait, in the little interface you and I are sharing right now, we are challenging this otherwise persuasive idiom: an author is being read and reappropri-ated. Perhaps you and I are agents after all. One sees that we too oscillate between praxiologies and mediologies of the contemporary. Such are the affective and epis-temic dialectics of our lives informatic.

The Life Informatic

Introduction

News Journalism Today

"The 'truthiness' is, anyone can read the news to you. I promise to feel the news . . . at you."
—Stephen Colbert, *The Colbert Report*

"The distracted person, too, can form habits."
—Walter Benjamin, *Illuminations*

Truth-seeker, Screenworker

Truth may seem an ever more plural and slippery concept in public and political culture today. But news journalism retains a certain romance for its dogged pursuit of all things factual. Even in a time of endless complaints about the growing sensationalism and ethereality of "the media," one continues to find journalists positioned in heroic roles in Hollywood films and bestseller fiction. We find the hard-nosed beat reporter, the relentless investigative journalist, the cantankerous desk editor, the fearless foreign correspondent, all fighters for the objectivity of truth against forces of deception and dissimulation.

There are so many examples one could choose from but one of the most memorable in recent years appears in Stieg Larsson's globally bestselling Millennium series.[1] Larsson, himself an investigative journalist and ruthless critic of social violence and right-wing politics in Sweden, gifts us the character of Mikael Blomkvist, an investigative journalist engaged in a series of high-stakes battles with corporate and governmental villains whose conspiracies are undermining the integrity and transparency of Swedish social democracy. Driven by conscience and passion to expose elite corruption, Blomkvist is the heroic truth-seeker par excellence. Even as he is hunted, shot at, beaten, and jailed, he refuses to yield or to compromise his principles. But, most significantly, Blomkvist exhibits unwavering faith in the power of journalistic publicity, the power of bringing facts into public circulation via media. He is convinced that publishing the results of investigative work will galvanize and unleash a collective public will to punish the spectral powers that oppose it. Concepts such as "political apathy" or "informational overload" play no role in Blomkvist's self-imagination. As it turns out, the Blomkvist type of journalist turns out to be considerably more than just a heroic fact-finder; "he" (for we see this is a demonstrably masculinist heroism) is a guarantor of democracy itself.

Larsson's portrait is typical of a contemporary desire to imagine virtuous guardians of the principles and powers of liberal democracy, guardians who are capable of turning back the global antipolitics of neoliberalism and its ravenous feasting upon the living flesh of all public institutions. Even unflinchingly critical portrayals of the institutional realities of news journalism today—for example, the fifth season of the brilliant HBO television series *The Wire*—leave room for characters such as Clark Johnson's Gus Haynes, the principled old-school editor fighting management's sacrificing of public affairs journalism for increasingly sensationalist "pseudo-news." The brilliant satirists of news media that have emerged in the past fifteen years—most notably Jon Stewart and Stephen Colbert—move between parodic ambiguity and clear signals that they feel the regime of public truth that news journalism once epitomized is still worth fighting for.[2]

This image of the journalist as heroic truth-seeker and guardian of public interest, while powerfully resonant, actually obscures the fact that (for a variety of reasons explored at greater length later in this book) if one were to speak of an "average" journalistic type today, it would no longer be a beat reporter, an investigative journalist, a foreign correspondent, or even a desk editor. No, the far more common type is that of the office-based screenworker. This is not an uncontroversial assessment. It is, however, an assessment that is reinforced by other recent ethnographic portraits of the practice of contemporary news journalism—a profession transformed, initially by the computerization of western news organizations in the 1980s, and then by the subsequent linkage to fast-time digital information networks in the 1990s and 2000s.[3] Barbie Zelizer has observed that much of the work of news journalism transpires outside newsrooms these days.[4] And yet, regardless of whether a traditional newsroom is the production environment, one of the most striking changes in the craft of news journalism is that it, more so than ever, transpires in front of computer monitors. Olivier Baisneé and Dominique Marchetti have coined the term "sedentary journalism" to describe this growing trend in news practice.[5] If we ask why this is so, we find that journalists are in no small part increasingly fixed in their seats because there is more and more action to be observed and managed on their screens. And, typically, there is now a smaller staff to cope with the rising workload.[6] As journalists themselves often say, newsmaking today is as much about managing multiple fast-moving flows of information already in circulation as it is about locating and sharing "new" news. In other words, news journalism in the digital era has become as much about navigating the complex ecology of news information already "out there" as seeking and revealing unknown truths.

This is not to suggest that the work of reporting is no longer an important aspect of newsmaking nor that many journalists do not still understand themselves and their authorship as vital to the defense of democratic institutions. In Germany, where I did the majority of the field research for this book, I found that news journalists were almost univocally committed to the principles of liberal democracy and saw their work as essential for the robustness of political and social *Öffentlichkeit* (publicity, or, "public sphere"). Likewise, it would be preposterous to suggest that reporting does not endure as a core practice at the majority of news organizations across the world.[7] But it is fair to say that reporting represents a shrinking proportion of news activity today relative to monitoring and repurposing news content already in circulation. Moreover, entire news organizations like Google News now exist (and are quite lucrative) without doing any original reporting. Certain forms of reportage, notably investigative journalism and foreign correspondence, are under heavy pressure across the world due to their costs, risks, and occasional legal complications. Other forms like business, entertainment, and sports reporting are thriving because they are politically uncomplicated and relatively cheap to produce, while their popularity guarantees consistently high advertising revenue. Meanwhile, office-based screenwork has quietly emerged as the norm of professional practice.

I do not assume that the rise of screenwork is either an intrinsically negative or positive development for news journalism. To paraphrase Raymond Williams, it is not (just) the technologies of media that matter but also the decisions that are made as to how to institutionalize them.[8] So, in the tradition of revelatory publicity that anthropology shares with news journalism, *The Life Informatic* seeks to highlight office-based screenwork as an aspect of news journalism today that remains relatively opaque to both popular imagination and scholarly commentary. Yet, the scope of my analysis is necessarily broader than screenwork. Ultimately, this is a study of the practices, institutions, and implications of newsmaking in a time that is equally imprinted by the hegemony of neoliberal politics and worldviews as by the diverse institutionalization of digital communications technology. We find news journalists engaged in the process of trying to redefine their senses of agency, expertise, and authority given the new ecology of forces that have transformed and that are continuing to transform their work environments and practices. Only time and Hollywood will tell us whether news-oriented screenwork can be incorporated into the canon of heroic images of journalism as an epitome and guardian of liberal democracy. What this book does show is that screenwork, as currently institutionalized, typically creates conditions of distraction that make paying attention to anything offscreen increasingly difficult. A narrowing of journalistic attentiveness is coming to exquisitely overdetermine the traditional news business of finding and circulating facts in the world.

News in the Digital Era

Some preliminary terminological definitions are in order. "News" is not a transparent concept and indeed we will shortly discover that what should and should not count as "news" is an important area of debate and disagreement within news organizations and among newsmakers today. There is probably general agreement that news is a matter of the communication of information, with "information" understood as a relatively generic category of relevant message. Likewise, the temporality of news is rarely disputed. It is accepted that news consists of messages that communicate some "new" event or issue and that the relative novelty of this information is a principle source of its value. The issue of relevance is the crucial area of contention. Those of us who came of age before the 1980s may still remember the Keynesian model of news centered on public affairs and public-interest journalism and transmitted to us by expert journalistic authorities. For some journalists and news organizations, this remains the proper normative model of newsmaking; that is, to expertly gather and select important information and to authoritatively disseminate it "in the public interest." Since the 1980s, in the United States and increasingly in Europe, this model of news has slowly ceded authority to a post-Keynesian (or neoliberal) model that engages the reader or viewer less as a public citizen and more as an individual consumer, with individual tastes and preferences in news information to which news organizations should cater. At an increasing number of western news organizations today, "news" is being redefined by managers and by many journalists as information that users themselves deem relevant. As one can imagine, this shift has destabilized the old model of journalistic expertise and authority in which journalists could imagine themselves as Blomkvistian guarantors of an informed democratic public. The neoliberal model positions journalism instead as a particular kind of informational service labor on behalf of sovereign consumers, perhaps involving some specialized expertise in the filtration and "curation" of relevant messages, but nonetheless robbed of much of its authority to define what issues and events are newsworthy and why.

The destabilization of both the meaning of news and the authority of news journalism echoes throughout the ethnographic studies that make up the core of this book. So too does the idea that this destabilization is fundamentally tied to the digital revolution in newsmaking. "Digital" operates as a gloss in this book, referring in a general way to the transformation of newsmaking in the wake of computerization, the popularization of the Internet and mobile telephony, and the rise of "lateral messaging" (see below) over the past two decades, perhaps most notably in the form(s) of social media. Although there are analytical disadvantages to bundling all of these developments together, "digital" bridges -emic and -etic understandings in that it straddles how journalists tend to interpret the transformation of their work environments and practices and how academic observers have typically chosen to periodize new media. "The digital era" (*das digitale Zeitalter*) for the journalists with whom I spoke has signaled above all the appearance and institutionalization of Internet-based communication technologies and information systems. But it has also meant, in a secondary sense, computerization itself and the proliferation of mobile media platforms and reception devices. Digitality (*Digitalität*) had a fairly wide semantic range—not infrequently it connoted "the conditions under which we practice journalism now." I find that digitality has a similarly open semantic range in academic knowledge as well. Surely, academic reference to a "digital revolution" in information and communication is as commonplace as it is unspecific.[9] That talk has established certain common truths about the social impact of digital mediation, some of which are confirmed and some of which are undermined by the portraits and analysis in this book.

For example, two of the more commonly repeated truths about the digital era that will be put to the test are: 1) that information, including news information, now circulates instantaneously in a "real-time" temporality; and 2) that there is now a global system of information transfer, including news information. Both of these truths invoke the prophecies of an early digital oracle, Marshall McLuhan, about the contribution of "electric media" to the creation of a "global village" in which information circulated at the speed of light, retribalizing a world riven by differences between the imagined nations of print communication.[10] Interestingly, later social theorists of globalization such as Arjun Appadurai, Zygmunt Bauman, and Manuel Castells have largely bought into this idea that digital media have deterritorialized and accelerated social experience as never before, blurring distinctions and creating new regimes of identity, connectivity, and alterity.[11]

While to the user digital news may well seem to unfold in a real-time blur, this book shows that digital news is constantly retemporalized by a complex field of technologies, practices, and institutions of newsmaking that range from nearly instant technical transfer of data to a variety of tempos of informational processing and planning. Digital news is certainly not best viewed as a network of instantaneous messaging. Rather than "real time," I prefer to think about it as "fast time," often very fast time indeed, but always subjected to professional and organizational forms of mediation.

Digital news is also not, I would argue, a system, in any meaningful sense of systematicity. I will not rehearse my criticism of "system" as a conceptual trope of unified exteriority as much fantasy as fact when it comes to representing "things as they are."[12] As the cover illustration of this book—an image of the organization of Internet messaging—suggests, digital news is better imagined as an interlinked constellation of differently scaled nodes (organizations) that interact via variously sized and speeded channels to connect a galaxy of newsmakers and newsusers. Digital news has no obvious bounded systematicity; instead, it has a dense, dynamic, and scalable network architecture in which powerful radial centers of messaging coexist with and overlap expansive peer-to-peer meshes of lateral co-information. To put this in terms of popular metaphors of informational liquidity, digital news has ocean currents, driven by the most powerful organizational nodes, sending certain messages coursing across the world. But it also has every imaginable wave, rivulet, pool, and runoff ditch in which other kinds of messages flow or drift on far humbler currents. Digital news is (like the ironically far simpler network architecture of the Internet) virtually unimaginable in its totality, which explains why those featured in this book—both analysts and practitioners—employ such a wide range of metaphors to represent newsmaking today. They are all struggling to find a language able to capture the experience of information passing all around and through them.

My use of terms such as "node" and "channel" to portray digital news in this book does not suggest the discovery of a more authoritative metaphoricity; it simply represents my attempt, once again, to find a fairly inclusive one. "Channel" can, for example, be understood materially and industrially as a conduit for carrying water or electric charge as well as informatically as a signal or data stream. "Channel" is also a processual trope; one could say that a channel exists to the extent that a process of messaging connects different partners. "Node" has informatic implications as well in terms of network architecture but also carries with it the botanical/corporeal meaning of a protuberance or "lump in the flesh." This connotation will prove to be quite apt in the sense that "nodes" of digital news are probably best conceived as complex knots of overlapping channels, dendritic lumps that epitomize Wittgenstein's wisdom that "the strength of the thread does not reside in the fact that some one fibre runs through its whole length, but in the overlapping of many fibres."[13] The strength and motility of a news node ultimately depends on its multiple fibers of connectivity.[14]

These are preliminary conceptual schemata, signposts for the ethnographic studies to come. As will rapidly become clear, the problem of how best to understand news and news journalism today became something of a shared analytical exercise between the ethnographer and his interlocutors. In each study, we explore different modalities of conceptualizing what news journalism is and how it is changing today. The power of informatic understandings proves to be substantial but not absolute as more materialist and humanist sensibilities resonate throughout the dialogues too. In the epilogue to this book, I focus at greater length on the oscillation between informatic and noninformatic understandings that emerge in the studies and discuss, in particular, how ethnographic contact with contemporary news journalism helps to surface a potent yet rather hidden legacy of informatic thinking (that I term "digital reason") in anthropology and the human sciences more broadly.

Background, Sites, Methods

Given the complex interconnected apparatus of news journalism and newsflow today, newsmaking is obviously an intrinsically translocal object for ethnographic research regardless of whether the actual research concentrates on one node or many. *The Life Informatic* focuses principally on three nodes but it is, at the same time, a profoundly "multisited" commentary[15] with all the advantages and disadvantages multiple locatedness entails for establishing the kinds of intimate understanding upon which anthropological ethnography thrives. Fortunately, I have also had the opportunity and luxury of being able to grow slowly into my understanding of contemporary news journalism over the past fifteen years, beginning with an earlier field research project in the mid-1990s, which took me into over a dozen news organizations in eastern Germany to discuss professional transitions from socialist to liberal democratic newsmaking. At that time, my journalist friends were already alerting me to their sense that the postsocialist transition, while significant, soon would be overshadowed by an even more dramatic transformation of news journalism with the widespread institutionalization of new digital information technology. I recall watching elements of this transition occur, for example, as one public broadcaster began the process of shutting down its paper archive and moving to a digital archive.

By around 2005 my research had shifted to focus more directly on the impact of digital information and communication technology upon contemporary news journalism in Europe and North America. With the generous support of a Humboldt Research Fellowship, I was able to gain my densest experiences of the channels, nodes, and practices of contemporary news mediation in phases of organizational field research (lasting from three weeks to three months) in Frankfurt, Darmstadt, Berlin, and Halle between 2008 and 2010. My interviews and background research took me even farther afield to other German news organizations based in Hamburg, Frankfurt, Berlin, Essen, and Mainz. At the same time, I also began interviewing North American news journalists on their experiences with digital media in Washington, DC, New York, Chicago, Toronto, and Santa Monica. I do not discuss these North American interviews and site visits at length in this book, but they helped me immensely in my ability to understand which aspects of German news practice were shared internationally and which were distinctive to Germany.

Although proportions varied somewhat from site to site, my office research broke down roughly as follows: about half of my time was spent observing news journalists at work (augmented by informal discussions, audiotape, and video captures of their screenwork). Another quarter of my time was spent in editorial meetings in which decisions about the newsworthiness of particular issues were debated but in which more often the focus of activity was the coordination and division of labor to improve efficiency and avoid duplications of effort. The final quarter focused on one-on-one interviews to develop a better sense of journalists' impressive analytical engagement with their professional practice and its recent changes. It is also worth mentioning that I developed a number of friendships during the course of the research such that some interviews and observations spilled over into lunches, dinners, and nightlife.

The ethnographic studies focus on work and office life. I rarely had the nerve to follow my own advice[16] to erode the *entente cordiale* between anthropologists of "cultures of expertise" and their expert interlocutors by critically engaging norms of intellectual professionalism. But, no apologies. The object of this book was to understand how the professional practice of news journalism is changing. And that professional practice takes place in offices, in front of screens, undertaken by professionals who have developed a habitus to insulate their expert epistemic labor from the distractions of private lives and loves.

Nachrichtenland Germany

One might fairly ask: why select Germany to center a study of the transformation of newsmaking in the digital era? Many observers of, and participants in, western news journalism today would say that the United States remains the trendsetter in all things digital. And, more than this, the United States has surely proved itself a global leader in all things neoliberal. But, as it turns out, its particularly intensive and unsettling confluence of digital and neoliberal vectors (what I define in chapter 4 as "digital liberalism") has also made the U.S. somewhat of an outlier to broader trends in western news journalism. For one thing, the weakness of the public broadcasting sector in the United States is remarkable as compared with other nations in what we now term the Global North. This weakness has surely accelerated the decline of public affairs journalism in the United States as compared with, for example, Europe, where political reportage and analysis remains on the whole more substantive and ideologically diverse. Second, the drastic crisis of print news journalism that the U.S. is currently experiencing has been moderated by the fact that European print publishers are typically less dependent on fickle advertising revenue and less exposed to international financial markets (and their short-term profitability expectations) than publicly traded news organizations in the United States are. Although northern news journalism is everywhere struggling to come to terms with the rise of online and social media, it seems to me that the transition is moving more slowly (and in some respects more successfully) in Europe than in the United States, even though the after-effects of the economic crisis of 2008 continue to undermine European news organizations, as is happening elsewhere. I frequently draw upon examples from the United States as a point of comparative reference in this book, but often it is to show a more extreme variant of a trend or condition present in German news journalism.

It is important to emphasize that there is no single "European model" of news journalism either. This is true despite the fact that in the era of cable and satellite television broadcasting all European countries have something of a "dual model" of public and private broadcasting, a model further augmented by the European Union's strong support for private broadcasting in its media ownership and regulation policies.[17] Print journalism typically remains stronger in European nations than in the United States although newspaper and news magazine readership is declining and use of online and mobile media news sources is rising. In Germany, consumer loyalty to print media remains quite high and most of the dominant national news organizations (or *Leitmedien*, "lead media") are newspapers (e.g., *Bild, Die Welt, Die Zeit, Frankfurter Allgemeine Zeitung, Süddeutsche Zeitung*), news magazines (e.g, *Focus, Spiegel* and *Stern*), and their affiliated online portals (e.g., *Bild Online, Spiegel Online*). Germany usually finds itself at the center of the pack in trans-European surveys of habits of news consumption such as hours spent watching television news and reading newspapers.[18] It has stronger regional-newspaper and broadcasting markets than most European countries and tends to score lower than average on evaluations of multimedia "meshing" (in which users engage more than one information medium simultaneously).[19] My journalist interlocutors in Germany frequently reported to me that they worked in the most complex and competitive news market in Europe, and perhaps in the world. At the time of my research in 2009, Germany had 134 newspapers with 1,511 local editions, two national public television channels with strong news commitments, nine regional public television channels with their own news departments, respected private 24/7 news television channels like n-tv and n24, over 350 radio stations, and twelve news agencies—all of which suggests a very dynamic news landscape. Add to this the fact that Germany also now has more Internet users (51.23 million) than any EU country and 70.9 percent of those users reported accessing news content online in 2011.[20] Although it is unclear on what basis one could quantify "the most complex and competitive news market" with any degree of certainty, it seems fair to say that German news mediation is a very diverse and vibrant domain of communicative and informational activity.

Thus, the short answer to the question, "Why Germany?" is that although there is no single national news industry that can be taken as representative of all the others, Germany's news industry is more representative of the majority than, for example, the United States' is. Germany is experiencing all the general trends affecting news journalism today in the Global North (e.g., pluralization of news channels across all media, the rise of online and mobile media as platforms for news use, the reorganization of commercial financing via advertising, a corresponding unsettling of the pre-Internet "business model" of financing news journalism, especially print journalism). But like other European countries, and unlike the United States, stronger public sponsorship of news and greater attachment to so-called old media are slowing Germany's institutionalization of digital news media and making this institutionalization seem less destructive of pre-Internet institutions of news mediation. Germany is an excellent place to watch the future of news journalism unfold because its unfolding is proceeding without a sense of dire panic and at a pace that permits both participants and analysts to occasionally suspend the phenomenology of transformation to reflect on its distinctive vectors, norms, and forms.

The Studies

The next three chapters of the book offer three different encounters with the lives and institutions of newsmaking today. Each study is meant to stand on its own ethnographically but the work of analysis overlaps the particularities of each study and affiliates them as a set. The division of labor in the news industry is complex and I have selected organizational sites that reflect some of the most important nodes in the contemporary ecology of newsmaking and newsflow. In chapter 1, I discuss the work of an international news agency which is increasingly responsible for supplying raw and finished forms of breaking news content to other news organizations. In chapter 2, I discuss what is arguably Germany's most broadly connected news organization, an online news portal that does little of its own reporting but which works assiduously at recrafting and recirculating news agency content. In chapter 3, I discuss a 24/7 news radio station housed within a regional public broadcaster which seeks to adapt the political publicity of traditional German broadcasting to the new exigencies of fast-time digital information.

The nodes I have selected all offer important and illuminating portraits of news journalism today. I have no illusion that they add up to a comprehensive portrait nor that other nodal configurations could not also have been illuminating. The nodes of contemporary news journalism are so many that a complete mapping would have been a quixotic and also I think repetitive exercise. By the same token, a single study would have been too organizationally and functionally specific to have served as the basis for a broader representation of the practices and institutions of news journalism today. I have sought, as noted in the prologue, efficiency in the organization of my analysis without oversimplification. These three studies offer, I would argue, key insight into many of the most consequential fields of tension in news journalism today: markets and publics, production and flow, originality and imitation, agency and automaticity. Together, these fields of tension provide the contour for what I term "life informatic"—a life that (as I have already disclosed) implicates other "information professions" such as anthropology as well.

The storylines that run through the next three chapters reflect the idiosyncrasies of different media, organizational contexts, and individual personalities, but they also highlight the common experiences, sentiments, and understanding of journalistic screenworkers, unified as they are by the opportunity and necessity of engaging fast-time newsflow, evaluating news content, and producing new texts and images. Each chapter has certain key attentional foci of its own. For instance, chapter 1 focuses closely on the challenges of managing (both personally and organizationally) vast quantitative increases in digital information and the challenges of defining news value on a fast-time basis. Chapter 2 investigates new modes of user feedback that are characteristic of online publicity and how the growing (spectral) presence of the end user in news organizations has unsettled traditional relations of journalistic expertise and authority. Chapter 3 focuses on how mid-twentieth-century political publicity is both being sustained and yet also subtly transformed by the new institutions of digital news-making and newsflow. These foci, needless to say, point to conditions that transcend any one news organization today. Yet, also needless to say, certain conditions are more visible and locally relevant in some contexts than in others. Likewise, analytical attention to questions of temporality, affect, practice, and understanding highlights resonances, analogies, and crucial differences among the case studies.

Chapter 4 orchestrates and amplifies these resonances between the ethnographic chapters and works toward a more general portrait of the state of news journalism today. Taking inspiration from Raymond Williams's brilliant analysis of the historical transformation of forms of electronic mediation, I offer five reflections on how news journalism has been impacted both by the development and institutionalization of digital communication and information technology and by the intensified legitimation of late and neoliberal worldviews in the past quarter century. I discuss in particular how the rebalancing of the radial (e.g., largely monodirectional, hub-and-spoke) and lateral (e.g., more often pluridirectional, point-to-point) potentialities of electronic communication with the institutionalization of the Internet and the popularization of mobile telephony has massively impacted and destabilized the mid-twentieth-century regime of news journalism. I also discuss how the "lateral revolution" of the past quarter century has coevolved with the "autological subjectivity" preferred by late liberal worldviews, reinforcing and extending the principles of "digital liberalism." Not contenting myself with the somewhat impracticable task of codifying the state of news journalism today, I also offer five reflections on its future. Signals of concern and despair abound, but there is little reason to believe that the end of news journalism is imminent. Still, it must (and will) change and evolve in the future.

The crucial question comes down to this: Will news journalism be able to stabilize a new regime of expertise and authority? The largely passive broadcast publics of the past are gone, likely never to return. The expansion and intensification of lateral messaging has undermined journalists' claims to serve as gatekeepers of truthful information. Yet, news journalists, like Hollywood, continue to believe strongly in the public necessity of their expertise. When I asked an editor at the *Wall Street Journal* what he thought of citizen journalism, the movement to encourage citizens to more actively participate in news production and circulation, he grinned at me and said, "I don't know. Tell me what you think about citizen surgery."[21]

Chapter 1

The Craft of Slotting

Screenwork, Attentional Practices, and News Value
at an International News Agency

From a conversation (in German) in October 2009 between the author and two Associated Press journalists at a Frankfurt music club:

AP1 [*to AP2, gesturing to DB*]: Guess what he is writing about now? "The *Craft* of Slotting" [*laughs*].

AP2: Hmm [*eyeing DB doubtfully*].

DB to AP1: Or, maybe I should have said "The *Kunst* of Slotting." Is it art or craft?

AP1: [*laughing*] Please not *Kunst*, that sounds too dignified [*veredelt*] . . .

DB: Or . . .

AP1: [*in English, laughing*] "The *Treadmill* of Slotting"!

Screens

There is no way to begin talking about the craft of slotting without talking about the screens. They are the centering point of a slotter's work, the alpha and omega as the Germans would say. To be sure, the taskscape of slotting is manifold and its interruptions and distractions are many—the news ticker scrolling across the large television monitor above, a query from one of the writers, a phone call, what has just been disgorged by the fax machine or the printer, the radio blaring out the top-of-the-hour news. Observing slotters at work, I tracked an average of ninety-seven different discrete activities every hour. That meant a change in focus or medium roughly every thirty-seven seconds. But, even so, no matter where the slotter's attention roams, it always returns to the screens in a magnetic, almost devotional way. When the slotter loses focus, just for a moment, he or she instinctively looks to the screens for cues as to how to resynchronize with the newsflow. All of the other activities of slotting deviate from this norm of remaining poised, inclined slightly forward in one's desk chair, focusing in on one of the screens.

At the Associated Press office in Frankfurt (the headquarters of AP Deutscher Dienst, or simply, AP-DD) where I did fieldwork in 2008,[1] the slotter screens came[2] in

1.1 The "slot island" at AP-DD (photo credit: Peter Zschunke)

rows of three, occupying the spatial center point of each slot desk, oases of order above shifting stacks of paper, ringing phones, rows of idle reference manuals, and the remains of whatever food or drink the slotter managed to find the time to gulp down during the shift. AP-DD had three slot desks (one for international news, one for national news, and one for business news) that were arranged as the sides of an equilateral triangle, creating in their centers a smaller triangle of nine screens. The *Slotinsel* (slot island) as it was sometimes described, sat in one corner of AP-DD's U-shaped newsroom where it had excellent sight- and shoutlines to several rows of desks where writers on shift worked at their single screens. Likewise, the slot island was positioned near to the glass-walled offices of the editor in chief and assistant editor in chief of AP-DD, who occasionally emerged from their own assignments to discuss events and coverage with the slotters. Overall, the newsroom was deceptively quiet. I made dozens of hours of tapes of the ambient sonic environment of AP-DD and these are dominated by the quiet click-click of dozens of hands word processing. Except for the phone calls. Except for a slotter shouting out a work assignment and a writer announcing he or she has sent a text in. Except for the automated "AP news alert!" which sounds whenever an *Eilmeldung* (the most urgent class of news bulletin) comes across the wire. Except for the quiet chatting between colleagues, mostly to coordinate and to comment on works in progress. Except for the not infrequent joke or ironic comment made by one of the slotters to break the work tension and the laughs and responses circulating, like a musical round, through the newsroom. Except for the editor in chief strolling through the newsroom, commenting on the themes of the day, nudging on the troops.

The office environment itself lay fallow, its white walls, slate grey carpets, taupe cabinetry, its light grey desks and filing cabinets, its fluorescent lights and blue chairs utterly mundane and unremarkable. Ditto the maps, the framed, neatly organized photographs on the wall, the bulletin boards, the plants. Occasionally the stack of daily newspapers was shuffled and one opened and scanned. More often, the fax machines and printers hummed into life. In my many observations of the AP-DD newsroom I did not once see a single journalist look out one of its many windows. Outside the vertical blinds there was not so much to see, a side street near the Frankfurt main train station, a sex emporium on the corner marking the edge of Frankfurt's red light district. As elsewhere in the office side of contemporary news journalism, the real action always took place on the screens.

Technologically speaking, the screens were ordinary flat panel LCD displays, with 40-centimeter diagonals. In each set of three slot screens, there was a center screen that the slotter used for word processing, for receiving, editing, spell-checking and sending news reports *auf den Draht* (on the wire), for sending e-mail messages and instant messages to their colleagues in AP-DD's other bureaus. There was a left screen which was known as the "smurf" screen because it contained several color-coded continuously updating message feeds called "smurfs" by their whimsical (American) programmer: a blue smurf for press releases from the police, a green smurf for all other releases which incorporated a news ticker, *News Aktuell*,[3] produced by dpa, AP-DD's main competitor in the German news agency market, and a red smurf for AP's own output. And then there was the right screen whose use was more personalized but which was normally reserved for open browser windows showing the websites of AP-DD's major news clients and competitors like Spiegel.de, n-tv, and bild.de. These are counted among the *Leitmedien* (lead media), the media organizations that powerfully influence the *Tagesthemen* (themes of the day) in German national and international news. These windows refreshed every minute or so, guaranteeing that the slotter knew exactly what messages were moving through the news channels that interconnected with the slot desk.

Together, the screens offered apertures into what Karin Knorr-Cetina has termed world-making "scopic systems."[4] They were certainly panoptica but more than this they were operationally flexible, scalable interfaces, allowing the slotters to compose and edit texts and to message locally as well as to track, organize and engage a multiplicity of translocal information feeds. Although the question might seem disingenuous given computerization, we might still ask why screens center the slotters' craft. Georg S., a junior but very talented slotter at AP, explained to me that *normale Slotarbeit*, normal slotwork, was the simultaneous combination of *Sichten* (screening), *Beaufsichtigen* (observation, surveillance) and *Texte rausgeben* (sending out texts). *Sichten* and *Beaufsichtigen* both find their nominal root in the Old High German *siht*, which is not coincidentally also the root of the English word "sight." Visual attention is enormously important in slotwork. The vast majority of the cues for engaging fast-time newsflow, both on- and offscreen, are organized visually. Indeed, slotters typically described the normative ideal of slotting as *Überblick zu haben* (having an overview), as being positioned somehow panoramically above the torrent below. *Überblick* (overview), any slotter would tell you, is however at best a fragile, fleeting condition, won only through concentrated multiattentionality and easily lost in the constant distractions of practice. Which is why the electronic co-location of incoming and outgoing newsfeeds on the slot screens is the best material approximation of *Überblick*. The screens are the slotter's primary attentional compass and navigational equipment as they chart a course through the fast moving waters of the news. If newsmaking today confronts the outside observer as a dizzying spectacle of circulation and flow, in other words if it appears as a space of intense informational *mediation*, screenwork was surely one of the slotters' most reliable techniques of *immediating* newsflow into forms susceptible to their professional agency.[5] The screens channeled "synechdochical power,"[6] assembling chaotic parts into flowing wholes, gathering up "a lifeworld while simultaneously projecting it."[7] They represented, as much as anything could, "the news." At AP-DD, I would often sit near the slot island—staring over shoulders at the clutter of overlaid smurfs, web browser windows, word-processing windows, and instant-message windows—and find myself thinking that three screens were almost too few.[8]

The Nodal Importance of Slotting in Contemporary News

The terms "slotter" and "slotting" are material metaphors themselves. They reference a predigital division of labor in newsmaking in which an editor distributed writing assignments by putting sheets of paper into wooden boxes, pigeonholes, or "slots." In print journalism this was a relatively low-status form of editorial activity often lumped in with copyediting. And, in the digital era of print and broadcast journalism, slotting has dwindled into a terminological archaism. But, in news agency journalism, the role took on greater significance because of the pressure to manage breaking news on a fast-time basis. Slotters operated as managing editors[9] whose job it was to survey incoming news, to assign tasks to their shift's writers, to edit their draft *Meldungen* (reports, bulletins) and to send these out on the agency wire. As agency news practitioner and analyst Peter Zschunke explains, "with the order to send out a report, the slotter creates the possibility for millionfold distribution. Given the immense responsibility the slotter has over news-output during his shift, he also inherits a correspondingly far-reaching decisional authority. Reuters' maxim, 'the slot is always right,' captures this well. And, no less important than sending out reports is the slotter's constant supervision over the general news scene [*Nachrichtenlage*] and the organization of the real-time news production."[10]

The decisional authority of the slotter is amplified far beyond the confines of the news agency as well. News media organizations have long relied upon news agencies like AP, Reuters and dpa to deliver maximally accurate, maximally fast, maximally factual information. Indeed, news agencies developed historically in the 1830s and 1840s as newspaper cooperatives (like AP) and private service agencies (like Reuters or AFP) sought to share the significant costs of foreign correspondence and to extend the scope of their international news coverage beyond what their clients could otherwise afford. By the mid-1860s, with the laying of transatlantic telegraphic cable that reduced message communication speeds from days to minutes, the business in international correspondence boomed and news agencies thrived in both Europe and North America. News agencies have thus long been important nodes in the production and distribution of facts and messages from afar.[11] But, in our current era of European and North American news, which has been marked above all by the powerful intersection of digital information technology and global (neo)liberalism since the 1980s, the core role of news agencies has, in certain respects, expanded.

I asked Friedrich H., the head of AP-DD's national news desk, to reflect on the changing position of news agencies in the twenty years he had worked in news journalism:

> DB: Can you say more about how news agency work has changed in the time you've been at AP?
>
> FH: Our *Themen* [themes, stories] used to be clearer or better defined somehow. The division of labor between the news desks was clearer and it was clearer what was worthy of being reported and what wasn't. The role of the news agency was also clearer. People didn't demand so much analysis, so many background stories, or service pieces. It was just expected that we would go to the press conferences and write reports about them. And that has *clearly* changed. . . . There's a tendency across the media to move away from the stiff news reports [*weg von den starren Nachrichten*]. Our clients don't want what appeared last night on the evening news from us. They want to present their readers the next day with a further development of a story with a background piece, something that embeds a political event in its context. That simply wasn't the case before. In the old days, we just reported a political event in the style, 'On Tuesday, the Federal Government in Bonn made this or that decision . . .' Today we write about the consequences of those decisions for consumers.
>
> DB: So, has that changed the importance of the news agencies in the news industry today? I mean, the fact that you're not just offering short news bulletins anymore but longer texts with more context?

FH: Yes, I think of these completely new formats that would have been unthinkable back then. These question-answer formats, these graphic infoboxes [*shakes his head*]. I *would* say that the news agencies are becoming ever more important. On the one hand in Germany we have what I believe is the most competitive news market worldwide. And this puts all news media into a slightly crisis-prone and shaky situation. So I would say, yes, the news agencies are gaining ever greater significance but what I don't know is whether our clients are actually ready to appreciate that significance and to pay for it. News agencies are becoming more important quite simply because almost all media organizations today right up to the big online media like *Spiegel Online* and *Focus Online* are operating with fewer employees. And so it's increasingly important for them to have the good news agency texts with their broad coverage. Look at a news agency like AP which has a correspondent in every federal state in Germany and that has excellent foreign coverage, with the largest correspondent network worldwide. That's something that no media organization can afford.

DB: So your clients' need for your service is growing, but you don't feel that need is being recognized?

FH: Our role is getting bigger but the tendency among our client base is to deny that ever more fiercely. For example, there are quite a few newspapers here that understand themselves as *Autorenzeitungen*[12] and they simply deny that news agencies are a very, very important foundation [*Grundlage*] for them. They think of us simply as a form of [*in English*] *backup*. But when you look closely at these newspapers, even the ones that operate overwhelmingly with their own bylines, you'll still find a huge amount of agency material that they are simply not acknowledging as a source.

Unacknowledged sourcing of news agency material certainly does exist, as I discuss further in chapter 2. But it is difficult to determine exactly how widespread the practice is. What is more easily verifiable is that news agencies are delivering more reports, longer reports, and more textually finished and publishable reports than they did in the past. German news researcher Jürgen Wilke calculates that, between 1989 and 2005, the four largest international news agencies increased their total news output by 50 percent to a combined average of over 1,500 *Meldungen* per day. The average length of an agency report meanwhile increased from 189 to 220 words during the same period, reflecting the rise in demand for analysis and background material that Friedrich noted.[13] News agencies are also increasingly delivering "ready-made" content designed to be directly transferred into clients' content management systems without the need for further editorial intervention.

The growing importance of news agencies is thus partly rooted in their easy availability and use. In the ten newsrooms that I visited during the research for this book, every one of their content management systems included access to multiple news agency feeds. These feeds were both extraordinarily efficient in terms of alerting journalists to potentially newsworthy events and offered a steady stream of source material that could be drawn upon for story composition. But, as Friedrich noted, there are also pressing financial reasons for the rising news agency dependency. News agencies maintain broad and expensive correspondent networks that would be largely unaffordable to individual news organizations, particularly at a time when the vast majority of news organizations are shedding staff.[14]

Intensified use of news agency content may be an increasingly common survival strategy in a transforming news industry, but it also creates new conditions of vulnerability. Although news agency material is much cheaper to use than self-produced reporting, the ubiquity of news agency texts creates uncanny replications of themes and texts, reducing their value to news organizations since they are more difficult to claim as "original content." This, I would emphasize, is truly *the* dilemma afflicting investment in original news content today: it is expensive to produce and increasingly difficult to commoditize profitably.[15] Under the current institutions of digital information, breaking news is proprietary at most for a matter of minutes, and often only for seconds. If a nineteenth- or even twentieth-century news organization with a correspondent in a remote location could have hoped to hold a monopoly on reports from that location for days or even weeks, the synchronization and translocal interconnectedness of digital news have drastically reduced these kinds of advantages. One could thus argue that the marginal value of original news content has diminished throughout the news industry since new content is so easily and rapidly republicized elsewhere, a condition that the rise of online news aggregators like Google News has only exacerbated. News organizations have also become so adept at watching each other's news output and at synchronizing coverage of major news events that reporting such events no longer appears to offer the basis for building a distinct identity in a competitive news environment. News organizations have reacted to this dilemma variously; some have emphasized user service, others local coverage, and still others (e.g., Fox News) a particular political orientation in which they feel they can specialize most efficiently and distinctively. News organizations that imagine themselves as serving translocal and elite audiences have often moved away from breaking news reporting and toward offering news analysis and background coverage, placing current events in context.

The desire for distinctiveness has been passed along to news agencies in the form of rising pressure to provide more content-heavy and client-tailored forms of news, for example, deep background reports and interactive multimedia. The slotters I observed at AP-DD all mentioned fielding daily phone calls from newspaper clients with a variety of individualized coverage requests ranging from follow-up reports to graphics. At the same time, news agencies continue to do a brisk business in "readymades" that can be reproduced with minimal intervention. The assistant editor in chief at AP-DD, Paul Z., confirmed that demand was rising across the board for finished forms of text and image bundles. In such instances, he noted, client organizations are literally "outsourcing" news production to news agencies. Paul noted that such outsourcing had been an aspect of agency-client relations since the beginning, "it is just that now our clients are offloading more of their journalistic work to us than in the past and that we increasingly do the finishing work as well as the raw content."

In sum, the nodal importance of slotting for news mediation is strong and rising. Slotters decide, on a fast-time basis, what stories news agencies will send out and how they will cover them. And, agency clients increasingly rely upon news agencies both to obtain fast-time channels of breaking news content and to reduce their own production costs for reporting, editing, and analysis.

But many of my interviewees at AP-DD wondered about the long-term sustainability of the current production model. Competition among news agencies is also escalating as the general financial unsteadiness of the news industry has caused clients to reduce the number of agencies to which they subscribe. Between 2007 and 2009, for example, the Associated Press was forced to reduce its rates for American newspapers to avert threatened unsubscriptions and to lay off approximately 10 percent of its staff globally. Oskar L., the business director of AP-DD until 2009, told me quite frankly that he feared for the future of news agency journalism: "In my view, the news agencies tend to be very weak in terms of innovation. We still have the idea more or less that we mirror what happens in the world, we produce image and text for wholesale, and then the clients take it and publish it. And maybe the clients would publish whatever we did. But we don't know as much as we should about how that relationship could be optimized. We're producing in a black box."

The editor in chief of AP-DD, Per G., was more optimistic that neither the public nor client news organizations would be able to do without news agencies in the era of digital information, simply because the rising volume of circulating news messages generated a parallel need for more labor-intensive, credible forms of filtering:

> "I'm sure you've heard the argument, now we have Google why do we need a news agency? First of all, we produce many of the stories that Google tracks but that's just part of the story. The bigger point is that it takes a huge investment of time and personnel to sort through the mass of information circulating today, trying to understand what is valuable out there and what isn't. We do the selection work, we do the sorting work, we do the evaluation. This gatekeeper function is incredibly important today—so that our customers don't have to wade through that mass of information alone. You need news agencies because you need credibility, credibility built through past experience. You're not paying us for the news per se but for the intellectual work [*geistige Arbeit*] we do. Of course, that intellectual work costs money."

At the Edge of Chaos: Learning the Slot

The heart of AP-DD's intellectual work was the slot island. Given their status but also their stresses, the three slot positions at AP-DD were shared and rotated among the more senior members of the editorial collective (*Redaktion*). Slotwork was considered to be so taxing that the collective's last labor contract stipulated that an editor could spend no more than five hours consecutively in a slot. Friedrich explained this to me during an interview:

> FH: When I started here [in 1993] we used to schedule the slot shifts for seven or eight hours but now we've capped them at five hours maximum because there is such an overflow of stimulation [*Reizüberflutung*], because it's not just the electronic press releases you have to go through, but also, at the same time, you are watching the news ticker, and keeping an eye on the competition. You have to go though the videotexts, and pay attention to what is scrolling above on the big news television stations like n-tv and n24. Then there are still the printed press releases, the faxes, and then you may be on call to do the backup for a big press conference at 8 p.m. and if there's an *Eilmeldung* in that, then you're going to have to do that here. As the central office for both the AP national and international news desks, you have to be ready to field queries from all the other bureaus across the country [*pauses, shaking his head*]. And that is such an overflow of information, so much juggling of parallel assignments, that it's often the case that a slotter here has two or three projects [*Arbeiten*] opened on his desktop at the same time but then has to push those to the side and open a fourth window because there's an *Eilmeldung* that has to be immediately edited and sent out. And then go right back to one of three remaining workspaces [*Baustellen*]. It really pushes you to the limit in a way that not every journalist can manage; it really takes a very special profile to do this work.

> DB: The problem being that you have to juggle so many tasks at once?

> FH: Exactly. You have to make decisions. That's the main thing. It's the kind of work that permanently demands that you make immediate decisions [*eine Arbeit dass permanent sofort eine Entscheidung erfordert*]. Because if you defer a decision, if you say to yourself, hold on, I'm not quite sure, you are going to lose the whole *Überblick* and you will sink into the chaos. That's why the slotter has to constantly click through these smurfs and feeds and he has to decide immediately: Do we need this? Do I need to inform one of the other bureaus about it? Do I need something from them? Or can I just throw this one out? You reassure your colleagues, you're making so many decisions, some of them are bound to be wrong ones. The most important thing is to be decisive. Otherwise, the slotter will just sink into the chaos [*Ansonsten versinkt er halt ins Chaos*].

Given the stakes, it was unsurprising to hear from other journalists that learning the practice of fast-time decision making was daunting. Isidora S., a slotter on the national desk, explained to me over coffee one day that slotting was a responsibility for which new journalists had to be extensively mentored before they were allowed to take it on. It was the informal rule at AP-DD that a journalist had to work as a writer for at least six months to learn the techniques and rhythm of news agency journalism before being integrated into the slot rotation. A slotter on the international desk, Anke H., explained that new slotters always started on the night shift (12 a.m–8 a.m.) because the newsflow was so much slower then. "It's such a huge rearrangement [*Umstellung*], when you are sitting here alone in the center of things, you just have to give yourself over to it."

Isidora confessed to me how terrified she had been during her first solo shift:

> "The first four times you do it, someone else is there with you and then you do it for the first time alone by yourself. And when you sit there in the slot you realize, '*I* am the Associated Press Germany' and it's terrible [*laughs*]. You're afraid to make an error. You're afraid you've left something out. You realize that for the first time you are going to send out texts that go straight to the clients and that no one else is going to check them over first. . . . I didn't sleep well the night after my first shift, and not for many months afterward. Honestly, it took at least two or three years before that feeling went away altogether, until you felt you had things pretty well in hand, that you had an *Überblick*. . . . Actually, when I did the early slot, I used to come home and go right to sleep. At one in the afternoon [*laughs*]. After only five hours' work because I was completely exhausted. Because you have to do so many things at the same time."

At some point in the process of learning slotwork, terror gave way to a sense of pleasure or at least confidence in being able to master the speed and dynamics of newsflow. All the slotters seemed to take genuine pride in their ability to maintain *Überblick* in the face of the dizzying pace and volume of news. All told me at some point that "this work wasn't for everyone" and that it required remarkable poise and stamina, the capacity for decisive accurate judgment, and a feeling for the *Aktualität* (timeliness; see below) of news, qualities which by extension were understood as central to the jurisdiction and expertise of news agency journalism. One journalist, although not himself *reif* (ready, mature) enough for slotting, compared an internship experience at a newspaper with his work at AP and said that he felt as though the acceleration of all news journalism in the digital era probably had less of an impact at the news agencies because "they have always worked in this real-time [*Echtzeit*] mode." Georg commented, "The thing that fascinates me about slotwork is the uncanny speed. I think you find that with a lot of us here, we need that 'kick' [*laughs*]. . . . It's very, very exciting when you have to be really fast but also have to be really precise. It's unimaginably stressful sometimes, but then at the end of your shift if things have gone more or less how you had imagined they would, then it's actually very satisfying."

Echtzeit: Attentions, Transactions, and Distractions in Normal Slotwork

Conveying a sense of "normal" slotwork is difficult, partly because the slotters assured me on many occasions that there is no "average news day." Nor are there average slot shifts in that the morning and afternoon shifts (8 a.m–6 p.m.) were invariably busier at AP-DD than the evening and night shifts. Moreover, the national and international slots, where the majority of my observations took place, each had distinct work rhythms and routines. Finally, and most importantly from an anthropological research perspective, so much of slotwork is silent and individual, a matter of what a slotter is thinking about and paying attention to, that it is only partially accessible to visual observation and to real-time querying, our standard tricks of the trade. I could observe, for example, where a slotter was looking and what he or she was typing but could only guess at how these corresponded to internal thought processes. I could and did ask as many questions as I felt I could about why they were doing what they were doing. Yet, pressures and distractions abounded and even when slotters were so inclined as to interrupt their practice to externalize their thinking and decisions for the benefit of a further distraction, me, they were often pulled away in mid sentence by the need to listen to one of the other slotters, to field a query from a writer, to answer a phone call, or by some fresh piece of electronic information that demanded their immediate attention. Given its norm of silent concentration, slotwork seems highly phenomenological to me and, in important respects, a "black box" (quoting Oskar) to observational engagement. But I will nevertheless reproduce my impressions of two of the "average" slot shifts at which I was present. In order to illuminate different edges and vertices of the black box, I offer two different ethnographic modes, the first more synthetic-retrospective and the second more real-time.

MONDAY, JUNE 23, 2008. NATIONAL DESK.

5:57 p.m. It has been a relatively tedious shift for Georg on the national slot, perhaps one that has not gone exactly as he had imagined or hoped it would. Despite the weekend's excitement over the German national football team's success in the European Cup, this Monday proved to be a relatively slow day with no breaking news of obviously strong appeal. So most of the day's effort was focused on minor reports with titles like "Saxony's CDU Strengthens Its Position in By-Elections" and "Subway Attackers Confess and Express Regret." Georg seems to me to be spending more time than usual trying to find titles that make the *Meldungen* attention-worthy before he sends them out on the wire. "Data Leaks Now in Germany Too" becomes "Personal Data of 500,000 Citizens Available on the Internet" before finally being sent out as "Embarrassing Data Leaks on the Internet." Early in the afternoon, perhaps as an act of resistance, Georg struck out on his own a bit to see if he could generate a couple of interesting story ideas through Internet research. Unfortunately, of the two ideas he came up with, one was already being done by the Berlin office and the other had to be put on hold because no one could immediately track down figure skater Katarina Witt's unlisted phone number. Meanwhile, the *Laufband* (treadmill) of slotwork rolled on. In the past four hours, Georg has edited or written eighteen *Meldungen*, made or received fourteen phone calls, read nine faxes, scrolled the latest news reports on Spiegel Online and dpa's news ticker five times, listened to the radio news four times, glanced at the television screen playing n-tv twice, sent out twenty-eight e-mail messages and instant messages, checked his smurfs thirty-four times, and printed and read dozens of press releases. This is to say nothing of the frequent chats with writers and his fellow slotters to coordinate works in progress, to fact–check, or to simply react to the newsflow. Georg, I have to confess, seems implacable, even good-natured, in the face of all this. When he talks to his fellow slotters and writers he slides quickly into witty banter. But he is almost constantly managing several tasks and exchanges simultaneously. He rarely chats or speaks on the phone without typing or scrolling through smurfs or the dpa news ticker at the same time. He reaches for his liter-bottle of Coke Zero and brings it to his lips without ever breaking his concentration on the screens. His word-processing program has remained open on the center screen the entire time, usually with two or three open windows for *Meldungen*, a spell-check program window, a window for Google for fact-checking, and a window for AP's internal search engine to access previously filed stories and his queue of *Meldungen* for editing. But despite his general good humor, I get the feeling that the shift has been wearing on him. Some of his e-mail messages have been a little testy and the hours have elicited one or two deep sighs from him as well as a rare admission to me that he sometimes wishes he had finished his thesis in American Studies. It couldn't have helped that Georg received a friendly but blunt dressing-down from the editor in chief, who was perturbed that twenty-seven reports were sent out over the weekend on only eleven *Themen*, some of which were, in his judgment, "completely unnecessary. Health care reform? I mean, nothing even happened. Why do we have three news summaries [*Zussen*] on it then? You need to look into some of these things a bit more to see whether there's anything worth sending out." Later, it took Georg almost ten minutes to determine whether the "Francoise" in one *Meldung* he was editing was a man. Just as he is sending the final instant message of his shift to one of his writers ("Let's cut the FDP[16] guy down to one sentence so we can keep this less than fifty words"), the editor in chief walks by with a watering can and remarks to me, "I'm sure you're wondering who waters the plants. It's me, I have to do it. We need the plants. Because the people spend so much time here that you want to give them a pleasant environment to be in. It actually raises production. I spend, I don't know, sixty hours a week here, certainly more time than I spend at home. So you want the place to feel homey [*heimisch*]." Not looking away from his typing, Georg quips to him, "Quick question: Does that mean I can wear shorts in summer then?" The chief editor and I both laugh and the chief editor continues, "That, of course, you *can't* do." "Then how can I feel at home," Georg asks laughing. "Well," the editor in chief says, gesturing to me, "At home you don't have totally unknown people showing up and finding you here in your boxer shorts." "You'll never catch me wearing underwear," Georg smirks back and we are again laughing. "Just as I suspected, just as I suspected," the editor in chief says, chuckling and strolling back toward his plants. Slightly animated, Georg logs off the slot, checks his datebook, and makes way for the next shift.

FRIDAY, JUNE 27, 2008. INTERNATIONAL DESK.

8:02 a.m. I sit down beside Paul at the international slot and quickly glance at his screens to orient myself to what is going on. On his left screen is the website of the California state government's air resources board.[17] On the center screen, he has AP's word-processing workbench program up and he is titling a story on climate change, "Ambitious Plan for Environmental Protection in California." And on the right screen, a feed that combines the output of all of the AP bureaus across the world, what Paul has described to me before as "the mother of all wires." I see that he has the daily openers[18] from the Paris, Nairobi, and Madrid bureaus opened in separate windows on his screen. The dot matrix telex machine to his right whines into action intermittently and scrolls out new stories from AP-New York. I note that he has two AP-NY stories printed out on his desk: "Changes in Energy, Transportation Are Seen as Key to California's Global Warming Law" and "US Court Rejects States' Appeal to Force Federal Decision on Global Warming." I ask Paul how it is going and he says only, "Well, we have Zimbabwe[19] as a bit of a top story [*Schwerpunkt*] today" and continues typing with speed and a certain blunt force.

8:04 a.m. Paul explains to me that when he arrived he checked over the stories that the night shift had left for him, thought over his "priorities for the day," and decided to do a *Paket*[20] on climate change beginning with the California *Meldung* since "the environment is always a *Thema* [the singular of *Themen*] of interest here." He shows me how he loads the text of English-language reports into his word processor and then translates the text into German a few sentences at a time, deleting the corresponding English passages as he goes. I have noticed that he also sometimes works from paper printouts or from the telex and props these next to his keyboard or holds them in his lap as he types.

8:05 a.m. Nadia, the sole writer on Paul's slot shift, arrives and he greets her as she gets set up at her desk. The international desk works with fewer writers than the national desk, which means that the international slotter spends more time writing than the national desk slotter does. The data feeds that need to be monitored on the international slot are also, thankfully, fewer since the primary task of the international desk is to select stories of interest to German news media from other AP national bureaus and to translate them. The intensity of the international slot is similar to the national slot but differently oriented, a trade-off between a reduced expectation for fast-time multiattentionality and an increased emphasis upon concentrated textual production. The national desk slotters were actually convinced that the international slot had it worse. Isidora, a national desk slotter, told me once, "Their work actually requires that you are able to hear yourself think and I think we make it rather tough for them sometimes since we talk so much over here."

8:17 a.m. Nadia asks Paul whether he received the correspondent report from Kenya and without visibly shifting his attention away from his center screen, he says it just came in. Somehow, the right screen is also in the corner of his eye. His concentration upon his story seems positively rapturous to me; he leans closer, pounding the keys without looking down.

8:26 a.m. "So, that's it," Paul says to me, leaning back and stretching for a moment. "It's fairly long, so I'll add a byline," he says and does so. Paul's German text stands at just under 330 words while the English original is over 530. "So you don't translate word for word?" I ask him. "No, not word for word, the important thing is to get the information across."

8:27 a.m. Paul reads over his *Meldung*, spell-checks it, corrects one typo, and sends it out on the wire in less than thirty seconds.

8:28 a.m. Paul jokingly complains to the national desk slotter, Michael, that he sent a correspondent report out at 8:21 instead of more properly on the top of the hour. Michael says, "8:21 is a fine time for a report any day" but then denies responsibility for the timing anyhow. "Dust in the wind," Paul mutters to himself.

8:29 a.m. "Having finished my first job [*Arbeit*], I will now turn to my pile," says Paul, and he sweeps up a huge roll of telex printout that lies on a tangled mess on the floor at his feet. He tears off a few meters of paper even as the printer gleefully spits out more. He uses a metal ruler to separate the stories and then goes through them with remarkable speed, reading only the headlines of some and scanning the full text of others. Nadia complains she's idle and Paul jokes to her, "Oh, you'll get something now, don't worry." He saves only one story about North Korea's nuclear program. The rest of the telex paper is consigned to an enormous waste-paper basket that Paul has described to me on other occasions as "our most important workstation."

8:31 a.m. Paul walks over to Nadia's desk, saying, "Nothing special, really" and then hands her the North Korea story to work on and they chat about it for a few moments. They decide that she will write an analysis of the North Korean political situation with a focus on nuclear energy.

8:33 a.m. Back at his desk, he asks me if I have heard anything about the *Waterfalls* art project in New York. I say that I haven't. Nadia chimes in that she saw the

Meldung too; it came in overnight. I ask if it might be something for them and Paul says, "Could be, I'll have to look at the photos first." And he begins to check in the AP image archive on his center screen.

8:37 a.m. Paul explains to me that since he doesn't see anything else taking precedence [*vorrangig*] at the moment, he is going to do the art story after all, "since the German media expects that we, with our headquarters in New York, are also going to be able offer interesting pieces on these kinds of topics." He opens a new browser window on his center screen and types in the title, "New York celebrates the energy of water."

8:41 a.m. An automated voice announces, "AP News Alert!" and a new red-shaded window automatically pops up on Paul's right screen. He glances at it, points, and says, "It's a news alert from the G-8 meeting in Kyoto about Zimbabwe." Paul does not immediately react to it, however, and keeps working on his *Waterfalls* story.

8:50 a.m. Paul explains to me that he is checking AP's internal archive for information on the artist Christo's Gates project to which the *Waterfalls* project is being compared in the AP report he is translating. "By just typing a few search terms into our own archive, we can basically google ourselves."

8:52 a.m. "AP News Alert!" This time Paul ignores it entirely, saying for my benefit, "It's just the longer version of the Kyoto alert."

8:54 a.m. "I'm just going to check that the URL [for the art project] works, we can also do that right here inside our Reporters Workbench program." The German version of the *Waterfalls* report is 190 words, as compared to the 620-word original.

8:55 a.m. Paul spell-checks and sends out the *Waterfalls* report, again in a matter of seconds.

8:56 a.m. Paul says, "Production is always the first thing for me, but now I'm going to work on the *Tagesvorschau* [daily preview; see below]."

8:57 a.m. Paul says aloud he's a bit irked that the preview item on the Zimbabwe election uses the term *Wahl* [election] instead of *Stichwahl* [run-off election] which is correct and the term they have used already. Michael comments ironically, "Well, he's being creative anyway." Paul is working on his *Vorschau* (preview) on his center screen and consulting the office's planning wiki (see below) on his left screen at the same time.

8:58 a.m. The business slotter arrives, asking how everyone is doing and chatting with Michael for a moment about the European Cup and the "great hopes of the Germans."

9:00 a.m. Paul adds the California climate story and the *Waterfalls* story to the *Vorschau*. He tells Nadia he's pulling out another story on Tallinn, to which she says, "Fine."

9:02 a.m. The national desk is talking over their top stories for the day; the office as a whole has become much noisier than when Paul's shift began.

9:06 a.m. Paul takes two phone calls in quick succession but says little on his end.

9:10 a.m. Paul tells Nadia that he's saved the *Vorschau*. He rips off a new roll of telex printout and processes it quickly.

9:12 a.m. He writes a quick-yet-formal-sounding e-mail message to the offending editor: "Herr B., Please be sure to use the terms we have already adopted. Greetings, P" and he cuts and pastes the Zimbabwe text into the e-mail and sends it.

The instrumentarium of slotting is complicated and its taskscape multilayered. I noted above the importance of visual attention for slotwork. More specifically, I would say that the slotting is enabled by disciplined attentional practices, both visual and aural, that permit concentrated work in a field of fast-moving high-volume informational channels. I was impressed by the slotters' ability to remain deeply focused on their center-screen projects while ambiently attentive to what was happening on their left and right screens, to other information feeds in the proximity of their desks (TV, radio, faxes), and to verbal interactions with their colleagues. It was, no doubt, tiring to hold focus for such long periods of time and they could only be selectively multiattentional to contextual stimuli. Attentional hierarchies existed as well with screen-based information feeds and screenwork dominating slotters' focus, and non-screen informational feeds (with the partial exception of phone calls) and offline interactions typically treated with secondary interest as distractions or amusements.

Although all of the AP-DD slotters and writers with whom I spoke maintained a normative orientation toward engaging spheres of information and politics far beyond the slot island and AP-DD, the intensity and organization of their labor made it seem to me that their most efficacious and reliable connections to the outside world were electronic: the internal AP archives and feeds, the smurfs and news tickers, the search engines, and the websites of clients and competitors. The interfaces of the slot island were thus insulated from a certainly overwhelming and possibly chaotic sea of events outside the newsroom by technical, institutional, and practical breakwaters that made slotting something like a manageable task even if it remained, to be sure, a taxing one.

Insulation was, however, a double-edged sword, as the slotters were well aware; what made the *Echtzeit* (real time) of slotting possible also left it prone to becoming locked into the orbit of information feeds processed by other news journalists, making the outside world of events seem often remote and secondary to the subset of event representations already circulating through the channels of news journalism. Of the many challenges that slotters faced, perhaps the greatest was how to extend their *Überblick* above and beyond the slot island and to think about what was actually worthy of being reported and circulated in the news. Slotters are by no means alone in this challenge; they simply epitomize a general problem facing all news journalists working in the era of digital information. The density and diversity of information news journalists are expected to engage today leaves them attentionally brimming with what appears on their screens and desks alone. With such a wealth (and burden) of information always already at hand, it has become exceedingly challenging for them to pay attention to what is not already on their screens.

Other Temporalities of the Slot: Planning and Coordination

Thus far, I have emphasized the intensity of slotters' fast-time information practices, especially how slotters manage the "overflow of stimulation" resulting from their need to manage multiple modes of attention and distraction. In this choice of emphasis, I have simply been following the slotters' own narratives regarding their work. The volume and intensity of information management and the struggle to maintain *Überblick* were always front-and-center in self-descriptions.

Yet, it became clear to me through my observations and interviews that a variety of temporalities coexisted in the slot. Some of them demanded split-second decision making over word choice or news value, others assumed slower rhythms and longer time horizons, measured in minutes and hours, even weeks and months. As noted above, an important feature of the discipline of slotting is the ability to dampen down the excessive qualities of news mediation to the extent that the slot's newsflow can be managed in a more craft-like way. This meant, above all, the effort to give thematic shape and substance to the day in advance of sitting down to the screens. "I'm not a *Chaosmensch*," Isidora said to me with a smile. "I actually behave much the same way at home that I do in the slot. I like to keep things orderly. Maybe because I'm so good at keeping things orderly, the slot doesn't put me out so much."

All the slotters described morning routines that helped them prepare for the slot. These varied in their details but all involved checking a variety of online, print, and broadcast news sources to get a sense of the *Tagesthemen* already circulating in news media. The most intense phase of planning began when the slotter on the morning shift arrived at the office. Georg explained,

> "Since the early slot also has the responsibility of helping to plan the day, when I'm on the early slot I usually show up a little earlier so that I can, in peace, read a little about what's running today, what came in last night. Watch a bit of Germany's version of the *Today Show*. And so I begin to get an *Überblick*. And I think about what's going to be a *Thema* for the whole day. It depends a bit on the newsflow, there are certain themes that come in, we talk them over, and then they flow back out again. When you figure out the *Themen*, you also have to consider whether they

are playing in Berlin or somewhere else. If they are playing in Berlin then we usually don't have so much to do with them because our Berlin office will cover them. And so what we plan for ourselves is basically the news for Germany other than Berlin, basically politics and general news [*Vermischtes*]. Business news has its own slot here. We look at the *Tagesvorschau*, think about what texts we'll be able to offer, think about which bureaus aren't too burdened with other projects already. This planning goes more or less from 8 a.m. until 10 a.m."

The slotters on the evening shift normally composed a preview outlining the likely top themes of the following day, along with the provisional plans for AP coverage. Their work in turn was based on preview wikis to which all journalists could contribute. In the event of a major news event that could be predicted considerably in advance, the wikis began to fill up with notes on press conferences and local contacts weeks or even months ahead of time. At several pages in length, the finalized *Vorschauen* typically gave a fairly full portrait of breaking, ongoing, and expected stories that would keep the office busy in the event that the day proved to be a slow one in terms of unexpected breaking news.

Figure 1.2 shows the first page of the completed preview for June 17, 2008. The top political theme is listed as the Berliner Rede, the major annual speech of the Federal President of Germany, then Horst Köhler. It lists the archival information for a report already written on the speech (APD7298), followed by the scheduled time for the speech to begin (14:00), the predicted timing of the first reports on the speech's themes (after 14:15), and the first and second summaries (*Zusammenfassungen*) of the speech (15:30, 17:00), followed by an expected correspondent report (*Korr*) normally containing an immediate analysis of the significance of the speech and quotes (*Wortlautauszüge*) at 17:00. Below the Köhler story we find several other important *Themen* organized by the bureau covering them as well as by time. It was quite common that the majority of the planning concerned events and coverage scheduled between the late morning and the early evening. Although AP-DD's clients include television and radio broadcasters and online news media, the *Redaktion* viewed their primary client base as daily newspapers and their production schedule reflected an interest in providing the majority of their reports in time for newspapers to meet their press deadlines later in the evening. Slotters reported feeling more freedom to do reports on unexpected or minor news stories in the evening shift. And the national desk's night shift (11 p.m–8 a.m.) turned to writing more short form reports that could be readily used by radio and TV news broadcasters that operate throughout the night.

I asked Friedrich if he could tell me what portion of AP's coverage on an average news day was planned in advance. He emphasized that news days could be very different but he estimated that for the national news desk perhaps 60–70 percent of the *Meldungen* they send out on a given day could be planned to some extent at least a day in advance. That rather large percentage somewhat diminishes the dominant image

Routing: [dsa brn did dad fru fruj frup]
Stichwort: [Vorschau/Politik RED.]
Titel: [T a g e s v o r s c h a u Politik]
¶   Associated Press erwartet am heutigen Dienstag,
¶   17. Juni 2008, im Ressort Politik Meldungen zu
¶   folgenden Themen
¶
¶
¶   Inland Thomas Seythal   069 27230102
¶   Ausland Nina Gödeker   069 27230107
¶   Berlin Michael Fischer   030 39992512
¶
¶   TOPTHEMA
¶   Bundespräsident Horst Köhler hält Berliner Rede
¶   --
¶   BERLIN   - APD7298
¶   Redebeginn   14.00
¶   Meldungen nach Themen   ab 14.15
¶   Erste Zusammenfassung   15.30
¶   Zweite Zusammenfassung   17.00
¶
¶   Stichwort Berliner Rede   14.00
¶   KORR (Winkhaus)   17.00
¶   Wortlautauszüge   17.00
¶   Stichpunkte   17.00
¶
¶   BERLIN   55. Jahrestag 17. Juni 1953
¶   Gedenkveranstaltung mit Jung
¶   Wowereit   11.30
¶   Meldung   13.00
¶
¶   BERLIN   Europäisch-israelischer Dialog
¶   Rede Steinmeier
¶   Meldung   10.30
¶
¶   STUTTGART   Streit über Altersteilzeit geht weiter
¶   - APD7252 Kobler
¶   Erste Zusammenfassung   in Vorb.
¶   Zweite Zusammenfassung   15.00
¶
¶   WIESBADEN   Sondersitzung Landtag zu Studiengebühren14.00
¶   Meldung   15.30
¶   Erste Zusammenfassung   17.00
¶   Grafik   gepl.
¶
¶   KASSEL   Verwaltungsgerichtshof entscheidet über
¶   Ausbau von Flughafen Kassel-Calden 10.00
¶   Meldung   13.00
¶   Erste Zusammenfassung   15.00
¶
¶   ESSEN   Pk Deutscher Kinder- und Jugendhilfetag
¶   zu soziale Lage in Deutschland   12.00
¶   Meldung   13.30
¶   Erste Zusammenfassung   nach Entw.

1.2 Page one of the AP-DD *Tagesvorschau* for June 17, 2008 of news agency journalism as a fast-time practice. Yet the reliance on planning can also be viewed as an organizational effort to abridge the quantity and plurality of news information into a more practically operational form. Planning also reflects the increased expectations for news production at news agencies—regardless of what a day brings in terms of unexpected news, news agencies consider it both desirable and necessary to maintain a high rate of output.

For their parts, the slotters felt that planning was an essential feature of their work and that no *Überblick* was possible without it. However, several also noted the disadvantage that a high proportion of planned production ate considerably into a news agency's resources, meaning that proportionally less attention and energy was available to handle unanticipated breaking news. Several cited September 11, 2001, as the kind of historical event that completely destroyed their *Tagesvorschau* and justly so. On the other hand, one slotter admitted, "a less significant story arriving later in the day once the plan is already in place is less likely to be covered than an equivalently minor story we had already planned for." For a relatively small agency newsroom like AP-Frankfurt, decisions had to be constantly made as to how to make the most of its staff. In my weeks at AP-DD, I witnessed days when slotters seemed anxious about having adequate staff to handle both unexpected and planned news and other days when they wondered about how to keep their writers busy when there appeared to be such a paucity of news of obvious national or international interest.

The practice of normal slotwork at AP-DD was disrupted only by a single editorial meeting per day. I say disrupted because the editorial meetings at AP-DD were exceedingly brief and focused compared to the editorial meetings that I observed in other news organizations (see chapters 2 and 3). The three slotters gathered at a conference table situated between the writers' desks for the national desk and the photo desk, usually less than a minute before the meeting was to begin. The photo department desk head would also join and then the conference call phone would ring with the Berlin desk chief on the phone, as well as representatives from the Berlin-based graphics department and the Am-desk (American desk), which coordinated coverage of special interest to AP-New York. Sometimes, the meeting was also joined by phone-ins from one or more of the regional bureaus if there happened to be a major news story anticipated in their jurisdiction as well. With little opening ceremony, what then transpired was rapid-fire coordination as each of the slotters and desk heads went over what their *Schwerpunkte* (top stories) were for the day. Although the national desk slotter often took the role of keeping the meeting moving, he or she did not exert any other authority over the other desks. Usually *Schwerpunkte* were presented as decisions already made and they were subject to little discussion, let alone criticism. For example, the editorial conference on the morning of Köhler's speech lasted scarcely seven minutes and started like this:

Berlin [*on phone*]: Over here, it's pretty simple. Our focus is Köhler's Berliner Rede and then we have the few other things you see on the list, but they are relatively small.

National slotter: Good, we're just sending an *Eilmeldung* out with the announcement of the recipient the Georg-Büchner Prize.[21] A certain Josef Winkler, an Austrian. Otherwise, as already discussed, we're going to do phased retirement [*Altersteilzeit*] again, but certainly smaller than yesterday. And we're preparing a *Korr* on it for tomorrow because that's when the decisive negotiation is. So we're going to do it today not so much in terms of the deep political debate, unless one of you gets something bigger, an interview, blah, blah. I still have to discuss the *Korr* on Wiesbaden with D. to see if he has something to offer. The special meeting on student fees—we *might* also do an *Eilmeldung* on that. Otherwise . . . football is still running as you see in the *Vorschau* and that's it. International?

International slotter: Internationally, we have something on the U.S. election—Gore just declared his support for Obama. In California, same-sex marriages are legal as of today, or as of yesterday, and apparently there's a rush to the marriage offices. In terms of general news, we're doing the floods in the USA and in China.

National slotter: Am-desk?

Am-Desk [*on phone*]: Nothing special [*nichts besonderes*].

Photo: We're covering the 17th of June celebration in Berlin and doing *Pakete* for Köhler, etc. Tonight we're doing the premiere of *Hancock* with Will Smith and Charlize Theron. Otherwise, we're doing Bielefeld and the PK [press conference] by the Oetker-Gruppe and we're in Dresden for the presentation of the new cabinet, we'll get the images of that out right away. And then we're in Erfurt for the 100th anniversary ceremony for the Gutenberg School. We'll do a bit of weather and we're keeping an eye on several possible warning strikes, potentially one in Stralsund, those are also about *Altersteilzeit*. And we'll be in Hesse for the student fees.

National slotter: Good, that's fine. Graphics?

For the most part, the editorial meetings stayed close to the script of the preview. Many individual points had been discussed earlier in the morning by phone or e-mail between Berlin and Frankfurt and these had already been incorporated into the wikis. Indeed, most of the participants in the Frankfurt office held copies of the *Vorschau* in their hands during the meeting and used the documents to follow the various points as they were presented. After the participants covered their *Schwerpunkte* for the day, they did, in the same order, an even faster round on their planned coverage for tomorrow. Interventions were fairly few in number and restricted to clarifying the division of labor between the various desks or to sharing news about events that might interest the other desks.

Every once in a while, however, some topic would spark a quick round of commentary or laughter. Two weeks after Köhler's speech, in the course of discussing the following day's news plan, the Berlin desk chief mentioned in passing that he had read in a newspaper about the planned reform of the *Schornsteinfegergesetz* (chimney sweep law)[22] which he judged "possibly not bad" in terms of its news value. "Stupid as it sounds it actually affects anyone with a chimney." When it came to the Am-desk's turn, the desk head, Dan, deadpanned, "Our *Schwerpunkt* is this *Schornsteinfegergesetz*," which immediately produced laughs around the Frankfurt table for the absurdity that a dispute concerning an arcane German craft monopoly law would be of any interest to the New York office.[23] The photo desk head, Britta, immediately promised to make it her *Schwerpunkt* as well and to give Dan as many pictures of chimney sweeps as he needed. "They're supposed to bring you luck," Dan quipped. "Oh," said Britta and paused for a moment, "for the European Cup final, right." The international desk slotter mentioned in passing that she actually knew a "very sweet" chimney sweep, to which Britta joked, "Can I have his number?" The innuendo evidently caught Dan off guard and he guffawed audibly over the phone, which in turn caused another round of laughter at the Frankfurt table. But, like a guilty indulgence, the laughter resolved into a collective sigh at which point the national desk slotter, with perfect timing, suggested, "Shall we move on?" and everyone shifted back into the regular routine of the meeting, the entire ludic detour having lasted thirty-four seconds, exactly.

Two things became clear in my observations of AP-DD's morning meeting. On the one hand, there was a relatively strong sense of desk autonomy and a relatively flat status hierarchy so the norm was collegial information sharing and synchronization rather than the competitive pitching of stories to a decision maker, which is more typical of news editorial meetings elsewhere. One slotter explained to me that the main purpose of the meetings was to integrate each desk's information flow "into a larger complex where you might hear something on your *Themen* you didn't know or perhaps the photo desk even has a contact which the national desk could use, something that could be a helpful addition." On the other, the brevity of the meetings was also clearly driven by the pressure each slotter felt to return to managing his or her own newsflow and workload. There simply was not a great deal of time to discuss any of the *Themen* in a detailed or open-ended way, a necessity that was also influenced by a sense that news value was a relatively transparent quality of information, that is, that it was relatively obvious to all the slotters by 9:30am which *Themen* would dominate the day's coverage.

Deciding News Value

But this sense of the obviousness of news value is itself not transparent. On average, AP-DD produced approximately 280–300 *Meldungen* of its own per day, with approximately one-third of those originating from the international slot and the other two-thirds from the national and business slots. But these reports represented only a fraction of the possible available storylines in a given day's newsflow. What fraction precisely is difficult to determine. No one could tell me exactly how many *Informationen* (pieces of information) a slotter had to process in a given shift. Friedrich estimated that the national news slot received anywhere between 1,500 and 1,800 press releases in the fifteen hours that it was active. Add to that thousands more reports from AP's news agency competitors (dpa alone, for example, releases approximately 650 *Meldungen* a day[24]) and from other *Leitmedien*. Some of these reports recapitulated press release material and some did not. Add to these radio reports, the television news tickers, the occasional faxes, and information received by phone and e-mail, and the entire number of *Informationen* a single slotter processed would probably be closer to 4,000 to 5,000 per day (although, again, certain stories always generated multiple *Informationen* across different media). It is also difficult for me to say exactly by what factor this information volume has expanded in the digital era. But older slotters who remembered news journalism before computerization were uniform in their opinion that the quantity and diversity of *Informationen* had expanded drastically since the days when telex, fax, and phone were the main channels of news information. Shaking his head, Friedrich answered me with, "I can't tell you precisely. But the amount of information has increased massively [*massiv zugenommen*]. There was just less news back in those days." Another slotter responded, "The amount of information has probably increased but the more important dynamic is that we're trying to process that information with fewer staff than back then."

Even were we to assume that each of AP-DD's 300 reports focused on an individual story (knowing that a *Topthema* like Kohler's Berliner Rede might actually generate several reports across a day), we might fairly estimate that that AP-DD was able to cover perhaps one in ten of the stories that reached it. Perhaps less. Georg informally estimated to me that 95 percent of what slotters receive "is just thrown away [*einfach weggeworfen*] because it's not important enough for us." And it is important to note that this 95% was already cleared of spam, junk mail, pranks, threats, and all the other signal noise of the digital era by the slotters' technical assistants (RTAs) before it was allowed to reach the interfaces of the slot island. Georg was clear that the remaining 5 percent did not all make it to the wire in the form of reports but that these *Informationen* were judged at least to contain content worthy of more serious consideration.

So what are the evaluative criteria at AP-DD? When I asked, for example, whether it made a difference who was sitting in the slot as to what reports would be sent out that shift, all the slotters invoked professional standards. Isidora said, "There are general rules [*allgemeine Regeln*]" and Georg confirmed that there was something like a collective perception [*kollektive Vorstellung*] of what was and was not report material.

Although Georg noted that these rules were neither codified anywhere in writing nor even explicitly discussed among the editors. The *Gefühl* (feeling) for newsworthiness, he said, was intuitive and one acquired the proper intuitions only through *Erfahrung* (experience) on the job.

In my interviews, five filtering principles were commonly invoked by the slotters. First, national relevance: since AP-DD is oriented to servicing the entire German national news market, slotters felt they do not have the labor power to send out reports on events judged of only regional or local interest. Second, social prominence: given news agencies' frequent engagement of press releases and attendance at press conferences, the perceived prominence of a speaking subject became a key principle for filtering. The slotters explained that the more prominent the politician, public figure, or expert in question, the more likely their public statements would be made into *Meldungen*. The federal chancellor would always be covered, for example, but even the pronouncements of various ministers might or might not be, depending on how politically powerful and relevant they happened to be at a given moment. The third principle, timeliness (*Aktualität*), was also decisive here. If an event or statement seemed to be temporally or discursively askew, in other words if it seemed to lack a certain presence in the news already, it was less likely to be taken up by the agency. The fourth principle, spectacularity (*Spektakularität*), was connected explicitly to accidents and disasters. The slotters were hilariously blunt, for example, about how many corpses were required to make an accident worthy of being reported. Georg explained, "If there's a car crash somewhere, one person dead, we rarely do it; two dead people, no; with three dead people, then okay, you look at it to see whether we can convert this into a *Meldung*. With five dead people then that's something, that's something we would certainly do." The fifth principle, extraordinariness (*Ausserordentlichkeit*), was the most miscellaneous, and was used to legitimate reporting on stories that would have been judged unimportant according to other relevance criteria. "Like the recent story about a porcupine that a driver saw wandering across the street in Hamm of all places. The police were called in to look for the porcupine [*laughs*], not something that happens in Germany every day," one slotter reminded me. "That story was probably inconsequential to the public according to the standard criteria we learned in school but it is just a nice story [*aber es ist einfach eine schöne Geschichte*]. We'll do those too sometimes—what's curious, what's bizarre, what's funny."

Doubts concerning newsworthiness did, of course, surface and these were often the catalyst for brief exchanges of opinions among the slotters or among the slotters and the writers. These were never, at least in my experience, framed as open-ended discussions of the news in general but rather focused on specific decisions about reports or ideas for correspondent reports. For example, the day after the German football team's European Cup victory over the Turkish team—a game that had gen-

erated a great deal of advance speculation within German news media about its potential to spark interethnic tensions in Germany—everyone seemed somewhat surprised that so little violence had taken place after the game. Friedrich had confided
in me the evening before, "I don't want this to happen, don't get me wrong, but I can
easily see fights breaking out or some *Dönerbuden* (kebab place) getting torched in
the East so we have to be ready for that." Having half-expected to do his follow-up
report on postgame violence, one of the writers, Stefan, approached the national desk
slotter, Ulrich, about fifteen minutes before the morning meeting to tell him that the
news from Berlin was that everything was pretty peaceful overnight. So he wondered what emphasis he should put on the correspondent report he was slated to
write. Isidora had been standing and talking with Ulrich already so she joined in the
discussion as well.

> Stefan: With it being so quiet, I don't really see how we can . . .
>
> Ulrich: Maybe we could do something focused on the reactions from the Turkish
> fans to the defeat, something on the mood in the public viewing areas where all the
> fans were mixed up together.
>
> Isidora: I haven't been following this closely but I wonder whether anyone is really
> going to be interested in "Disappointed Turks" tomorrow.
>
> U: Yeah, but as a portrait of their mood [*Stimmungsbild*] . . .
>
> I: No, I mean in general, that the *Thema*'s through [*durch*].

The slotters batted their sense of the news value of a reaction piece back and forth
a few seconds with Nadia, the international slotter, joining briefly in the discussion as
well. Finally, Stefan offered a new idea:

> S: We could also spin it a bit in the direction of "Will the Turks Cheer for Us
> Now?"
>
> U: Yes.
>
> I: Yes, that's exactly right. I'd suggest looking into that more.
>
> N: For example, in Frankfurt you saw Turks with German flags in the *Autokorsos*.[25]

They discussed possible image and text sources for a few minutes longer, at which
point the business slotter, Angelika, walked back to her slot and Ulrich stopped her
to ask, "What do you think of 'Will the Turks Cheer for Us Now?'" "Sure," she said,
"with some nice photos, but you'll need good photos so people can connect with it."
That seemed to satisfy Ulrich who resolved, "Then that's how we'll do it" [*Dann machen wir's so*] and he presented the new correspondent report idea a few minutes later
at the editorial meeting. At less than five minutes, this exchange was one of the longer
ones regarding news value that I heard during my observations at AP-DD.

Just as the criteria of timeliness and spectacularity converged decisively if implicitly in this conversation, the five principles were activated variously in different situations of evaluation and thus never fully integrated with one another. But there was something like a dominant meta-principle that intervened in all decisions over news value in the practice of slotting. One slotter remarked that he and his colleagues would frequently ask themselves, "What is an issue right now?" (*Was ist gerade Thema?*) both in the context of fast-time decision making and in the context of daily news planning. In this way, it became perhaps *the* dominant principle of news value—at least the one that could trump any of the others. *Thema* signaled, at least in AP-DD slotwork, both what issues were under public discussion at a given time (and thus worthy of news interest) as well as what issues were judged to already be present in news circulation. In most cases, the latter was allowed to stand in for the former since the slotters' main opportunities to judge newsworthiness came through their constant surveillance of what topics other *Leitmedien* were publicizing and in the post facto evaluation of which of AP-DD's own reports their clients chose to republicize. Some issues were considered to be powerful but transient and possessing a short life span (a victory of the German national soccer team) whereas others were considered to be *dauerbrenner* (slow-burners), sometimes quiet but always ready to quickly reignite like the occupation of Iraq or conflicts in the Middle East. *Thema* was a quality that certain issues inherited and that others needed to earn. More importantly, *Thema* was presented to me as a consensus condition in the newsroom; journalists could certainly differ in their estimation of the importance of particular issues, but whether something was a *Thema* or not, in other words whether a topic was a subject of news mediation and/or public discussion, was treated as a more factual condition. *Themen*, needless to say, were not likely to be ignored by slotters. Once a topic was collectively judged to be a *Thema*, that status normally operated as a legitimating factor to support further reporting on it.

When I asked slotters how they could tell what counted as a *Thema* some eyed me curiously or simply shrugged at the obviousness of the condition as though I had asked them how they knew they were sitting on chairs. Others, however, spoke to their parallel observation of other news media, to their past experience reporting on similar issues, and to their gut sense of what would interest an average citizen (often instantiated in the form of an older family member or nonjournalist friend). Because of the significance that other news media (especially clients and competitors) were said to play in determining *Thema* I asked Isidora whether she ever worried that there was a gap between actual public interests and what was circulating in news media. Could news media, in other words, generate the newsworthiness of an event simply by publicizing it intensively, even in an uncoordinated way? She saw what I was getting at right away:

"You mean this situation where one of us elevates a *Thema* and then we all go and do it? Although it is perhaps not a *Thema* at all? Yes, that happens and I find it very concerning because there are times when one creates an artificial *Aktualität*. Simply through our communication with one another. All the media people are revolving around themselves and forgetting for whom they are actually doing this job. We're very influenced by each other. You go out in the morning, walk by the newsstand and the *Thema* is there. You turn on the TV and the *Thema* is there. Then you come to the office and do that *Thema* yourself. The question is how you can withdraw from that. *Should* one even try to withdraw from that? Because if the *Thema* is everywhere, then we actually have to be in on it too."

A sense of the ubiquity of *Themen* in news, as well as a sense of the inevitability that slotters would have to authorize reports on issues that they felt were being overplayed or even truly insignificant, was widely shared throughout the *Redaktion*. I asked Georg about the life span of issues and how he knew when a *Thema* was on its way out. He replied, "You just notice after a while that the media are losing interest in it, when you see something appearing on page five instead of the front page, then you know a *Thema* is beginning to slowly die off. You notice when after a few days you get less prominent people weighing in, organizations that want to make a public statement but got to the topic too late. When fewer people are making statements or when less *significant* people are making statements then we'll spin down our coverage too. But the biggest consideration here is whether a *Thema* interests our clients or not. You can't protect yourself from that and sometimes it isn't pretty. You can feel like you've chewed through [*durchgekaut*] a *Thema* but if our clients disagree then we have to find something more to offer them whether we think it's sensible or not." Indeed, most slotters agreed that they tended to err on the side of republicizing stories already in news circulation in order to avoid the embarrassing situation of not sending out reports on topics that continued to be of interest.

All the slotters had memories of mistakes they had made in the slot and almost inevitably these concerned times that they had thrown out [*weggeworfen*] a story that later was widely circulated. As Friedrich suggested, this was an anxiety that inhered in the job, that since one processed so much information, important stories were bound to slip through the cracks. AP-DD institutionalized a post facto evaluation procedure that was meant to help orient the *Redaktion* to how their understanding of news value compared with those of their competitors and clients. Every day, the editor in chief or assistant editor in chief (or more occasionally a desk chief) would prepare what was known as the *Tagesplay* on how AP-DD's previous day's coverage had played in a select group of major newspaper clients compared to the offerings of their news agency competitors dpa, AFP, Reuters, and ddp. One slotter described this to me as their daily "report card," an accounting of what topics their clients actually chose to run as well as a tabulation of AP-DD's relative successes and failures relative to the other major press agencies.

Figure 1.3 shows a typical *Tagesplay* from May 26, 2008. In addition to the raw numbers of the table, the *Tagesplay* normally included a few short paragraphs in the form of a cover e-mail, which sought to briefly summarize and analyze the results. Perhaps inevitably, the competitive dimension of evaluation dominated the textual portion of the *Tagesplays*, with a language slightly reminiscent of sports coverage. For example, the international desk paragraph for May 26, 2008, concluded, "As evidenced by the table, not a good day. . . . Overall dpa was far in the lead," and the national desk paragraph stated, "A mostly evenly matched day with two fine successes with the *Katholikentag* and Eurovision." The business desk paragraph noted, "We were there with the two big themes, we took the Telekom story from dpa, and W.'s byline was printed with it."

The slotters uniformly found the *Tagesplays* valuable for assessing the *Grundtendenz* (fundamental tendency) in the media regarding dominant *Themen*. But none of the slotters seemed too worked up over the results of the plays and they were referenced mostly as justifications for whether to proceed with coverage of a certain *Thema* or not. Still, performance had an emotional valence. Georg commented, "When I first started in the slot and I had a defeat of 2–5 on some *Thema*, I really got pissed off, or conversely I probably would have been too happy about a 9–2. With time, I've become a bit more relaxed about them." The breaking news emphasis of news agency journalism certainly contributes strongly to its competitive character. News agencies typically strive to be credited as the first to break major news stories and the memories of these victories and defeats, even when they are measured in seconds or minutes, live long in the memory. I recall a poignant moment with Paul from a day trip we had taken to visit the Gutenberg Museum in Mainz. While we were slowly walking through an exhibit on freedom of the press in Germany I heard him whisper, "Oh shit" and I looked over to see his grimace reflected in the glass of a display case bearing the title "1989." When I asked him what was wrong he pointed into the case at a piece of graying telex paper so washed out that I had to squint at it to make out its text. "It's the announcement of the opening of the Berlin Wall," Paul explained, "And you see they put the dpa *Meldung* in there. But do you know that AP actually got that out first? I still have a copy of our report at home." By how long, I asked him. "By at least a couple of minutes," he said rather testily.

Paul was also the member of the AP-DD *Redaktion* with whom I had the most extensive discussions about long-term trends in news value. Like many other news journalists, he was particularly concerned by the growing mainstreaming of entertainment and celebrity news coverage. "The way that news media are chasing these inanities [*Nichtigkeiten*] about various popular figures is a very disturbing trend," he once noted, and then smiled, "but we are resisting it." He drew my attention for example to a remarkable AP news bulletin in which they reported not having reported

Freitag, 26. Mai 2008	AP	rtr	afp	dpa	ddp	spec
1 Rangun: Geberkonferenz für Birma	7			10		
2 Beirut: Suleiman zum Präsidenten gewä	1			7		3
3 Johannesburg: Ausschreitungen	1			2		1
4 Washington:Wahlkampf	1	1	1	5		1
5 Harare: Oppositionsführer kehrt zurück	1	1				1
6 Chengdu: Schweres Nachbeben in Chin	4		1	5		
7 Kopenhagen: Prinzenhochzeit	2			6		
8						
9						
	17	2	2	35	0	6

	AP	rtr	afp	dpa	ddp	spec
1 Berlin: SPD stellt Schwan auf	4		1	8		5
2 Osnabrück: Katholikentag	4			4	1	7
3 Cottbus: Linkspartei	5		2	8		4
4 Berlin: Merkel zu Artenschutz	1			1	1	
5 Frankfurt/Berlin: Armut	5			1		1
6 Berlin: Steuersenkungsdebatte/Ölpreis	3			5	1	1
7 Berlin: DGB-Sommer zu Mitgliederschw	1					
8 Berlin/Rangun: THW-Team in Birma	siehe Ausland 1					
9 Frankfurt/Belgrad: Eurovision	5			5	1	5
10 Zwickau: Tillich/Sachsen-CDU	3		1	4		3
11 Bremerhaven: Jugend forscht	1			4		
12 Dortmund: 5 Tote bei Unfall auf A2	1		2	3		
	33	0	6	43	4	26

	AP	rtr	afp	dpa	ddp	spec
1 Frankfurt/Bonn: Telekom-Spitzelaffare	10			9	1	3
2 Frankfurt: Gaspreise	2	1	1	5	2	2
3 München: Vor Siemensprozess	1			2		1
4						
5						
	13	1	1	16	3	6

1.3 The *Tagesplay* for May 26, 2008

on Paris Hilton to see if anyone noticed.[26] By all accounts, no one did. But his greatest concern in terms of trends in contemporary news mediation was what he termed, in English, "self-referentiality." Paul explained,

> "Foreign coverage is the most independent of this tendency because there the emphasis is on factual events. In Monrovia if there are people on the street who are shooting at each other, that's an event that we report on regardless of what other media are doing.... In the domestic coverage, however, this tendency of self-referentiality is much more influential. We're speaking now of *Leitmedien*. [The news magazines] *Spiegel* and *Focus* send out interviews on the weekend and thereby influence very strongly the 'agenda-setting' for the upcoming week. For example, whether a debate over pension reforms will spread across Germany without necessarily anything concrete having happened, other than perhaps some backbencher has seen fit to give an interview. And then all the media react to it and we, as a news agency, feel then that we have to report it as well."

Craft or Treadmill?

Once upon a time, in the first generation of sociological ethnographies of news journalism, the brilliant works of Gaye Tuchman and others,[27] it seemed relatively clear who made news: journalists. And perhaps needless to say it seemed clear that news was "made," a crafted object, some *thing* in the world recognized by human senses, analyzed by human reason, and then "made public" by further human operations like reporting and editing. Tuchman and her colleagues held no illusions that this human agency was free and voluntary. They discussed the powerful institutional forces that influenced newsmaking and observed that journalism was governed, like all collective social action, by a great many rules, rituals, and routines. Yet, their central ethnographic narratives were built around the figure of the journalistic *newsmaker*, a praxiological[28] subject who possessed at least a significant degree of agency to shape his or her social environment through his or her professional practices and, by extension, a significant degree of influence over public knowledge through the craft of journalism. This portrait of news journalism doubtless drew upon, and reinforced, in subtle ways, the popular praxiological images of news journalism cited above: the fearless foreign correspondent, the hard-nosed desk journalist, the relentless investigative reporter.

But what I heard in my interviews and saw in my observations and what I have sought to convey here is a different vision of news practice than that which Hollywood offers us. Slotting is heroic, but in a different way. I asked Paul once how many words he wrote each day and I gasped a little when he calculated for a moment and told me: 6,000. Every day. Perched in front of his computer or the slot screen, with hawk-like concentration and purpose. Slotters took pride in their achievements along these lines, in their impressive mastery of fast-time information practices that intimidated even other digitally enabled and digitally confident information practitioners.

The journalist as professional, as craftsperson, as praxiological subject, remains even at the heart of sedentary journalism. Yet, as one hears in their narratives, slotters were also acutely aware of themselves as *mediological* subjects, that is, as mediatic operators within a complex, fast-moving mesh of information flows and intra-institutional relations. Their work life was also informatic, overflowing with stimulus, exhausting of their attentions and all too often unresponsive to their intentions. AP-DD's journalists struggled with the implications of electronic immediacy and informational automaticity for their decision making; they were worried about being caught in a world of self-referential news mediation gradually hiving off from the genuine *Öffentlichkeit* (publicity, public culture) they strived to serve and to influence; they felt sometimes disempowered by how clients and competitors defined *Themen* and by how the synchronization of contemporary news media, in Anke's words, made them *zwangsläufig miteinsteigen* (necessarily climb on board).

The slotters, in other words, did not or did not always narrate themselves as the praxiological protagonists of their newsworld; they were well aware of the contingencies and vulnerabilities of their professional agency, of the stupefying circulation of news messages that made any claim to perceive the news as a series of crafted, controlled objects an improbable assault on the truth. Georg had a perfect answer for my impossible question as to who or what made the news today: "I mean, who knows really. All I can tell you is that we're somewhere in the mix." Everything that transpired across the screens of the slot island suggested the same: a dense, vibrant, mediatic mix.

And, yet, the slotters had institutional routines and powerful strategies of attentional and epistemic *immediation* at their disposal with which to constitute a flowscape of news that could coexist with a sense of praxiological subjectivity. What other choice, after all, did a news*maker* have? They had, for example, the filtering principles of their craft. They had their complex and powerful digital information technology. They had planning and evaluation instruments like the *Tagesvorschau* and the *Tagesplay*. They had a faith in good news decisions made elsewhere in the *Leitmedien*, the authority and objectivity of whose news output offered a desirable counterpart to the sometimes harried and anxious experience of slotting. They had their colleagues with whom they could negotiate what constituted a *Thema*. They had an entire praxiological language of *machen, geben, senden, nehmen, werfen* (making, giving, sending, taking, throwing) with which to discursively transfigure the stresses and contingencies of their work into more sedately objectified forms susceptible to craft. With the assistance of so many epistemic prosthetics, it was entirely possible to sustain a sense of praxiological subjectivity on the slot island.

Yet, in conversation, the hard armor of immediation could be turned over or inside out to reveal the soft belly of self-doubt or the supple skin of market supply and demand. And, suddenly, once more the overwhelming flood of information was there, the anxious choices, the exhaustion. Georg told me, "If I'm going back and forth about whether to do a *Meldung* on some topic, I'll look at whether it is out there somewhere else already and, if it is, that will usually sway me to do it." Mediology seems to hold the upper hand. But then Anke said, "It's stressful to come to terms with the flood of information [*Informationsflut*] that's for sure. But the work itself is fine, I seldom find it stressful. I mean, the environment is stressful, the TV, the three computer screens, the e-mail messages, the competition, the telephone. But the work of reporting, sorting, and distributing, that's easy to get used to." What is so interesting about her statement is that she defines an immediated sanctuary—her work, her active self—within an environment of informational stress and distraction. In this, she was not alone among the slotters. Praxiology, too, holds an upper hand.

So what do we make of all this as analysts of news journalism in the era of digital information? Slotters both accept and do not accept the vision of the news as ceaseless liquid flow. Indeed, they constantly oscillate between visions of craft and treadmill. On the one hand, we have excessive overflow, the *Informationsflut*, and on the other hand the frequent material metaphors of *Baustellen* (construction sites) where one puts in *Arbeit* (work); for every aquatic metaphor, I heard computational talk of operations with "interfaces," "circuits," "inputs," and "outputs." We find a sense of news mediation as a vast, unknowable domain and on other hand little mystery regarding the *Meldung* as a textual artifact created on a workbench, and then edited, sorted and sent off on a wire. The slotters, unlike Karl Marx for example, could narrate circulation without specters of extraction and domination clouding the production of value. The flowscape of information might well seem daunting but it was only judged overwhelming by those who did not accept the premise that only 5 percent of the circulating content really warranted close attention anyway. When I asked Isidora once whether she could really find the time to be reflective given the intensity of slotwork, she lowered her eyes and shoulders and then raised them again, meeting my eyes firmly, "It's a good question, but I know *I* can do it." And, of course, she did. The only reasonable conclusion is that both praxiology and mediology inhere in, and are constitutive of, news journalists' understandings of their practice, their agency, and the environment of news. News is made but it is also flow.

What makes these understandings incessantly oscillate, I would argue, is that their pairing is not only adequate but actually necessary for capturing (in discourse and knowledge) the phenomenological experience of news journalism in the digital era. The concentrated attentions of screenwork enable disciplined practices of judgment and articulation, thus sustaining the praxiological imagination of newsmaking as craft. At the same time, the speed, density, and diversity of digital information as well as the constant distractions of environmental noise (both sonic and informatic) signal the limits and contingencies of craft and the mesmerizing fluidities of medium. Wherever attentional focus is directed, there one finds making. In the attentional peripheries, there one finds flow. Digital information has not only filled the peripheries to excess, but it has also elicited greater awareness of just how much periphery (literally "moving around") exists outside our immediate praxiological powers. The polarities of praxiology and mediology thus express practical intuitions attuned to the experience and conditions of newswork today. The lesson for academic theory here is that we need to recognize how formalized, verbalized understandings and knowledge emerge from the bundling of more inchoate attentions and intentions. As Maurice Merleau-Ponty once put it, consciousness does not possess the power of "giving a form to the stuff of experience"—consciousness *is* that power.[29] Praxiological and mediological discourse are examples of such epistemic form-giving, such grappling with the stuff of experience. They render experiential understandings into language, the medium for making experiential knowledge and putting it into motion.

We analysts are by no means exempt from this process. We have to recognize (and seek to explain) a parallel rise of mediological discourse and imagination within the human sciences in the postwar period. That story, which I discuss at much greater length in the epilogue, also involves computerization and the ecologies and institutions of digital information. Today it is commonplace in the humanities and social sciences to schematize the contemporary in terms of flow, media, circulation. The famously "postmodern" collapse of the Enlightenment's individuated rational human agent is a related trope. And yet for all the reports of its doom, academic praxiology endures, thrives even, living on in anthropology for example in the form of a busy industry of analysis focused on humanity's "construction" of this or that feature of their social experience. Nevertheless, academic mediology is also surely here to stay—so many of our theoretical luminaries today are oracles of medium and flow.[30] Just as in news journalism, the increasing experiential intuitiveness of mediological understandings has not displaced or crippled praxiological understandings, it has only recalibrated them for coexistence in the making of truth claims. Is this because we human scientists are also now principally screenworkers operating in dense flows of digital information? It is an intriguing thought. At the very least, our lives informatic are becoming more thickly intertwined with those of other "information professions," like news journalism. Given what we now share in terms of informational experiences and environments, analytic engagement with news journalists can produce uncanny harmonies and doublings, especially when we seek to apply mediological theories to explain native mediologies (or when we lacquer praxiology upon praxiology). My phenomenological attentions in this book do not offer a higher level of truth; they are just designed to temporarily jam these feedback loops so that different signals can get through.

Orchids

One of Paul's favorite hobbies is photographing orchids. Not the spectacular tropical varieties but the smaller, more demure wild orchids that grow across Europe in areas that have not been processed for agriculture. He told me that he first developed an interest in flowers when his children were younger. They would take walks together in fields or forests and ask him what the names of various flora were. So, like any good father, he bought himself a book on flowers, read it, and found himself drawn to orchids. Now he plans his summer vacations to visit the remote places around Europe and the Mediterranean where wild orchids still flourish. He connects with other orchid-lovers via his own websites and he has even set up an impressive digital archive of his and others' orchid photography.

Why, I felt I had to ask him, orchids? "Orchids are relatively new in the evolutionary ladder, only about 30 million years old. So their forms are less stable than other flora, they are still evolving. For example, dandelions and clover grow together in the same fields everywhere but you'll never find any hybridization between them because their structures have stabilized. But with orchids, when you see different kinds of orchids growing near each other, you can also find all these transitional forms [*Zwischenformen*] there as well. I'm especially interested in the transitional forms."

I find the *Zwischenform* a compelling metaphor for news journalism today, as a practice evolving between professional tradition and new media, between technological automaticity and human agency, between attention and distraction, between *Öffentlichkeit* and market, between producer and client, between praxiological and mediological modes of understanding. There are multiple *Zwischenformen*, of course; slotting is just one node among many. But slotwork captures for me many of the crucial trends that inform contemporary news journalism, particularly how journalists are increasingly working with and through screen interfaces and trying to come to terms, both in practice and in knowledge, with what seems to them (and to us) increasingly fast and dense channels of digital information. Slotting is therefore a good point of departure for assembling our own understanding of what contemporary news is, how it is made but also flow. In other words, we are also chasing *Zwischenformen*.

Chapter 2

Click and Spin

Time, Feedback, and Expertise at an Online News Portal

From the author's first conversation with the editor in chief (Max S.) and assistant editor in chief (Markus V.) of T-Online news in Darmstadt, June 2008.

MS: Our basic publication rhythm is to change the site every two hours. If there's breaking news we try to do that as quickly as possible. We can also measure what the user does with the material we make available to him. And if we see that our journalistic decision was false, because the numbers aren't right, then we'll spin our total visualization of the story teaser—that is, headline, subtext, and optics—to try to optimize it. If that doesn't work, then the story will go and something else will replace it. It's hard-nosed. And there's only one thing that speaks against this: *relevance*. There are *Themen* (stories, themes) that no one wants to read anymore although they are incredibly important. Like AIDS, one of the most pressing issues facing humanity. But it wouldn't work for us.

MV: Or, let's say, the run-up to elections. After a certain point, we see that users aren't interested in those stories anymore.

DB: How do you measure the resonance your stories have with users—through clicks?

MV: Yes, we have all kinds of ways. Clicks, visits, and page impressions are the going measures. We have a tool that tells us what happens on the site every quarter hour: where people were on the site, where they clicked, how many clicks and page impressions they made.

DB: Every fifteen minutes. So, continuous feedback.

MS: We are inside a permanent feedback loop [*Wir sind in einer permanenten Feedbackschleife drin*].

Broken News: AF 447

Sometime shortly after 2 a.m. UTC on June 1, 2009, Air France Flight 447 from Rio de Janeiro to Paris lost contact with air traffic controllers somewhere between Brazilian and Senegalese airspace and disappeared into the depths of the Atlantic Ocean. At the time of writing, the circumstances of the crash remain a matter of debate, long-distance forensic science, and lawsuits. The plane had flown into an area of significant, but seemingly not atypically severe, thunderstorm activity three and a half hours after takeoff but there was no communication from the pilots to indicate trouble. About fifteen minutes after encountering the thunderstorm formations, the plane's automated maintenance data link issued two dozen alerts concerning problems with multiple aircraft systems ranging from the autothrust system to the cabin air conditioning to the air speed sensors. One of the final alerts was a chilling "cabin vertical speed warning." Thereafter no Mayday call or other communication from the plane or its pilots was received and it was surmised that whatever had happened, had happened very quickly. The aircraft had either exploded mid-flight or had plummeted from 38,000 feet within a matter of a few minutes. Although fifty bodies (of the nearly 230 passengers and crew) and over 400 pieces of debris were recovered from the area of the crash, it took over two years of intense deep-water searching and a minor miracle for the French government to locate the main fuselage of AF 447 as well as its flight data and cockpit voice recorders, all of which remained intact.

Early speculations as to the ultimate cause of the crash ranged from a terrorist attack to a lightning strike that had caused engine failure. However, after the recovery of the recorders, the French accident investigation bureau BEA released its third interim evaluation in July 2011[1] that suggested that the crash had resulted from an equipment malfunction resulting in inaccurate air speed data and pilot error to correctly manage a high air stall.[2] BEA's reports suggest that as much as we now know about the crash of AF 447, the reason why a technically salvageable situation turned deadly is still ultimately unknown. The *New York Times* was thus prescient in writing only hours after AF 447's disappearance, "As a search for wreckage began over a vast swath of ocean between Brazil and the African coast, experts struggled to offer plausible theories as to how a well-maintained modern jetliner, built to withstand electrical and physical buffeting far greater than nature usually offers, could have gone down so silently and mysteriously."[3]

I arrived at the Darmstadt campus of T-Online—the Internet subsidiary of Deutsche Telekom AG, the largest Internet service provider in Germany—on June 2, about twenty-four hours after AF 447 disappeared but before the crash had been officially confirmed. Over the past year, I had done several informational interviews with journalists working on T-Online's *Startseite* (homepage), http://t-online.de, and was beginning the observational phase of my research in T-Online's news department.[4] As I walked in the door to T-Online's main office, one of the *Chefs vom Dienst* (CvDs), or assistant managing editors, Jürgen K., who had been charged with getting me settled and making introductions to the other T-Online *Ressorts* (desks, departments), greeted me by asking if I had heard about the Air France story, which he predicted would be their *Schwerpunkt* (top story, focal point) for the rest of the day. As it turned out, AF 447 was a story with unusual presence and duration within the *Redaktion* (editorial collective), a coincidence that offered insight into how an online news portal handles a news event of global resonance. Indeed, another CvD, Bertram T., remarked to me a few days later that the last story T-Online had covered for such a long time and from so many different angles was 2004's tsunami catastrophe in Asia.

AF 447 was an unusual global news event in that it combined, from the point of the view of the *Redaktion*, obvious sensational news value with a frustrating trickle of actual factual information. The crash occurred in the middle of the Atlantic Ocean; there were no witnesses and little data upon which to ground plausible theories of what had happened. It demanded both patience and resourcefulness to cover such a story, qualities that strained the informational capacities of a news organization that depended on other news organizations and external information sources for its content. Moreover, the unpredictable flow of new information ground against the forward momentum of a news medium in which frequent updates (or *Drehs* as they were termed in the *Redaktion*) to main storylines were expected by newsmaker and newsuser alike.

The problem of finding *Weiterdrehs* (serial updates) and of anticipating *Nachdrehs* (future updates) for AF 447 thus proved to be more difficult than in a great majority of breaking news stories, eliciting obvious frustration from several of the journalists assigned to manage the main story line. But AF 447 was unusual in one further respect as well. Like other Internet-based news organizations, T-Online utilized a fast-time feedback loop of web analytics to evaluate what percentage of visitors to its homepage clicked on various story links. These *Abrufzahlen* (page view data, including data on site visits and page impressions) and CTRs (click through rates), automatically calculated every fifteen minutes, were a powerful presence in the *Redaktion* and were invoked by journalists continuously to judge whether various stories and the portal overall *funktionierten* (worked) or not. AF 447—a global news event covered by every news agency, front-page news on every German newspaper, and top-page news for every major German online news portal—was a *Thema* whose news value was exempted from routine metrical surveillance for an unusually long time. As Jürgen told me that first morning, pointing at his screen, "I don't need to see the numbers to tell me that this is our top story [*Aufmacher*] today." And yet, I observed that Jürgen did look at the *Aufmacher* numbers frequently during the first few days after the crash and discovered, happily confirming his initial judgment, that AF 447 had generated precisely the extraordinary user interest he had expected.

The extra journalistic labor, attention, and coordination that AF 447 demanded also illuminated more routine issues of sourcing, timing, feedback, competition, and audience that are vital for understanding the normal rhythm and practice of online news journalism. This chapter thus comments more broadly on the practices, self-understandings, temporalities, and interfaces of an online news department. Not unlike news agencies, online news departments and Internet-based news organizations operate to a great extent on a "breaking news" model in which the perceived novelty of a story significantly impacts its news value. At T-Online the entire homepage was "rethought and refreshed," as the editor in chief described it, every two hours between 8:00 a.m. and 10:00 p.m. This meant reviewing the click metrics for the entire homepage, comparing the promise of new *Themen* to the performance of old ones, and rotating content accordingly. Older *Themen* were sometimes retitled with new headlines (known as "teasers") or rewritten to enhance their performance. Nevertheless, the half-life of a news story at T-Online was short. Although AF 447 managed to retain its *Aufmacher* status for eighty-two hours straight and even more remarkably held a spot on T-Online's homepage for ten days, I rarely saw stories enjoy longer than four hours of unbroken homepage presence.[5]

By positioning T-Online's reportage of AF 447 as a red thread within a broader discussion of its news practice, we can explore the intersection between Internet-based journalism and "breaking news" in two senses.[6] First, in the sense of how breaking news is handled by an online news organization with only indirect access to the frontlines of reporting and interviewing[7] that is nevertheless facing the expectation of constant updates to main storylines. Second, in the more metaphorical sense of "breaking," I discuss how the fast-time temporality and informatic feedback procedures characteristic of online news are affecting (and some would say afflicting) traditional practices of news journalism. But before delving into these questions in more detail, some further data on T-Online and on online news journalism more generally will be helpful.

Of News Portals, News Aggregators, and Values Added

The sheaf of marketing material[8] I was handed on my first visit to T-Online describes t-online.de as the number one "General Interest Portal" in Germany with 14.39 million unique visitors and 2.93 billion page views per month. These figures may seem modest as compared with global Internet giants like Facebook (with 900 million active monthly users as of March 2012) or Google (which surpassed one billion unique visitors in May 2011). But t-online.de is one of the most trafficked nodes in the German-language Internet, buoyed by the strength of its Deutsche Telekom parent in landline, mobile, and Internet services, by its offer of free e-mail accounts, and by its multiple service online portal. T-Online's marketing brochure further describes the t-online.de user base in very desirable demographic terms to potential advertisers and business partners. The average T-Online user is loyal and frequent (90 percent likely to use the site more than once per month), of prime working age (63.6 percent are aged 20–49), and professional (67.3 percent), has or is pursuing secondary education (66.8 percent), partnered with or without children (86.3 percent), and earning over €2,000 per month (57.7 percent). What these statistics connote is that t-online.de has not only a firm hold on Germany's social elite but also on its diverse *Mittelschichten* (middle strata). These broad and favorable demographics allow T-Online to position its Internet news service as an addressee of a national public and as a forum for national publicity.

In the *Redaktion* itself, I often heard journalists characterize T-Online as the largest news provider in Germany. This is, I should emphasize, a highly controversial claim among German news media organizations but it is a claim with some empirical basis in independent measurements of web traffic. Statistics from IVW,[9] a German organization that tracks print circulation and online traffic data for the advertising industry, show that t-online.de significantly leads all other German online content providers in terms of *Redaktioneller Content Visits* (RCVs), a measure of traffic to pages with content produced by a media organization as opposed to, for example, traffic associated with user-generated content, e-commerce, or search engine use. In the month of March 2012, T-Online received 239,448,875 RCVs as opposed to 165,047,697 for *Spiegel Online*, which is widely regarded within the German news industry as the most influential German-language online news source. Strikingly, the web outlets of major national newspapers such as the *Frankfurter Allgemeine Zeitung* and *Die Welt* lagged even farther behind with 24,015,434 and 39,290,720 RCVs respectively. The page view data unfortunately gives no indication of how thoroughly users read or digest any of this news content, let alone how "informed" they become as a result. Moreover, since online news organizations guard their internally produced web analytics data jealously,[10] there is no shared pool of data upon which T-Online (or any other online news provider) could compare the effectiveness of their coverage of particular *Themen* with that of their competitors'.[11]

Even taking the gaps and limits of web traffic data into account, it would seem reasonable to conclude, with the hundreds of millions of views of its news pages every month, that t-online.de is a powerful node in the online circulation of German-language news. However, I discovered that T-Online was, among German news journalists at any rate, granted little legitimacy as a member of the German *Leitmedien* (lead media). This privilege is still awarded almost exclusively to print and broadcast media like the daily newspapers *FAZ* and *Süddeutsche Zeitung*, the weekly *Die Zeit*, the news magazines *Spiegel*, *Stern*, and *Focus*, and the public broadcasting networks ARD and ZDF. Nor was T-Online even acknowledged to have a leadership position in online news, a field dominated in Germany by the online divisions of newspapers, magazines, and broadcasters, especially *Spiegel Online*, Welt Online, bild.de, sueddeutsche.de, and ard.de. Arguments based upon web traffic were entirely invalidated, several journalists told me, by the fact that T-Online operated "parasitically" rather than productively in its news operation. Rather than producing news, T-Online was viewed as being in the business of recycling news content produced elsewhere, presumably by news agencies. When I mentioned my research at T-Online in casual conversation with Paul from AP-DD, for example, he asked me the size of their *Redaktion*. When I told him that they estimated the size to me at 120–130 full- and part-time employees, he winced and looked visibly annoyed. "You realize that's more staff than we have [at AP-DD] don't you? And what are they doing with their time, all these *Re-dak-teure* [drawing out the word to indicate his scorn], I wonder. Brilliant investigative reporting? No, they are just republishing news agency material! It's unthinkable!"

The massive potential to circulate and republish news content in the digital era is indeed unsettling to the point of being unthinkable for a great many news professionals in Germany and elsewhere. Anxieties, often well-founded, about the deleterious financial and informational consequences of uncontrolled news recirculation frequently spill over into negative imaginaries of parasitism and value extraction that invariably center on online news providers.[12] These negative imaginaries are, in my experience, considerably starker among German news journalists than American journalists, for reasons that I discuss below. I found that even journalists working in the online divisions of German newspapers and radio broadcasters tended to make few distinctions between different kinds of online-only news providers, interpreting them all, as Paul did, as robotic middlemen that trawled advertising revenue by reposting the content of news stories generated elsewhere. Another (radio) journalist commented, "Okay, in my view, journalism consists principally of bringing new news and commentary to the world. These online providers essentially take news that is already out there and try to repackage it somehow to gain extra advertising revenue. So they're in the information business, sure, but they're not doing journalism. They're the journalism aftermarket, like used information dealers."

The editor in chief of t-online.de, Max S., told me that he was very aware of his site's poor reputation among other German news journalists and said that he viewed such criticism as a defense mechanism foremost: "We are basically the big fish in an aquarium taking a lot of food away from our bowlmates. So they say to us, you have no business being in this aquarium anyway. You do mail, you do telecommunications, so go sell your cables and phone lines and telephones or whatever, just stay out of our media business. That's why everyone says we're nothing." When early on I once innocently suggested a comparison between their news department and Google News or Yahoo News to t-online.de's assistant editor in chief, Markus V., he lost his usual witty composure and replied vehemently, "No, that's not right *at all*. What *they* do is pure aggregation. Nothing self-produced [*selbst gemacht*]. They just turn the content over to get revenue. There's no *Mehrwert* (value added), they have nothing of their own." Jürgen contributed his own opinion later on: "Google is fully automated, and although we are also based on news agency material, we don't just take someone else's content and then send it out again. We actually *read* and *evaluate* the material from the agencies and we decide what of it is the most important. And that *is* a sign of quality [*Und das ist schon ein Qualitätsmerkmal*]." All the senior editors at T-Online emphasized to me repeatedly that although they operated a web portal, in most other respects their work was *klassische Redaktionsarbeit* (classical journalistic activity) in terms of its labors of *Themenauswahl* (selection of themes), *schreiben* (writing), *redigieren* (editing), and *informieren* (communicating information).

Supporting this interpretation, I observed differences between the generic negative imaginary of parasitic aftermarketers and how T-Online actually operates, differences that make it a relatively unique and illuminating *Zwischenform* (transitional form, see chapter 1) of contemporary news journalism. This is to say that T-Online was neither, strictly speaking, a news "aggregator" like Google News nor the online publication center of a print or broadcast news organization. Like a news aggregator, T-Online subsists ultimately upon content produced by news agencies and other major news organizations. But unlike Google News or Yahoo News—which use search algorithms and news agency feeds to locate and organize headline news stories and then repost that content verbatim or offer hyperlinks to source stories elsewhere in the Internet—T-Online employed a large staff of journalists to monitor and select news agency stories, and to rewrite them into partly original (the proportion varied from story to story) texts, which frequently included material drawn from additional online background research. Like other news journalists portrayed in this book, T-Online journalists constantly monitored news agency feeds, paid close attention to the news stories posted by the German *Leitmedien*, had daily editorial meetings, and organized a steady stream of news output. The noteworthy difference was the absence of original reporting at any of T-Online's desks.[13]

Nevertheless, T-Online's news staff was typically quite adamant that they were real journalists and not just "content managers," a term that carries a much more negative valence in German news journalism than in the United States. As Jürgen explained to me during my first few days of orientation, "Look at what we are doing with the Air France story. This absolutely is journalism, bringing together the diverse sources that are available to us, always looking out for a new *Dreh*, making sure the story stays interesting [*Spannung erhält*], even though it hasn't really become clear what actually happened. Even if we don't speak directly with officials from Air France or with family members, bringing together the different sources is very much journalistic work." Not everyone in the senior ranks of the *Redaktion* felt that T-Online's work was truly equivalent to the practice of news journalism elsewhere. One CvD who shall remain nameless commented to me under his breath, "I mean, I don't think there's any question that any of us here would drop this job to work for an elite newspaper [*Qualitätszeitung*] if given the chance." Although not unaware of such skepticism,

Jürgen stressed the evaluational and compositional dimensions of news journalism that existed at T-Online just as at any other news organization. And he said of his own position, with considerable emotion and conviction, "The CvD has the job of distributing work, but that's not just an *organizational* task, that's a *journalistic* task as well. Because he's the one who decides if something is a *Thema* for us or not a *Thema* for us. And whether we'll do a big story or just a short report. Whether we need additional background research for the story or whether what's there is sufficient. Correspondingly, this *is* real journalistic work, we provide *Mehrwert*."

The invocation of *Mehrwert* (value added) here echoes classic praxiological labor theory of value.[14] Like Adam Smith and even his critic Karl Marx, T-Online journalists frequently justified the social value of their news products by outlining the human time and energy that went into remaking content for the benefit of their users. Like the slotters at AP-DD, who coordinated incoming and outgoing newsflows for their news agency, T-Online journalists frequently discussed the social importance of their work in helping a distracted, informationally overwhelmed audience find their way to the issues and news most important to them. By contrast, news aggregators' perceived lack of *Mehrwert* was grounded in their supposed algorithmic automaticity and absence of human epistemic intervention in terms of decision making and composition. This did not lead T-Onliners to claim that they were originating new news content. What they argued was that their labors of evaluation and adaptation added value to others' news content by helping that content to be communicated more effectively to online news consumers and thus to reach a wider audience. The *Mehrwert* was considered primarily *extensional* of values generated by other journalists' work at reporting and writing. Yet, this dominant discourse concerning the vital complementarity of T-Online's role in the ecology of online news was also accompanied by a related practice of critical differentiation. The journalists frequently mirrored back their lack of professional acceptance as legitimate news journalists by positively differentiating their medium-specific expertise at understanding the environment of online media and the specific needs, habits, and desires of online news users.[15]

One afternoon, for example, Markus joined me for lunch in T-Online's bustling canteen fresh from a meeting with two sales representatives from a news agency. I asked him how the meeting went, and he sighed and rolled his eyes before digging into his pork loin. A minute later, he set down his fork and said, shaking his head, "They were trying to sell us on greater personalization of content." "And?" I prompted. "Well, for one thing, it doesn't work anywhere in news. It's a shopping model so maybe it works for Amazon but not in news. Even if we wanted to be in that business, we couldn't effectively personalize content with the amount of user data we're currently able to collect." Markus laughed, shook his head and picked up his fork again, "The agencies would be so much better off getting real numbers on how their content is being used. They rely too much on unproven assumptions like 'personalized content is the future!' But sadly they can't afford to commission their own studies. So instead they rely on these lobbyist studies, which are always connected somehow to the online advertising market. You know, personalized content ultimately means new opportunities for advertisers. That's fine but the *Lobbyismus* (lobbying) is terrible. Video is another thing. You keep hearing, 'Video is the future of online!' Sure, maybe, more video could be a great thing. But where are these studies coming from? Largely from the two largest German private television companies who have *tons* of video content that costs them nothing because they've paid for it already. And they want us to pay again for their video even though we can't run advertising of our own on it. I mean, some asshole runs over someone on the street and you've got great video but what company wants their advertisement embedded in that? Or, 'Air France Tragedy as Brought to You by Mercedes' [*chuckles*]. I don't think so. I'm not saying the news agencies or even the TV companies are ill-intentioned, just somewhat clueless as to how the online medium actually functions."

Although criticisms of news agencies and other content providers occurred on a daily basis, they tended to signal superior expertise gently. And, they did not seem to, as Friedrich feared in chapter 1, suppress recognition of the increasingly central role of news agencies in the digital era. Indeed, all of my interlocutors at T-Online recognized their fundamental and absolute reliance upon news agencies for their livelihood. But they also recognized that this reliance undermined their legitimacy as news professionals, given how frequently and intuitively all online journalism was defined through mediological tropes of aggregation and automaticity. Since "unique content" has emerged as a yardstick of organizational and professional value everywhere in news journalism in the digital era, it was particularly important for T-Online's staff to articulate special forms and zones of online expertise that their colleagues in agency, print, and broadcast news journalism had not yet been able to master. Efforts at differentiation also obscured a deeper convergence, however. Since reporting staffs have shrunk rather dramatically at most western news organizations over the past two decades, the pressures faced by online-only news providers to provide unique content while relying on a shrinking stream of original news input are becoming less and less particular to them.

Between Copy/Paste and Unique Content

Thomas K., the entertainment desk head, said it irritated him how other news journalists tended to take the copy/paste functionalities of word processing as the epitomizing practice of online newsmaking. "In Germany, the print journalists are always saying that online is just copy/paste [*makes a dismissive brushing gesture with his hand*].

[They say that] onliners aren't real journalists and if newspapers go under, there'll be no journalism any longer. Personally, I don't believe that at all. Okay, so we don't do any investigative journalism here, we don't uncover data scandals or some case of economic espionage. But in print journalism, how many newspapers actually do that either? What, 3 percent of them? Most of the small newspapers in Germany, when you look closely at them, are 95 percent composed of reports from dpa. And it's not as if printing them out on paper makes it somehow more intellectually noble while reposting agency reports online automatically makes us morons. I think you have to judge the total work [*gesamte Arbeit*] of a *Redaktion.*"

The spatial and social organization of T-Online's *Redaktion* indeed resembled print, broadcast, and news agency *Redaktionen* in many respects. Like AP-DD, for example, T-Online possessed a central editorial group (known as the *Schlussredaktion*) consisting of the editor in chief and his assistant managing editors (CvDs) whose primary tasks were to manage the homepage and to continuously monitor, coordinate, and review the work of the thirteen desks (news, sports, business, cars, computers, games, lifestyle, entertainment, travel, shopping, parenting, mobile, and video, listed here roughly in order of their relative prominence within t-online.de). Each desk was managed in turn by a desk editor on duty (*Redakteur vom Dienst* [RvD]) who was responsible for maintaining the desk's *Unterseite* (subpage) and for supervising the desk's writers, who could number from one to several depending on the desk and the shift, many of whom were part-time employees. Although the desks enjoyed considerable autonomy in terms of which *Themen* they pursued and adapted for their own subpage, it was a widely understood priority that each desk focused its energy on providing content that was *startseitenrelevant* (relevant to the homepage), since the CTRs and page views for the homepage were typically several times higher than for any of the desk subpages. Three daily editorial conferences (at 8:45 a.m., 12:45 p.m., and 4:30 p.m.) brought representatives from all of the desks together with a CvD to pitch new story ideas and to coordinate coverage. These meetings typically lasted between thirty and forty-five minutes and occasionally elicited fairly extensive and lively discussions of the likely popularity and news relevance of particular *Themen*; certainly more extensive discussions than had taken place in AP-DD's editorial conferences. Throughout the day, the CvDs remained in close telephone contact with the RvDs (especially of the news, sports, and business desks that delivered the majority of stories to the homepage) to discuss *Themen* in their jurisdiction, how the most recent *Zahlen* (numbers) for their stories looked, and what possible *Drehs* each story had.

As in the other studies in this book, office-based screenwork was also the dominant mode of journalistic practice at T-Online, even though its specific forms varied. Multiple screens were, for example, relatively rare; only at the news desk did two-screen configurations seem to be the norm. But having numerous browser and word-

2.1 newsLINE IV, June 2, 2009

processing windows open on one's screen was entirely unremarkable. To streamline and concentrate external newsfeeds, T-Online used newsLINE IV software[16] to integrate forty different news agency feeds into a single composite agency feed that connected to all the PCs in the office via a local area network (LAN). Figure 2.1 shows the newsLINE IV feed for June 2, 2009, the morning after AF 447's disappearance and how the Air France story absolutely dominated the news agency wires. Much like AP-DD's slotters, the CvDs and RvDs checked newsLINE IV, referred to locally as *der Ticker* (news ticker) several times each hour, processing between 5,000 and 6,000 agency reports each day. They also reviewed their competitors' homepages only somewhat less frequently, often leaving a series of browser windows open on their desktops that could be quickly paged through to look for *Neuigkeiten* (new developments). Like other news organizations, T-Online further maintained an extensive searchable database of its own output and a specialized content management system (CMS) for producing and editing texts and images. T-Online's writers seemed to me to work just as intensively as other news journalists, switching frequently between the ticker, the

CMS, and their search engines as they sought to complete their assignments, often forgoing meals and breaks to file texts with their RvD or CvD in advance of the next *Dreh*.

So, both technologically and organizationally, T-Online operated much like the *Redaktionen* of other news providers. But T-Online's legitimacy within German news journalism was not questioned on technological or organizational grounds. Instead, they were questioned for the supposed automaticity of their republication of texts derived from elsewhere. In my observational experience, copy/paste was certainly a widely utilized word-processing function throughout the *Redaktion*. On the other hand, the textual practices and discursive explanations for textual practices I encountered at T-Online stressed editorial intervention and transformation over automaticity. Although practices differed from journalist to journalist and from story to story, copy/paste was more often utilized as a means to developing unique content rather than as an end in itself.[17]

For example, on my first afternoon, I was beginning my observation of the news desk where a RvD, Carsten, and two writers, Freda and Uli, were busy updating the top stories on their subpage. I asked Uli why they did not seem to be concentrating on the Air France story and he explained that nothing new had come across the wires for hours and what little relevant background information they had been able to find themselves was already incorporated into the main story text on the homepage. Everyone was still awaiting what was felt to be the inevitable sighting of wreckage by the rescue teams in the Atlantic. We started talking about the textual forms of agency reports and the kinds of edits he did on agency texts before reposting them on t-on-line.de. "In essence, we send them out [as is] [*Wesentlich geben wir schon rüber*] but we also fuse together content from more than one report, we optimize the text for search engines and naturally we always change the headline and teaser." Like many T-On-line journalists, Uli commented that writing the teasers could be the most challenging part of the process: "They have to be juicy [*reizvoll*] to get the readers' attention, and there's an art [*smiles*] of, let's call it strategic overemphasis [*strategische Über-treibung*], to get the user to click through to our page."

Interrupting him, as if on cue, the phone rang from the *Schlussredaktion* and Carsten answered it, listened for a moment, slammed the receiver down, and called out, "Wreckage 650 kilometers northeast from the coast!" Immediately, everyone else in the vicinity called up newsLINE IV to look at an *Eilmeldung* (urgent news bulletin) that had just appeared from AFP. A minute later a similar *Eilmeldung* appeared from dpa. Carsten and Freda immediately began to discuss which report they should *hochschiessen* (shoot up [to the homepage]) and opted for dpa's. Carsten quickly opened a new text file in the CMS and copied the body of the dpa report from newsLINE IV into it. Within a few minutes he had a new teaser written and the attribution of the story to dpa placed with the text: "Vermisster Airbus: Wrackteile gefunden" (Missing Airbus: Wreckage located). He forwarded this immediately to the CvDs to post to the homepage. Freda commented to me that while it was important get the new information out as quickly as possible, she would now write an entirely new *Zusammenfassung* (news summary) that would merge the new information into the story line for AF 447 that they already had.

This was not untypical of how copy/paste operated within the life span of *Themen* at T-Online. Usually the first iteration or *Dreh* of a story would have the greatest proportion of content copied verbatim from a single agency report. Much depended simply on the day or on impending deadlines. One writer admitted, "If I have multiple assignments or if the next *Dreh* is coming up immediately, I'm much more likely to take the agency text more or less as it is. If I have more time, I like to read around it [*die Sache umlesen*], see how the competition have covered it, whether there's other information I can find that they have missed." If a story lasted more than one *Dreh*, the core text would become increasingly mosaic as additional elements were either copied from other agency reports, summarized from competitors' coverage, or added from the *Redaktion*'s own additional background research. On several occasions, I witnessed Max, the editor in chief, urge his team to develop more research-based content. He opened one afternoon editorial conference by chiding his assembled RvDs with, "Look, it *won't work* if you click on something on our homepage and find just a paragraph with three sentences in it. That is simply too little. A plane crash is another matter entirely. We'll do a report and then keep adding more, more, more, as new information comes in. But if this is something else from sports, news, entertainment, then there's already a whole world of information out there. Even Wikipedia has a background on this whole Rolf Eden story[18] that is twice as long as our contribution. If something is on the homepage then it is a *Thema* and it needs as much lining with content [*inhaltliche Unterfütterung*] as we can deliver."

Given more *Drehs*, the content lining of *Themen* typically did thicken from its various gathered sources not unlike the sedimentary production of a bird's nest. Given the lack of materially or temporally imposed restrictions on text length in online news, new content more often intertextually fused with old content than replaced it outright. It was often the case that new information would be added in the form of new paragraphs to the top of a story page. Older content would then drift down, perhaps receiving a light edit to reduce redundancies and contradictions with the latest *Dreh*, such that it came to function as background material that could be absorbed after the latest news was processed. As in the case just mentioned, frequent full rewrites of story pages were not uncommon for top stories like AF 447. As *Aufmacher* these stories were judged to warrant greater investments of journalistic time and energy. So, for example, in the first forty-eight hours following AF 447's disappearance, the *Redaktion* generated several significant unique content augmentations of their own which were hyperlinked to the main Air France story page, including maps of the crash area, a chronology of events, a question-and-answer page on typical causes of airplane crashes, and a photo series (drawn from news agency images) on the disappearance and rescue efforts. To this they added further hyperlinks to content drawn from partnerships with other providers including reports on the weather in the region of the crash from a German online weather service and an animated graphic on airplane black boxes taken from AFP.

All this is to say that the *Themen* and a great majority of the textual content that appeared on t-online.de had their origins elsewhere in the digital ecology of news. Journalists could only recall a handful of times, all of them on the sports desk, when T-Online had actually been in a position to produce unique breaking news content itself. This would seem to confirm opinions of the "parasitical" character of T-Online's newswork. Yet, copy/paste lacked automaticity at T-Online. That is, copy/paste was certainly an integral procedure in the production of every story and every *Dreh* but it never amounted to the totality of the text work that journalists performed. Discussing angles and emphases, balancing different sources and authorities, rewriting for T-Online's audience, finding additional background information were indeed all, as Jürgen had explained to me on my first day in the *Redaktion*, important aspects of their work.

It is worth noting that although additional research to enhance unique content was encouraged in principle, it was frequently limited by available time and by the active policing of external online sources by the *Schlussredaktion*. Often additional research simply meant reviewing multiple agency or *Leitmedien* stories and synthesizing them selectively. As one of the CvDs explained to me, "I have no problem with a writer *supplementing* [*ergänzen*] an agency text or a text from another reputable media organization with some additional facts; indeed we encourage this in most cases. But there's always a question of reliability with material you find on the Internet. If there's any doubt whatsoever, I wouldn't approve it." Journalists rarely if ever criticized this policy, telling me that they also preferred to work with news agency material because of its higher level of credibility. Bernd B., the RvD of business told me:

> "Our core work [*Kernarbeit*] here is with the news agencies. There is a lot of terrific content out there, great blogs for example, but the CvDs don't take them seriously as sources. And, there's a reason for that. For example, if I find a certain statistic in a dpa report, I don't feel I have to go back and research it, I can assume that if it's dpa, it's correct. That is what the blogs lack, it's a matter of trust. . . . Here in business maybe more so than in the other *Ressorts* (desks) having correct figures is important. And getting information from blogs just isn't efficient when you have to spend a lot of time going back to double-check where their information is coming from. I've

had cases where I've traced a single statistic back through four or five hyperlinks before finding the original source. And then it turns out it's from a Finnish newspaper and I can't read the original text [*laughs*]. We just can't afford that time."

I was interested but not surprised to note that copy/paste was rarely discussed in the *Redaktion* except in the context of discussing other journalists' prejudices against online journalism. Copy/paste was, after all, an utterly routine feature of digital information technology and a thoroughly unremarkable aspect of the *Redaktion*'s informational practices. But there were journalists at T-Online who were concerned about what the proliferation of similar *Themen* and similar texts augured for both news journalism and German public culture. Like Isidora in chapter 1, these journalists were concerned about the ease with which news organizations in the digital era were able to subtly influence each other's *Themensetzung* (story selection) through the presence of constantly observed and frequently synchronized newsfeeds.

When I asked Bernd late one afternoon about how he decided *was Thema sein soll* (what should be a *Thema*), he replied with a certain bitterness:

> "Well, it is all very, very driven by the ticker [*tickergetrieben*]. Very, very treadmill [*Laufband*]. And it's like that everywhere, when you look at the news that is online, you find the same images and texts, more or less [*he demonstrates this by clicking rapidly through the browser windows he devoted to the online* Leitmedien]. Very, very many online media have the same news, often one-to-one the same texts. The end effect is that the news is everywhere the same. And this is a difficult issue because, I'll just be politically incorrect, once upon a time in Germany we had something called *Gleichschaltung*,[19] which meant that one place steered all the information that appeared. If now it is the case that a certain news agency text is suddenly taken verbatim by 200 other places, then we're pretty much back to that situation again. There's been such a unification of information [*Informationseinheit*] that you can even find the same errors appearing verbatim in hundreds of online publications. They're even landing in the newspapers now which is a terrifying trend."

Given his generally easygoing demeanor, I was a little shocked to hear Bernd liken the nodal power of news agencies today to the Nazi propaganda apparatus. But the end effect of thematic and textual homogeneity clearly unnerved him. I asked whether he felt the unification of information, as he put it, had political effects. "That's one thing," he replied grimly. "The people who run the locks [*Schleusen*] earn a certain importance this way because they control the content that flows down the channels. Those who control how the news circulates earn a certain distinction that way. The agencies are gaining more power through their texts. It's only a matter of time. And the stories the agencies don't choose to cover are becoming ever more difficult to get hold of."

This was a moment of mediological reckoning, a grappling with the external presence and power of information channels over which the *Redaktion* had no control but which determined to a great extent what *Themen* they chose and how they covered them. There were certainly other similar moments of reckoning as well, idiosyncratically motivated and articulated as one might expect. At the same time, T-Online journalists seemed to maintain an extraordinary degree of faith in their praxiological powers, extraordinary given the apparent fact that so much of their journalistic labor involved repurposing themes and texts derived from elsewhere. There is, as I argued in chapter 1, no simple calculus to the oscillation of praxiological and mediological judgments; their conditions and expressions are deeply situational and phenomenological. At T-Online I was constantly impressed by how journalists were able to infuse even the most seemingly minute textual operations and genres of writing with vocational purpose. Writing and rewriting teasers was, for example, always invested with considerable time, attention, and craft. Lively discussions would erupt when a CvD would read a teaser out loud for a trial of its impact. At twenty-one characters per line, two lines maximum per headline, the teasers' degree of lexical precision was haiku-like. Berta W., the RvD of the video desk, laughed, "It might sound easy to write so little, but these little teasers, they are really . . . [*pausing to reflect*]. To tell people in so few words what's going on is always the greatest challenge, always these games of formulation [*Formulierungsspiele*], counting letters, all for it to collapse sometimes on just a single letter that breaks the line. You often just sit there and think and think."

But perhaps the deepest and most secure field of praxiological investment at T-Online were the ceaseless conversations and planning that surrounded the updates, the *Drehs*. Many journalists told me that preparing new *Drehs* was the most challenging and intellectually invigorating aspect of their newswork. *Drehs* generated a sense of urgency through their anticipation but also gave online newswork its journalistic depth: "You have to always think in advance," Jürgen explained. "You have to develop a feel for when a *Dreh* is played out and whether a *Thema* has yet another *Dreh* in it or not. This requires both a chain of experience [*Erfahrungskette*] and a subtle feeling for the flow of news."

Zeit und spin

From my first morning at T-Online, I heard this "thinking in advance" everywhere. Given the expectation that the homepage would be updated every two hours between 8:00 a.m. and 10:00 p.m., and on a selective basis even more often, there was more or less continuous discussion in the *Redaktion* of what the next *Dreh* should contain. Although the individual desks maintained their own pages in addition to their contributions to the homepage, the organizational emphasis on fresh homepage *Drehs* was understood and, at least in my experience, unquestioned. The *Drehs* for homepage stories also received far more discussion than any of the other *Themen* appearing on the subpages. At the same time, once the next homepage *Dreh* was determined, discussion quieted down and the *Redakteure* returned to scanning newsLINE IV and *Leitmedien* websites, either searching for updated information on existing stories or to find new story ideas to pitch at the next editorial conference. In the *Schlussredaktion* meanwhile, the CvDs followed the competition, reviewed the web analytics reports, and chatted with each other about the current homepage stories and which were worth further serialization. *Dreh* was as much an epistemic touchstone at T-Online as *Thema* had been at AP-DD. Indeed, for T-Online there was no discussion of *Thema* that did not involve a discussion of *Dreh*; that is, of how a *Thema* would play with one emphasis or another, or of where it could go next.

Like its closest English equivalents, "turn" and "spin," *drehen* has a rich semantic range and indexical efficacy that helps secure its position as the key metaphor for what Markus once termed T-Online's high "rotational frequency." Beyond online news, *drehen* peppers the German lexicon of turning or rotating machine elements. Its popular semantics meanwhile conjure the image of spinning, swiveling, revolving motion. Terms like *Dreh* and *Weiterdreh* suggest turns on a dial, but at T-Online they merged, like the English "spin," into a metaphorical sense of one's "take" or "angle" on a particular story. A very common question in the *Redaktion* such as "*Wie sollen wir das nachdrehen?*" thus translates roughly to "What angle should we take on this [story] in the next update?"

The angle one took on a story was said to epitomize the fast-time expertise of the online journalist and, to a more variable extent, the values and communicational strategies of the journalist's organization. It was a way of constituting personal and organizational differences within a field of content shared by all. Jürgen felt that as a "pure agency story," AF 447 was a perfect example of the importance of the *Dreh* in online journalism. On the morning of June 2, Jürgen's first lesson in the art of spinning was to show me how t-online.de and other *Leitmedien* had covered this crash, which was not even yet confirmed as a crash. It was a lesson in differential strategies for publicizing common information but also in the praxiological power of news coverage, its aesthetics, and occasional errors in judgment (see figures 2.2–2.5).

JK [*pointing to the teaser photo on their homepage*]: Here you can see the image we have, probably from France, of the people still waiting to hear news. It's a very dramatic image. Let's look at what *Stern* has [*types in their URL*]. It's the same basic idea, people waiting, but it looks to me like it could be any airport on any day, it could be delays because of bad weather. Our picture, at least in my opinion, is more emotional, and let's compare it with *Spiegel* now [*types in their URL*]. And they have just this . . . this file photo from Airbus . . . it's not even really a photo, some kind of promotional image of this 330-200 aircraft . . . [*trails off in disbelief*].

2.2 http://t-online.de, June 2, 2009

DB: Why would *Spiegel* use this photo?

JK: Very hard to say [*shaking his head incredulously*]. I wouldn't think *Spiegel* would be capable of this . . . maybe because for so long it wasn't clear if it had really crashed, so maybe to convey a certain sense of hope for survivors? [*shrugs*]. See, at *Stern* they also have an Airbus picture there, but at least an Air France Airbus. It

2.3 http://www.stern.de, June 2, 2009

can't be the exact plane but at least it's an Air France plane. That *Spiegel* is using a promo image for their *Aufmacher* is incomprehensible . . . and [*clicking on their teaser image*] . . . *Spiegel* still has an old story from last night. There's not much new, of course, just this point about another pilot having perhaps seen some "orange-colored dots," on the water, which according to the radio, has helped to narrow the search area. *Spiegel* doesn't have that. *Stern* has it in addition to the normal story,

2.4 http://www.spiegel.de, June 2, 2009

2.5 http://www.focus.de, June 2, 2009

"Everyone's waiting" and our take is basically, maybe someone saw wreckage but basically searching, still searching.

DB: And where did your photo come from?

JK: [*checks this*] dpa. [*checks* Spiegel *again expectantly*]. Well, it's still there. It's morning, I suppose they don't have a lot of staff yet, but I'd almost guess they are experiencing some kind of IT problem. The fact that they let *that* photo stand overnight is a catastrophe [*catching himself*], a *media* catastrophe, I mean. The fact that an airplane crashed, *presumably* crashed, is a genuine catastrophe. This is just a question of how the media go about covering it. Here you have bad example from *Spiegel*, a reasonable example from *Stern*, and you can judge for yourself the one from us. We are the closest to it, though, the most emotional in terms of the photo and the text. And that's what counts for us, that we get very, very close [*sehr sehr nah dran*] to the topic, and are very up to date. That's our value added, whereas this *Spiegel* one has no *Mehrwert* whatsoever . . . [*types*]. Let's look at one more. You see here a similar *Dreh* from Focus, very emotional. Although they don't have anything yet about the possible wreckage. For us, that's still speculation so we are working with a question mark.

DB: So, everyone's operating with the same information but the *Drehs* are nevertheless different.

JK: Exactly, that's what so interesting about this particular case. *Even though* the sources that all of us are using are almost exactly the same. There may be a couple of supplementary things here and there but the story is basically just an agency story. But nonetheless one sees these *extremely* different ways of covering it.

The extremity of difference may have lain in the eye of the expert beholder. But Jürgen's sense of the tremendous importance of how one chose among the stock of images offered by the news agencies captures the epistemic seriousness with which *drehen* was invested in the *Redaktion*. It truly was the locus of expert practice and judgment in the *Redaktion*. In our epigraphic conversation, Max described the *Dreh* as a means of "optimizing" content for the audience and also as a way of bringing "journalistic decision making" into better alignment with "the numbers." Other journalists saw *drehen* as foremost a creative exercise, a way to put one's own mark on a story that was otherwise universal. *Drehen* thus captured both the light and the dark of online journalism; it could both affirm and subvert journalistic agency. Everyone agreed that *drehen*'s dominant characteristic was that it was ceaseless. Although particular acts of optimization/creation had their beginnings and ends, the process of alignment itself never stopped.

At the end of my first week at T-Online, I asked Jürgen if he ever found the constant rotation of *Drehs* tiring. He immediately contrasted the experience of being an "onliner" with his several years of past experience in newspaper journalism:

"At a newspaper, at least in my experience, you always have a point that you're working toward. And that is when the paper goes to print. In an emergency that can change but as a rule there is a specific point at which the day is done for you. You can breathe deeply and relax. And then you take care of a few minor things and go home. At a newspaper you can plan. At a magazine, I don't have personal experience but I have friends who do, at places that publish once a week or once a month it's even more blatant. You can work in a very relaxed way, at least some of the time. Of course it can be very stressful just before you go to press. But the point is *that you are working toward a point*. There's no experience like that in an online medium and that means that the journalist is constantly standing under a certain tension [*unter eine gewisse Spannung stehen*]. This makes online journalism, at least in my experience, the more stressful form, since there are simply no breaks. Because you can simply never switch off [*weil einfach die Pausen fehlen. Weil einfach dieses Abschalten zwischen drin fehlt*]."

The absence of endpoints, the continuity of content rotation, cultivated a certain quality of time, a temporality of continuous anticipation. Jürgen termed this feeling in the *Redaktion* as *eine ständige Erwartungshaltung* (a constant state of expectation). Next-ness exerted a massive influence over the *Redaktion* and conjured effects ranging from stress and exhaustion to joy and satisfaction, depending on situation, personality, and mood. Laughter and relief would course through the *Schlussredaktion* when T-Online was able to get a *Dreh* with a piece of vital information out in advance of the competition or when the first analytics report on a new *Dreh* arrived a quarter hour later with positive numbers. "These are the little highlights [*kleine Highlights*] of this job," one of the CvDs noted.

Sometime after AF 447 had finally disappeared from the homepage, I happened to mention to Jürgen how a friend of mine who worked in the (hopelessly understaffed) online department of a German regional newspaper described his work to me: "You know, I sit there in front of my computer sometimes feeling like a junky looking for my next fix." Although I had perhaps been expecting a laugh from Jürgen or perhaps a wink of *communitas*, instead his eyes lit up and he leaned in to me, saying with great earnestness, "That's a very good description actually. There are these experiences of success [*Erfolgserlebnisse*], you see. I know them from the world of newspapers because I spent a long time there myself—ten years of my life I spent working for newspapers—and there you can have the success experience where in the morning you see no one else has your story. And it will be that way for the whole day. In online journalism, that success experience might only last a minute, so you come down off the high much faster. I think that one has to develop defense mechanisms so that you can walk away from your computer and have a conversation. So that you don't stay just a minute longer to look at what *Spiegel* or *Stern* have on their pages. So that you can say to oneself: it's fine [*das geht*]. But that's something where you have to protect yourself, where you have to admit that this is stress, not just pure fun." "So it can become something of a habit [*Gewohnheit*]," I commented. "Yes, I can only speak for myself," he replied, "but I can say that when I go home I still go online, and not just for a minute or two. Instead I find that I am basically going through my work process in my private life [*imitating himself*]: 'Aha, that's what *Spiegel* has! That's what *Stern* has!' I see myself doing it and I resist. I find that I have to protect myself from myself."

This sense of the addictive quality of constant anticipation was described to me in similar terms by other *Redakteure* as well. They agreed that defense mechanisms were needed to preserve a sanctuary of immediated *Privatleben* (private life) from the sine wave of highs and lows they associated with the restless search for *Drehs* and *Nachdrehs*. But at work little sanctuary was to be found. I did, more than once, hear a CvD tell a RvD on a slow news day that he or she could rest on a *Thema* for a few hours unless something obviously better came along since it made sense to stretch things out a bit. In such moments, the logic of the *Dreh* could, like the planning mechanisms at AP-DD, actually work to create short spans of respite that held a purer logic of *Echtzeit* (real time) at bay. But more routinely, phone calls from the *Schlussredaktion* to a RvD would end with friendly reminders of the insatiability of rotation like, "No rush on it, any time in the next fifteen minutes would be fine."

Portrait of a *Dreh*

AF 447 was an unusual story in that its numbers remained high for several days, signaling strong user interest, despite the fact that new information on the story never exceeded a trickle and very often came in the less-than-desirable form of expert speculation rather than fact. In editorial conference after editorial conference, no one questioned the *Aufmacher* status of the story. The numbers were high. All of the *Leitmedien* were granting AF 447 top-story status as well. And it was a thematic *Schwerpunkt* for all the news agencies, even when they had little to no new information to report. These conditions created an obvious warrant for further serialization (*weiterdrehen*). Yet developing new and distinctive *Drehs* was exceedingly difficult given the paucity and generality of available information. Spinning AF 447 required imagination and tenacity as well as close coordination between the news desk and the *Schlussredaktion*. This led to not infrequent minor conflicts between the desk staff and the CvDs as to the pace and substance of rotation. What follows is excerpted from my fieldnotes and audio recordings:

THURSDAY, JUNE 4, 2009. NEWS DESK.

11:32 a.m. I am sitting behind Freda, observing her morning shift. The current *Dreh* on AF 447 concerns the aircraft's automated maintenance reports indicating major systemic problems just before contact with AF 447 was lost. The *Dreh* has been on the site since 8:00 a.m. this morning and the news desk staff are restless to find a new update. But nothing compelling has presented itself this morning which is feeding a growing sense of resignation that the *Thema* is losing steam despite its high CTRs. Often a RvD herself, Freda is talking with Carsten, the current RvD, about whether it is time to scale back their investment in AF 447. As she chats with Carsten (who is sitting several feet away to her right) she never takes her eyes off her left screen, which is currently displaying newsLINE IV. Hunting through the stream of agency reports she simply calls out to him, "We don't have anyone specially assigned to the airplane, right?" "No, the wreckage is probably kilometers deep by now . . ." Freda interrupts him to say, "But we have just as much to do now as before. We have to endure it a bit longer." Paging through their competitors' websites, she calls out to one of the writers, Christina, and begins to ask her if she'll take over AF 447 for a while.

11:34 a.m. But Freda locates something and says softly to herself "not fast enough." She swiftly actualizes her newsLINE IV screen to look for the original report and quickly spies a dpa *Meldung* filed at 11:04 a.m. titled "Unglücks-Airbus flog mit falscher Geschwindigkeit" (Crashed Airbus flew at the wrong speed).

11:35 a.m. With her eyes still glued to the dpa report, she grabs her phone and calls the *Schlussredaktion*, asking for Jürgen, who's not there. So she talks to another CvD, Christian H., instead: "Hi Christian, I'm calling because of this report in *Le Monde* that the airplane wasn't flying fast enough . . . [*listening*] . . . hmm, okay, good, bye." She replaces the receiver.

11:36 a.m. Carsten spies the dpa report too and shouts over to Freda with some excitement, "Look, an *Eilmeldung*, "Unglücks-Airbus flog mit falscher Geschwindigkeit." Freda sighs, still scrolling through newsLINE IV, "Yes, I just called up to see

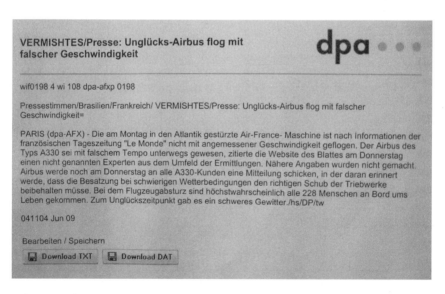

2.6 dpa report, "Unglücks-Airbus flog mit falscher Geschwindigkeit," June 4, 2009

if they wanted it but Christian wanted to stick by this *Dreh* instead. I think it will be our next *Dreh* though." Carsten grunts his assent. Freda opens an offline copy of the main story line, adds a few carriage returns to create the space for a new paragraph and pastes the line "nicht mit angemessener Geschwindigkeit geflogen" (did not fly with adequate speed) into it.

11: 40 a.m. Christina directs Freda's attention to a TV monitor on the next row of desks. n-tv's breaking news ticker has just started running "CRASHED AIRBUS FLEW AT THE WRONG SPEED." Freda turns around to smile at me, "Now we *have* to do it."

11:41 a.m. Freda comments to me that they are bit short-staffed this morning but that she's going to double-up tasks and start working on the new *Dreh*, "just to have it on hand."

11:42 a.m. I ask Freda whether it's more urgent to actualize the story now because other news media are carrying it. "Well, I called up front to the homepage to ask if they wanted a new *Dreh* immediately and they said no, it's okay the way it is. I could wait to actualize our story but I'm going to do it earlier and put it on our subpage. And put in a new link at least, because I think it's important that we have it somewhere online." "You're concerned about *Aktualität* (timeliness)?" I ask. "Yes, it's about the timeliness but they could also call me up in five minutes having decided that they want the new *Dreh* after all. The story can change in the shortest amount of time, the page can turn, if you will. That decision will come from above [*von oben*] and it could be that they'll put in an order to change the *Dreh* in five minutes." Looking away from her screen briefly, she reflects, matter-of-factly, "Nothing is eternal."

11:43 a.m. Freda announces to no one in particular, "Okay, we can start preparing this. I've found a decent photo." Carsten asks her if she wants to write it. Freda replies, "Sure, I'm on it, but I'm just looking at another report about an intensive lightning strike in the region of the crash. Carsten sounds interested, "Oh, yes? Should we do that *Dreh* instead?" Freda is reading the new AFP *Meldung* intently, murmuring "lightning strike" to herself. "But I think they're probably going to want the speed *Dreh* right away."

11:44 a.m. Carsten has walked around the desk to read the new report over her shoulder. "So, *all of a sudden*, another pilot recalls he saw a lightning strike three days ago in the area of the crash," Freda muses doubtfully. Nevertheless, she copies a short text block from the report into the new *Dreh* she is working on.

11:45 a.m. Carsten asks, "So can we get it all into the new *Dreh*?" Freda reacts a bit irritably, saying, "that's *just* what I was doing. I'll call up again to tell them about the lightning." Carsten signals his approval with a salute and grin. On the phone to the *Schlussredaktion*, Freda says, "Hello, me again, I now have *another* report, new speculation about the cause of the crash. The weather experts confirm a strong field of lightning and a Spanish pilot is reporting that he might have seen a lightning strike in the area. A bright flash of light, which could mean that it was some kind of bomb explosion too [*listens for a minute*]. No, those were the orange-colored dots; this is different. Okay, okay, if you don't think there's a hurry, no problem, bye."

11:47 a.m. Freda says to Carsten with more obvious irritation now, "*Very* laid back, this Christian; he's not at all interested in any of this because the current *Dreh* is running well." Carsten calls back sympathetically, "That's Christian." Freda imitates the offending CvD, "Oh, just pull that all together and bring it to the conference." Sitting upright in her chair, Freda declares firmly, "But it's interesting for us nevertheless" and begins to review images for the new *Dreh*. Carsten asks gently, "Are you going to do it as an extra?" "Yeah, as an extra," she replies, "unless they decide they *do* want it after all." Freda begins typing aggressively, developing a new teaser for the news subpage, which, after a few trials and errors, becomes "Drei Tage nach dem Absturz der Air France Maschine gibt es weitere Spekulationen über die mögliche Unglücksursache" (Three days after the Air France crash, there is further speculation about the cause of the accident).

11:50 a.m. Carsten walks over to comment that he thinks Freda's selected photo looks "really good." They grumble a little more about the CvD's attitude. Freda throws up her hands and says over her shoulder to me that "By the time we get around to it, everyone else will have the new *Dreh* already." Carsten shrugs, "True, but there will be another *Dreh*."

Measuring Success (and Failure): The Impact of Clicks

That there would be another *Dreh* was, of course, a certainty. How a story would spin and when it would cease to spin were questions that depended largely upon clicks. Click performance was an organizationally important and palpably present form of knowledge at T-Online. Web analytics were very often described as one of the "great advantages" of the online medium because of their capacity to deliver fast-time feedback on performance and their potential for optimizing communicational strategy and informational content. This lent analytic instruments like CTRs and page view data a certain sacral status in the *Redaktion*. The only condition on which I was granted access to the staff and organization of t-online.de was not to publicize the specific web analytic data of t-online.de and I do not do so here. As Max explained to me on my first day, "The *Zahlen* are the only sensitive thing, otherwise we are a completely open shop." The daily editorial conferences could be, as noted above, lively affairs, especially once the presentations of the news, sports, and business desks were completed. But everyone turned quiet and focused, picked up his or her pencil, and listened carefully as the most recent CTRs were read out at the end of each meeting. CTRs were the single most important factor in determining what stories were allowed to remain in the prized *Aufmacher* and "topbox" slots on the homepage and which stories would rotate. Between conferences, in the *Schlussredaktion* and at the desks, CTRs were a frequent point of reference for more informal conversations concerning *Themen*, *Drehs*, and *Mehrwert*. Even though the analytics reports were available to all the *Redakteure*, it was not uncommon for someone to call out the latest CTR rate for a story that was being covered, especially if it was strikingly overperforming or underperforming its target. A former employee whom I interviewed spoke of a "real click obsession" at T-Online, "because ultimately the clicks affect the advertising revenue."

I was struck that the *Redaktion* meanwhile made little use of another potential electronic feedback mechanism, user comments on stories (*Kommentare*), a feature sometimes promoted elsewhere in online journalism for its potential to bridge the gap between journalists and readers and to create dialogical relationships between them. It was apparently only rarely that journalists reviewed user comments on stories they had produced (I never witnessed it happen myself but was assured it occurred "every now and then" by more than one journalist). This lack of engagement with what would seem to be a more substantive (if open-ended) form of user feedback was explained to me as largely a matter of the pragmatics of time and attention. "Every day, we have four university students sitting over there who do nothing else other than review the user comments and release[20] them for the site," Alexander D. from the sports desk told me. He continued:

> "The commentaries arrive in a central spool and the ones that are filled with curse words, you can get rid of them. The ones filled with too many grammatical and spelling errors, sometimes those too. But everything else gets released. It's simple work but quite exhausting for the people who do it, sitting there all day long, reading what comes into the users' heads. I can't imagine what my job would be like if I had to read them myself. Sometimes you'll get a hundred posts within the first five minutes and 600 or 800 in total. We don't respond to their commentaries. I don't think that is what the feature is for. The readers are usually reacting to the story, not engaging us in dialogue."

Although the lack of time was certainly a persuasive argument on its own, Alexander's "I can't imagine what my job would be like" also suggests a certain resistance to deeper epistemic intimacy with the users and their frequently imperfect, even obscene comments. Part of the sanctity of CTRs was that they offered rules of engagement between journalists and users that were governed by another field of professional expertise: web analytics.

For this reason, I asked and received permission to interview Lorenz M., the head of T-Online's web analytics department, which handles the generation of the quarter hourly reports as well as more infrequent, longer-term analyses of site performance and traffic optimization. In a discussion heavily peppered with the German ontological marker *wesentlich* (essentially), Lorenz explained how web analytics allowed online to be a *wesentlich flexibler* (essentially more flexible) medium than other news media, especially print, since it allowed for experimentation and nearly immediate feedback effects. Lorenz noted, however, the technical potentialities of web analytics were framed by legal codes:

> "In essence, when a user calls up a page, he automatically retrieves the source code that builds the page. In that source code is a JavaScript code we have written which is in effect a pixel-sized element that the user cannot see. When that code is retrieved, it is recorded in our data banks that a 'page view' has taken place or that a 'session' has been originated. . . . For reasons of German data privacy laws, we are not allowed to generate 'Unique User' profiles here. That is to say, as a telecommunications company that sells DSL [digital subscriber line] connections we could, *purely theoretically*, cross-correlate ISP [Internet service provider] client data with Internet usage data to create 'Unique User' profiles but we do not do that. These data are archived separately here. What we do instead in my department is to generate 'Unique Client' profiles that are a mixture of a user's web browser type, the version of that browser, and his operating system. These are all technical elements that are communicated when the user surfs online. We have no way of knowing whether one person or several are using this computer but we can create an image of what is happening on the computer itself."

Lorenz said he was quite satisfied with his department's own performance and obviously very enthusiastic about several new projects they were undertaking, including an experiment in the passive personalization of content that recorded keyword data on page visits into a Unique Client's "cookie"[21] that then activated keyword tailored content in sample areas of the site. "For example, we know whether a client is more often in transit [*unterwegs*] in the entertainment part of the site or in the news part of the site and can react accordingly." Echoing Markus's doubts about the viability of content personalization for online news, Lorenz admitted, "It's just an experiment at this point and we are still fairly rudimentary. They are more sophisticated about this in T-Online's service and sales department." Lorenz ended the interview with the cautionary note that the future viability of web analytics was becoming more uncertain with greater public awareness about data security and privacy issues. "As a result of the competition between Internet Explorer and Firefox, it's becoming increasingly easy for users to safeguard their own data privacy. That has an essential effect on what kind of data we can record. We really count on the fact that only at most 2–3 percent of users don't accept JavaScript and at most 8–10 percent block cookies. If those numbers were to rise dramatically our data and analysis would be proportionally weakened."

Concerns about limits and contingencies of web analytics did not seem to have circulated back to the *Redaktion*, where "the numbers" remained a seemingly inviolable source of truth. The *Schlussredaktion* set explicit target CTRs for every box containing journalistically produced content on the homepage, targets which were well known throughout the *Redaktion*, if nowhere explicitly formulated. *Themen* and teasers that exceeded their targets were described in editorial conferences and more informal conversations as "successes" (*Erfolge*) and those that failed to reach their targets were labeled "failures" (*Mißerfolge*). In the many discussions of *Thema* and *Dreh* performance that I listened to, there was little further qualification of successes and failures, let alone an obvious third performance category.

The determination of success and failure was made quickly. Jürgen commented to me that he could usually tell "almost immediately" whether a teaser would work or not based on the time of day and the numbers in the first analytics report. Teasers could be changed relatively quickly and usually were if the *Thema* seemed a good one. Axel, another CvD, explained to me that he would sometimes work up two versions of a teaser from the beginning to have an alternative ready to go if the first teaser did not perform well. "Sometimes I'll put something online for an hour or so just to test it. Meanwhile, perhaps I'll be inspired [with something better]. For example, here's the teaser I inherited earlier, 'Operation on Rolf Eden's head: Fall down cellar steps' and here's the one I came up with, 'Emergency operation, great concern for Rolf Eden: Old playboy falls badly.'[22] Now you tell me which one is better." I had no chance to respond because Axel's fellow CvD called out instantly, "The second one!" "Correct!" Axel replied. Why, I asked him, because it contains more information? "No, not at all, both tell us about the operation. The difference is that by adding in 'emergency' now you know that this head operation was something serious. So I find it more precise. But it's also a bit more dramatically conceived. It *was* a dramatic event, however, so that's appropriate. I put the new teaser up on the site and it's running better now."

Still, sometimes changing the teaser could not correct underperformance. A story, for example, that fared disastrously in terms of its CTRs in its first few reports would very likely be replaced before it lasted a full two-hour *Dreh*. There was a slight shame involved in having selected an underperforming story for the homepage but nothing that could not be deprecatingly laughed away with colleagues. I never heard a CvD directly reprimand a RvD for poor story selection; this made sense because CvDs knew they were always complicit, having been integrally involved in selecting homepage stories throughout the day. Failure seemed to involve little affect and little mourning. But, as Jürgen once explained to me, cultivating emotional detachment from click performance was a designated part of the mentorship of younger journalists at T-Online.

"Listen, overall based on my experience working for newspapers, I would say that the numbers are a very positive advantage we have over other media. Success [*Erfolg*] is not measurable there. You have the total circulation, maybe the cancellation of subscriptions, every once in a while you may get a letter from a reader, but very little direct feedback on what you are doing. As an experienced journalist, I find that feedback very helpful. But if a journalist is still in their developmental phase [*Entwicklungsphase*], and in online you generally have younger colleagues than at the newspapers, where one's feeling of self-worth [*Selbstwertgefühl*] is not so stable and they have little to look back on to know that they can do this, then when they are confronted with bad numbers it's hard for them. What I do and what I think other CvDs do as well is to read the stories of junior colleagues more closely so that, if the numbers come back badly, then we can say, 'Hey, I really liked reading it, it was fun, well-written, too bad that it wasn't successful.' When you have that additional feedback, it feels more humane than when you just have the numbers."

Jürgen suggested an editorial pastoralism that helped younger journalists understand that bad numbers did not automatically mean bad journalism. But, of course, they could. Here again was a black box. Clicks appeared to all involved to be a meaningful index, and yet they were frustratingly ambiguous. What did they really indicate? Had the user clicked because of the story itself, because the teaser text was compelling, because the carefully selected image attracted attention? What aspect, if any, of journalistic expertise did clicks really evaluate?

Although such questions and concerns lingered, they were not foregrounded in the work and talk of the *Redaktion*. With web analytics very publicly positioned as the dominant mode of evaluating collective journalistic performance, it seemed very likely to me that routinely bad numbers would eventually be equated with, if not an absolute lack of journalistic skill, then at least an individual's lack of ability to adapt to the specific contingencies of online journalism. The pastoral interventions that Jürgen outlined were thus perhaps closer to what Caitlin Zaloom has described in the context of pit trading as training in the acceptance of loss as a means of not losing the confidence and focus to achieve future victories.[23]

But, given the temporality of *Drehen*, the overarching hegemony of next-ness in the *Redaktion*, the pleasure of success was fleeting too. The performance indicators that the analytics reports offered were so fast flowing that they never coagulated into a mobile value form, like a currency, against which journalists could be measured (or measure themselves) in a more absolute sense. Specific CTRs were quickly forgotten and journalists did not claim CTRs as their own or invoke them competitively with colleagues. There was (mostly) friendly competition among the desks for choice spots on the homepage and the analytics reports played a role in that struggle. However, there was little memory and no obvious pride taken in specific past successes—only the memory that one had had many successes, individually and as a desk, in the past.

Bernd explained to me that the best way to "outfox" (*austricksen*) the "fifteen-minute principle" which governed their work was to hope "always for success but to prepare always for failure." One afternoon I watched as he grimaced when he checked his latest numbers. "I'll get a call," he predicted, drumming his fingers on his mouse pad. And he did, several minutes later. After listening mostly in silence to the CvD for a minute, Bertram hung up and leaned back to me, laughing:

> "That was a pretty typical conversation. The CvDs did what we did and saw that our top *Thema* wasn't working so they checked the numbers for the other stories we had on our page and they looked bad too [*shrugging*]. That's why there isn't much point in doing stories for your subpage that aren't relevant to the homepage because if something runs poorly, you need a quick replacement and that's where they look first. Replaceability [*Absetzbarkeit*] is very important. And having a steady stream of replacements. Because once a *Thema* has been tested on the homepage and failed, there's no second chance. It's [*in English*] No-Go Material. Unless something really earth-shaking happens, then it's burned out [*es ist dann verbrannt*]."

The analytics reports thus allowed *Themen* to be given an audition or test marketing. In a sense, this practice transferred accountability for performance failure to the *Thema* itself and I often heard that some *Themen* (for example, HIV/AIDS, as discussed in this chapter's epigraph) were known based on collective experience not to function with T-Online's users and thus were rarely tested again. A journalist's failure would be to select a known underperforming *Thema*, perhaps with the hubris that his or her carefully assembled teaser might make a positive difference. But journalists who described themselves as *erfahren* (experienced) would not make such a mistake. To be "experienced," as Jürgen put it, was precisely to know which *Themen* "are guaranteed to run well, which will never run well, and how to spin the others to produce the best chance of success."

Web analytics could easily have been interpreted as belonging to the mediological forces of automaticity that constrained journalistic agency. Yet, I more often heard them claimed as an instrument for praxiological perfection. Still, toward the end of my time at T-Online, I met a RvD who offered a provocatively gloomy minority report on the impact of clicks on news journalism:

> "Yes, I look at the click numbers. Constantly. And let me say this. My personal experience and opinion is that they lead to shallow coverage [*flache Berichterstattung*], because the shallow themes naturally play better than the serious themes. We have a lot less politics, fewer real stories [*echte Themen*], because it's not the journalist who is really making the decisions but rather the reader. The journalist is only the

means of passage [*Durchreise*]. I see a real danger in it. Like today in Great Britain there's a very, very interesting political story going back and forth but that's precisely the kind of thing that falls away. That's a tendency I see everywhere online, also with the *Leitmedien* like *Spiegel*, which are going more boulevard too. Everywhere it's more boulevard, spectacular headlines, puffing some side aspect of a story out to get a juicy line. Just a lot of panorama and very, very little real news."

An Economy of Attention

The RvD quoted above was not alone in his feeling that T-Online suffered a tension between "the serious and the scandalous" poles of news coverage which was often resolved in favor of the latter. Berta confirmed to me that, at her desk anyway (video), political news just did not work:

"Today, it's the 20th anniversary of the student uprising in China. And I've got good video. The problem is that many videos don't run well when they take place in another country. People's interest stays very close to home except when it's something really extraordinary, like this plane crash for example. If there had been video of the crash it would certainly have run well. Protests in other countries don't interest people unless it's something very extreme. Or, let's say, conflict in the Middle East. At first those videos worked. But there have been too many of them. Now people think, 'Oh, another bomb, how many dead, well, that's doesn't sound like so many' [*DB laughs*]. *Really*, that's how it is. Interest fades and then unfortunately the videos don't work. *Die kann ich gleich aussortieren*. [I can toss them out immediately]. Or Obama has a speech. Not interesting. Political themes as a whole are very, very tough. I don't even present them [at the editorial conference] unless it's obvious that there's something radical there."

Journalists at T-Online felt comfortable voicing the preferences of t-online.de's *Durchschnittsuser* (average user); at least they did so frequently. But journalists did not claim to be able to offer a concrete rationale for these preferences. Instead, I typically heard that users were *abgelenkt* (distracted) by the great abundance of informational options while surfing the Internet. Distraction seemed to disable the user's powers of rational judgment, placing them instead into a state of reflex and reaction. Journalists told me it was a difficult business to gain and secure their *Aufmerksamkeit* (attention), even for seconds at a time.

I asked what the consequences of user distraction were and what strategies the *Redaktion* had developed to minimize its impact on the use of the site. Lorenz spoke of a constant process of site "optimization" to make sure that visual presentation was clear, "that signals do not get crossed." Max criticized at length the trend toward "animated forms of online advertising, increasingly with sound" since users and journalists alike found them "incredibly distracting and annoying [*nervig*]." Axel just shrugged, "This is why entertainment *Themen* are our bread and butter [*Schwarzbrot*]; for whatever reason they attract readers' attention most predictably."

Jürgen explained to me that appealing to emotion was another strategy to gain and hold the fleeting attention of users because it helped to generate a personal, affective investment in news that might otherwise not concern them:

> "Most stories are very general in their implications, and thus may not be able to generate much specific interest for people. The user wants to know, 'What does this mean for me?' Such stories succeed or fail based on our ability to connect them to the individual's experiential field [*der Erfahrungsfeld der Einzelnen*]. They always work better if you can find the use-value [*Nutzwert*] for the individual. So with this story [*gestures to the* Aufmacher *image for the AF 447 story*; see figure 2.2 above], when I show emotion in this image, where those involved don't know exactly what has happened, I have the right *Dreh*. Everyone can imagine this situation at the airport. It hits home, surely it makes one wonder, 'What would *I* do in that situation?' It's surely something subconscious, but nevertheless effective. I've made an emotional connection for you, the user, to a story that otherwise probably doesn't have anything to do with you."

But the appeal to emotions was general in its own right; one appealed not to a specific individual's set of emotional investments and detachments but rather to what was imagined as the "emotive individual" in the abstract. There was an unsettling paradox at the heart of T-Online's journalistic practice (and it was not a paradox distinctive to them). Users' interests exercised a strong influence over the *Redaktion*'s work of news (re)publication, particularly regarding the selection of homepage *Themen*. However, users' interests could not be understood beyond the informatic record of their actions on the site's pages. Lorenz used the term *Clickfaden* (click threads) to describe these records, which conjured for me the image of Theseus, only in reverse. Here, the threads only led one deeper into the Minotaur's labyrinth of user intentions. "Tracking the user," as Lorenz described it, was like retracing a path in the strange hope of anticipating future twists and turns.

User behavior could be modeled, of course, and it is hard not to shake the impression that the common image of mobile, distracted, and ultimately fickle users at least partly draws upon journalists' own experience of fast-time informational abundance as discussed in chapter 1. Pablo Boczkowski has written of the "crowded economy of attention" of online journalists in Argentina,[24] and T-Online's own attentional economy similarly teemed. But although journalists often sought to give voice to users, the limited and generic quality of such acts of mediumship only further stressed that the user was Other, a spectral presence not fully assimilable to the predictive and ventriloquistic powers of the journalist. As Jürgen put it aptly, "These users are also a mystery to us. We know only what they click on but not their actual motivations and interests. Or what will make them come back to us." Where motivation and interest could not be known, journalists worked different angles to capture attention (and clicks), ranging from the commercial (e.g., service) to the informational to the affective (e.g., emotion) to the erotic and ludic (e.g., seductive teasers and playful themes). Yet, none of these strategies dispelled the mysterious quality of users entirely. Since the paradox was structural to the conditions of news production and circulation at T-Online, it could not simply be wished away. And to *not* look at the analytics reports did not seem to be an option. Advertisers were reported to watch the data carefully. The balance of power between user and journalist shifts in an online news organization that takes, as most do, informatic feedback seriously. But the paradox could be deferred,[25] at least temporarily, by invoking the communitarian horizon of nation.

Imagined Community 2.0: User, Journalist, Nation

Toward the end of my time at T-Online, Max became increasingly interested in asking me for my views on how the *Redaktion* operated. I detected a slight embedded anxiety in these conversations about whether I had indeed come to recognize their journalistic *Mehrwert*. I always told Max that I honestly felt that T-Online's journalistic standards and achievements were comparable to those of its peers, and that T-Online's reliance upon agency content and its continuous feedback loop of web analytics were, in my view, more differences of degree than kind from other *Redaktionen*, especially online *Redaktionen* that I had observed in Germany and the United States. Max seemed pleased with this evaluation; it was not unlike his own discussion of the strengths and weaknesses of t-online.de at our first conversation the year before.

One of these exchanges merged into an informal pep talk for the *Schlussredaktion*. Although Max and I were standing by the editorial conference table chatting, he raised his powerful baritone voice and half-turned to his left, toward the CvD desks, opening his arms as though to embrace his team. "Look," he said to me/us, "what we do here is classical journalistic work [*klassische Redaktionsarbeit*]. What we are doing here is not just offering an attractive portal for the products and services of Deutsche Telekom. Instead we are offering a mirror of what is going on in the world. The world is spinning and so that means quick turnover. But even as a middle-sized *Redaktion*, even on our worst days, I see us delivering *Mehrwert* based on how we orchestrate things." I asked him to tell me who was receiving that *Mehrwert*. "You mean, our users, who are they?" he asked, and then continued, now facing me again but still speaking loudly enough for everyone in the room to hear:

"Our user is forty-two, likely male, likely married, likely a good earner, likely a father or mother. But those are just the statistical averages; [*with great emphasis*] our target audience is Germany [*Unser Zielgruppe ist Deutschland*]. We have readers from nine to ninety-nine. We have more students and intellectuals in our ranks than the *FAZ*[26] even has readers. We have more . . . more buffoons [*laughs*] reading our content than *Bild Zeitung*[27] does. We are able to reach *everyone*, but we cannot bore anyone and we cannot overstrain anyone."

A little later, when I was reseated, observing the work of the *Schlussredaktion*, two of the CvDs, Axel and Bertram, ambled over to share, in quieter tones, their reactions to my conversation with Max.

A: When you were talking about the users, I was thinking that there are so many different kinds.

B: Yes, but I understood the question as who we have in mind as our audience. And Max said it right, we speak to all Germany. We're the only ones who speak to both the *FAZ* people and the *Bild* people.

A: Right, it's just that this statistical image of the average user: forty-two, male, well-earning family dad with a house and a garden and two kids, that's not an image that I necessarily have in mind when I do my work.

B: Exactly, it's about Germany.

T-Online's *Redaktion* had no generic user in mind, rather its aspiration was to engage the German national public as a whole. Given the complex history of German regionalism and more recently of political federalism, there are only a handful of newspapers, news magazines, and broadcasters that seek and claim a truly supraregional (*überregional*) audience. But, as has been discussed at length by other scholars, the Internet enables new scales, temporalities, and, perhaps, modes of publicity.[28] As the most trafficked general interest portal in Germany and as a branch of Germany's national telecommunications company, t-online.de saw itself as a news organization with a naturally holistic relationship to Germany, one that cut across not just regions but across political ideologies and social strata as well. T-Online's user base was frequently described to me as Germany "in microcosm" and journalists frequently stressed that t-online.de was singular in this regard.

I felt that the appeal to nation was something more than a marketing strategy, however. It was also a way of reorienting the relationship between journalist and audience in the context of online publicity. Online media have clearly challenged the authority of the journalistic expert, long known in German-speaking Central Europe as a paternalist "educator of opinion."[29] It is often claimed both by practitioners and nonpractitioners that online media have already dissolved (or will soon dissolve) the authorial sovereignty of professional journalists and disperse the power to create, edit, and circulate news information across a more lateralized network or web.[30] Although such claims frequently, in my opinion, underestimate or ignore the nodal power of large media organizations and the inertia of professional traditions, they correctly identify how the widespread availability of electronic feedback has very significantly impacted the practice and self-understanding of news journalism. As Jürgen noted, "When you write for a newspaper, there is no way to know who has even glanced at your article, let alone read it. With us, you know almost immediately what the reaction is, even if you do not, strictly speaking, know why the reaction happened."

The immediacy and continuity of feedback juxtaposes a sense of unprecedented propinquity and intimacy between users and journalists with a confrontation of "autological" limits.[31] In a sense, the more that is known about the user, the less that remains unknown seems knowable. Users can be profiled as "Unique Clients" with perceptible individualized behavior patterns yet they remain imperviously mob-like in the analytical aggregate, bruising the integrity of journalistic authority with a massive crush of nonexpert interests and desires. Under these conditions, to make of this mob of semiknown ungovernable users a nation was a matter of safeguarding what Michael Jackson, following R.D. Laing, terms "ontological security."[32] Germany was an abstraction too, of course, but an abstraction of indexical us-ness in which the journalist too could take shelter. The imagined community of national publicity thus helped to assuage anxieties over the still mysterious qualities and powers of users. The data of the analytics reports could be framed not in terms of the unanswerable question—*Was will der User?*[33]—but rather in terms of the security of their punctuality. Every fifteen minutes one felt not the outstretched hands of the encircling masses but rather the steady pulse of the nation's beating heart, the response of the national audience to the call of the *Redaktion*, a pattern that soothed if never fully silenced the murmurs of mediological self-doubt.

Figuring the user audience as Germany even allowed for the remaking of expert paternalism in the heart of the allegedly antihierarchical online revolution. Clicks, after all, could not speak beyond binaristic patterns such as desire and aversion, or attention and inattention. The yes/no of CTRs was the language of children, of easily distracted creatures of simple interests and desires. Users were portrayed not as reasoning beings but as affective subjects, collections of "trajectories and circuits,"[34] that could be nudged this way or that. There was still a strong need, the *Redaktion* was convinced, of journalistic expertise to aid such creatures in broadening their awareness and deepening their capacities of understanding and action. How exactly this need was to be fulfilled was unclear given the apparent hegemony of user feedback over journalistic judgment but its promise nonetheless hovered in the air. Lorenz and the CvDs, for example, discussed the architecture of t-online.de as though they were urban planners and the site itself something like a cityscape. The user was constantly tracked *unterwegs* (in transit) there, moving through a rich deictic environment of front and backs, aboves and belows. T-Online designed and implemented signals for navigating that environment, and for guiding users to the attractively positioned vital information assembled on their behalf. The visual pollution of advertising was minimized to the extent this was possible, permitting the necessary communication of market information without cultivating semiotic blight and user alienation. The website was *wesentlich* a controlled environment, a city of information designed to acknowledge the expertise and authority of the online journalist.

If I had any doubts as to T-Online journalists' capacity to maintain a praxiological ideology of professional privilege in the face of a regime of publicity that seemed destined to subvert their authority, these thoughts were dispelled by Max's booming laughter. Once I asked him whether he thought there was any value to the kinds of "citizen journalism" experiments that were popping up in news organizations in the United States. "Well, I can tell you one thing," Max chuckled with obvious disdain, "We're not going to act like *Bild Zeitung* and encourage so-called *Leser-reporter* [reader-reporters] to fan out across the country. Which has led to fire departments and police departments across Germany complaining to *Bild* that their so-called reader-reporters have hindered rescue and recovery efforts. Because just as they're about to break down a door, someone asks them, 'Wait a sec, let me just snap a photograph of you. I'm from *the press*' [*shakes with laughter*].That actually happened." The most amusing thing for Max seemed to be the idea that a citizen could have deluded himself into believing he was a journalist. Of course, laughter sometimes, but not always, signals authority. At some point, the laughter of diminishment can also be construed as a hysterical form of displacement and denial.

Die Zukunft gehört uns: Ends, Fears, and Loops of Online News

Most *Themen* come to an end. On the afternoon of June 5, 2009, AF 447 had finally reached the point where it was beginning to burn out. I sat with Bertram and Wolfgang in the *Schlussredaktion* listening as they debated whether it would be possible to squeeze one more *Dreh* out of the story. The shock and excitement surrounding the breaking news of the crash was long gone. Although more questions than answers remained about what had actually happened, the trickle of incoming new information did not seem to be particularly enlightening. The holy grail of the search effort at this point—AF 447's flight data recorders—seemed in all likelihood unrecoverable from the depths of the Atlantic Ocean. The current teaser, "Marines find only sea debris," had begun with solid numbers at 8:00 a.m. that morning but had lost almost 50 percent of its CTR since. Wolfgang commented, "Reporting on a failed search for new information gets tedious after a while. It's becoming a forensics story." Meanwhile, both of the CvDs had invested a good chunk of time and energy that morning scouring the agency reports for something around which a *Weiterdreh* could be built. Wolfgang had found a report on a storm expert who claimed that the thunderstorm front that AF 447 flew into might have been worse than previously estimated. "Might have been . . ." Wolfgang sighed quietly at his screen in typically phlegmatic fashion. Bertram had meanwhile found an agency report from AFP that the aircraft might have sent contradictory signals in its last automated transmission and another *Meldung* that reported the official confirmation from the French accident investigation bureau BEA that the plane had been flying at the wrong speed. The former piece of information was speculative and inconclusive; the latter simply an official confirmation of a report that had been circulating since the day before. Bertram agreed that all this was not much to hang a new *Dreh* on. But there was nothing else obviously more compelling in queue to become the next *Aufmacher*. The following exchange took place between 2:34 p.m. and 2:40 p.m. with neither Bertram or Wolfgang ever taking their eyes away from their monitors and newsLINE IV.

B [*to W*]: So now we have to see whether we can do another *Dreh* on the contradictory signals . . .

W: As I see it, I'd be glad to get rid of the story, our *Aufmacher*.

B [*quickly, seeking conciliation*]: Yes, yes, no, of course we can also do that. But didn't you see that *FAZ* has just sent out the contradictory signals?

W [*still seemingly unpersuaded*]: Hmm. And we don't have anything more for Obama? Or, on Gordon Brown?

B: We could perhaps do Gordon Brown as a *Schlagzeile*.[35]

W: On the special zone in Switzerland?[36]

B: Isn't that over? I thought the referendum failed [*pointing to an AFP report*]. Meanwhile there is also new evidence that the Airbus had speed problems.

W [*quietly*]: But haven't we heard that already?

B [*not hearing or pretending not to hear W., picks up the phone and calls the news desk*]: Hi, are you the one responsible for the Airbus story or . . . because we're just debating now how we might *weiterdrehen* the story. There was just a report on mounting evidence of speed problems . . . It was AFP, twelve minutes ago . . . We've had this *Dreh* since early this morning that what they found actually didn't come from the aircraft and now we absolutely need something new. In the latest summaries there's more on the speed problems. Came in around noon today. And then another report that the aircraft sent out contradictory data. So those are at least two new angles we can use [*chuckles*] . . . It's all the same to me but . . . Why don't you let me know if you can make something out of it . . . Doesn't matter, send it in twenty-five minutes or thirty-five, just so that it's done in the next little while, thanks [*rings off*].

W [*to B*]: Did you order something?

B: Yeah, a new *Dreh* for the Airbus story: the speed problems, that they were confirmed, and then the irregular data angle. Both point in the same direction, same angle. Good, and then we should decide whether we should make the GM-Opel story the *Aufmacher*, whether it's *wesentlich* starker [*shrugs*]. I don't know.

W: I'm not sure it [the GM-Opel story] would be any better.

B [*somewhat noncommittally*]: Well, I'm no oracle [*chuckles*]. If we're wrong, we can just bring it down. Let's give it one more shot.

The new *Dreh* for AF 447, "Crashed Airbus transmitted contradictory data," appeared at 4:00 p.m. and remained the *Aufmacher*. But Bertram and Wolfgang's ambivalence already suggested that the end was in sight. AF 447 lost its top-story status the following morning, replaced by a report that the Bayer Leverkusen football club had hired a new coach. Although AF 447 remained on the t-online.de homepage until June 10, it did not return to the *Aufmacher* slot except briefly when the first human remains were located on June 6. The *Redaktion* spun onward to new *Themen*.

I have little doubt that my portrait of the work of the T-Online *Redaktion* would only confirm the opinion of many news journalists who doubt their claims to practice journalism. But Max told me he could also sense the desire in T-Online's competitors:

"They run us down, say we are nothing. Fine. But there are so many who would lick their fingers to be in our position. Over fifteen million 'Unique Audience.' Every kind of person in Germany represented. And we are not in the position of having to adapt ourselves to the online medium like the newspapers are. We grew up organically in this medium. So you could say for those of us who are helping to shape this medium that the future belongs to us [*die Zukunft gehört uns*]. I think that all of our competitors realize this whether they approve of it or not."

For Max, the disdain of other journalists, however painful, should be viewed ultimately as a sign of their own anxieties. If it is indeed a matter of anxieties then we should recall Jacques Lacan's bon mot that anxiety is the one affect that does not lie.

Online news captures, perhaps even epitomizes, many of the conditions, understandings, and apparent paradoxes of news in the era of digital information more generally. T-Online's *Zwischenform* signals broader tensions between automaticity and agency in contemporary journalistic practice and the tensions between generativity and (re)circulation within digital newsflow. At T-Online, the *Redaktion* normally emphasized the positive aspects of digital information. The new scales, speeds, and sensitivities of online publicity were routinely lauded. It was generally felt that online journalism exceeded all other news media in terms of its capacity to "optimize user experience." Even though this capacity was more often put in terms of commerce rather than citizenship, journalists stressed that web analytics created a kind of fast-time participatory feedback unknown to other media. But, at the same time, as we have heard, some journalists expressed concerns about the hegemony of CTRs and the treadmill of news agency dependency. The pleasures of a national audience were offset by anxieties that the influence of users was metastasizing, dissolving the public sphere into a mass of private interests, and negating the epistemic authority of journalists.

This delicate balance of praxiological and mediological understandings made perfect sense within the organizational environment of T-Online but was seemingly less credible outside it. I had, for example, great difficulty discussing t-online.de with other news journalists because it quickly became clear that they knew little about the organization and did not think it worth their while to learn more. When I asked a regional newspaper journalist who did admit having visited t-online.de whether he agreed with Max's point that "the future belongs to them." He laughed drily, "Well, one hopes not, those would be dark days for journalism." I asked him to expand and he quickly slid from the specific case of T-Online to the false promises of the Internet for news journalism.

> "The big promise of the Internet was really supposed to be 'user-generated content,' no? Everyone thought that as the Internet came into itself, that all the people would want to become journalists themselves and start writing and that it would be so easy for people to express themselves and to share important information. But I don't see it that way. There are certainly portals where discussions and exchanges are taking place, but very, very few portals where discussions are at a level of quality [*Qualitätsniveau*] that anyone would want to be involved in them. Basically, the portals are operating on a *Stammtisch* level.[37] To put it brutally, when you leave people to themselves, at least in terms of politics, then what you get is 'Look at all this crap, manipulation, and corruption' over and over again. It's not just that they need orientation, it's also that they need some input, they need real political information for example. Otherwise it very quickly devolves. . . . That's where you have to grab them and say, 'Okay, let me give you the details about what is going on in Kosovo what are the various options that we have.' I'm not saying we need to go back to the nineteenth century, to the literary editor sitting amongst his books writing 'I shall explain the world to you!' in twenty-five installments [*laughs*]. The main thing is just to find ways to keep people in these democratic discussions, to give them the basic knowledge [*Grundwissen*] they need to participate. Otherwise, you just have people listening to the recirculation of their own opinions. That's no *Öffentlichkeit* [publicity, public sphere]. That's no political culture."

The invocation of *Öffentlichkeit* is a telling sign of the concerns and desires associated with online news providers. German news journalists often exhibit a strong native Habermasianism in their faith in a sanctuary of communicative action and critical rationality maximally insulated from commercial or governmental influence. Although Habermas himself was skeptical about professional journalists' use of "display and manipulation" to "exercise a privileged influence" within contemporary publicity,[38] German news journalists themselves more often feel that they are defenders and enablers of true publicity and political culture. Indeed, they often position their commitment to publicity and informational exchange as the core of their professional jurisdiction and value to society. Though Max may well have been correct that a plurality of affects circulated in the imagination of T-Online's competitors, the clearest locus of anxiety seemed to me the devolution of news journalism into consumer-driven infotainment, thus rendering German citizens increasingly bereft of the *Grundwissen* they needed for democratic participation and thus, perhaps, open to manipulation or seduction by political ideologists.

This is precisely why Bernd invoked the specter of Nazism in his discussion of informational unification and imitation. In German public discourse, as I have discussed at length elsewhere, democracy is often treated as a fragile political sympathy and one prone to collapse without constant nurturing care.[39] Yet those who felt it their duty to defend the integrity of the public sphere also felt their strength sapped by a feedback-driven model of publicity. T-Online's *Redakteure* understood the conditions and constraints t-online.de faced as a news organization and were keen to make of it something as close to a "classical *Redaktion*" as they could. Not only as a matter of professional reputation, I would argue, but as a part of their intricate effort to maintain expert authority in the context of online publicity. As a *Zwischenform* of publicity in the era of digital information it is perhaps unsurprising that T-Online could appear both as a classical *Redaktion* and as a simulacrum of the same, or, seen differently, as both a news aggregator and a producer of *Mehrwert*. T-Online absorbed elements from both categories but fit neither perfectly, not least because such categorical distinctions make less sense in an era in which most news organizations share the same fast-time information streams and in which the sometimes acknowledged, sometimes unacknowledged repurposing of agency content is rising in every "classical *Redaktion*."[40]

The same logic could be applied again to the question of automaticity and agency. It would indeed be entirely possible to analyze the situation at T-Online in "negative dialectical"[41] terms of overformalization and informatic dispossession and to take the journalists' narratives about performing "classical journalistic activity" as a not particularly persuasive mode of false consciousness. Yet, it is also possible to take their praxiological intuitions seriously, to recognize that journalistic agency did exist, although perhaps in different techniques and at different scales, even in an environment widely suspected for its wholesale automaticity. The analytic challenge, as noted in the conclusion of chapter 1, is how to see the practice of news journalism through both lenses at the same time. Both mediology and praxiology must lead us forward.

The agentive and the automatic, the praxiological and the mediological, the expert and the mob. Much in the spirit of online publicity, it seems that we have entered our own feedback loop. As they would say at T-Online, time for a new *Aufmacher.* Thomas once sighed to me, "Sometimes, I find it a bit depressing that people are ten times more interested in some singer who can't sing on *Deutschland sucht den Superstar*[42] than the fact that Obama is giving an important speech in Cairo. And I think to myself: strange people. On the other hand, I have to say that we're no public broadcaster, we have no educational mission [*erzieherischen Auftrag*]."

We head now into the heart of German *Öffentlichkeit.* The impact of digital information in the context of German public broadcasting is our next and final *Dreh.*

Chapter 3

COUNTDOWN

Professionalism, Publicity, and Political Culture in 24/7 News Radio

From a conversation between the news chief (Rudi B.), and the assistant news chief (Marc H.), of mdr info and the author in Halle, October 2009.

DB: Is there special stress involved in digital news radio? In a sense, you have to produce a news program every fifteen minutes.

RB: I know many news radio journalists whose sleep suffers, who have bad dreams . . .

MH: Because of the pressure . . .

RB: There's a common anxiety dream where the seconds are ticking away toward the quarter hour and your *nachrichten* [news reports] are not ready yet . . .

MH: [*raising his hand, smiling*] Yup, I've had that one . . .

RB: This striving [*Anstreben*] is not at all uncommon. I find the dream image quite indicative of the feeling that one can't stop this clock, that one is running after it, that one has used one's allotted time and yet not completed [one's work] . . .

MH: Of course, it's not just about the digital era, it's about working in news radio. I had that same dream twenty years ago.

Background Report: Agenda 2010

The 2009 national elections marked the nadir of the New Left in Germany. Like most political crises, this one was years in the making. In 2003, Chancellor Gerhard Schröder—a politician whose combination of market-friendly centrism and televisual charisma prompted frequent comparisons with Tony Blair and Bill Clinton—pushed his Social Democratic Party (SPD)-Green coalition government to support a major campaign of economic growth-oriented social reforms: Agenda 2010.[1] Schröder argued that Germany's high unemployment (9.6 percent in March 2003) and economic "stagnation"[2] could not be cured without "courage for change." The ultimate goal of Agenda 2010 was, the chancellor said, "to improve the structural conditions for better growth and for reduced unemployment."[3] The measures Schröder's government recommended included a familiar neoliberal cocktail of reduced tax rates, health care rebalanced in favor of insurance companies, restricted unemployment benefits and workfare mandates, more "flexible" hiring and redundancy practices for employers, and discursive broadsides against traditional bureaucratic mind-sets and privileges. In a country whose welfare apparatus has long been considered a matter of national distinction and pride, however, Agenda 2010 represented a fiercely contentious political issue. The outcry from Germany's still-powerful trade unions was predictably immediate but also remarkable for the venom of its accusations regarding the government's betrayal of social democracy. Large public demonstrations then spread across Germany in 2004 after the controversial "Hartz IV"[4] labor market reforms were enacted. Schröder faced near rebellion within his SPD but the core elements of Agenda 2010 proceeded smoothly into law, supported as the policies were by the opposition Christian Democratic/Christian Socialist (CDU/CSU) union and by the more ardently neoliberal Free Democratic Party (FDP).

At the end of 2010, the economic impacts of Agenda 2010 remained open to interpretation. Unlike the dismal results of "Washington Consensus"-style interventions elsewhere in the world, Agenda 2010 appears to have helped boost a variety of growth indicators and lowered official unemployment statistics (6.6 percent as of December 2010). And yet critics noted that income inequality and the ranks of what in Germany are termed *das Prekariat* (unprotected workers and the unemployed; literally, "the precarious") had grown substantially during the same period.

The political consequences of Agenda 2010 for the SPD were, by contrast, relatively clear. The SPD membership was deeply divided by Schröder's policies and many, especially in the trade unions, were quite alienated from the party leadership. Some of Schröder's fiercest internal critics defected to form a small splinter party, the WASG (Wahlalternative Arbeit und soziale Gerechtigkeit), which advocated a more traditionally welfarist politics. In 2007, the WASG fused with the former East German communist party to create a new "Left Party" (Die Linke) whose antineoliberal platform has exercised a strong impact in German politics, especially in the states of the former East Germany, over the past five years.

Thus, after serving as midwife to the formation of a so-called "neoliberal consensus" in mainstream German politics, the SPD experienced a rapid decline in political relevance, often overshadowed by the growing political energy of smaller parties such as the Left Party, the Greens, and the FDP.[5] In 1998, the year that Schröder became chancellor, the SPD won 40.9 percent of the vote, the best performance of any party. In 2005, the SPD received only 34.2 percent of the vote and Schröder lost his chancellorship to Angela Merkel of the CDU (although the SPD remained the junior partner in a grand coalition government). In 2009, lacking both charismatic leadership and an economic platform that differentiated itself clearly from the neoliberal agenda advocated by the CDU and FDP, the SPD plummeted further to 23.0 percent of the popular vote, its worst showing in the history of the postwar Federal Republic. Following the national election of September 27, the SPD found itself adrift, in search of new leadership and new ideas.[6]

The week after the election, I traveled to Halle to begin the observational phase of my field research at mdr info,[7] a 24/7 news radio channel belonging to Mitteldeutscher Rundfunk (MDR), a regional broadcaster within the German public broadcasting network, ARD, which serves the eastern German federal states of Saxony, Saxony-Anhalt, and Thuringia. The aftermath of the election was a constant *Topthema* (top story) in the weeks that followed. Not only the SPD's collapse in Berlin but also their unwillingness to form a coalition government in Thuringia with the Left Party emerged as key story lines. Beyond this, mdr info's staff devoted considerable time to ruminating over the broader implications of the election for national and regional politics. On my first morning, Hagen R., one of the journalists in the news department, looked around the table at the morning editorial meeting and voiced one of the more perplexing ironies of the election: "Does anyone else find it curious that at the same time that so many people are abandoning the SPD because of Hartz IV that more people than ever are voting for the neoliberal FDP? I find that completely illogical. What is happening to politics in this country?"

One of the reasons that I sought to observe postelection coverage at a public broadcaster was that in my experience, even outside of election cycles, political themes are given unusual time and attention in their newsrooms. This is not to say that German news journalists do not, on the whole, pride themselves on their political awareness and expertise: they do. Across Germany, the venerable image of the journalist as *Meinungsbildner*, as elite educator of political and social opinion, still animates journalism's sense of vocational purpose. I mean to argue only that news journalists working in public broadcasting exemplify this broader tendency because the education of public opinion is, as I discuss below, literally written into their job descriptions and thus represents a touchstone of their daily practice.

Although a good place to observe the intersection of media and political culture, a public broadcaster might seem a less obvious choice for a discussion of informatic trends and fast-time temporalities in news journalism today. Public broadcasters have a distinct reputation in many parts of the world, not least the United States, for traditionalism, even for allochronic lag. Yet, digital information has saturated and reconfigured the practice of news journalism at public broadcasters just as fundamentally as it has at the private news organizations investigated in the chapters 1 and 2. mdr info is a particularly intriguing *Zwischenform* (transitional form, see chapter 1) for our purposes because its round-the-clock model of news journalism explicitly seeks to adapt the educational service mission of traditional public broadcasting to contemporary conditions of fast-time informational abundance. This chapter examines how journalists at mdr info interpret trends in newsmaking and newsflow today and how they envision the place of public broadcasting in the new ecology of digital information. I focus especially on their invocation of professionalism as antidote to perceived threats of digital news mediation even as journalists' sense of the specific content of their professional expertise is clearly shifting.

German Public Broadcasting in the Digital Era

The distinguishing feature of public broadcasting seems to be its "publicness," but what does that mean in Germany today? The first thing to emphasize is that this is not Habermas's ideal-typical sense of *Öffentlichkeit*[8] (publicity, public sphere) for the simple reason that German public broadcasting is a governmental enterprise, even though it may offer sanctuaries for communicative rationality and critical reason and an alternative to the ebb and flow of commercial mediation. The legal charter of broadcast publicity in Germany, as elsewhere in western liberal democracy, emphasizes informational and educational service and support of the arts and culture. Contributing to the formation of public opinion is crucial. For example, Article 6.1 of the treaty that established MDR in 1991 outlined the new broadcaster's objectives and responsibilities as follows: "In its programming, MDR will give an objective and comprehensive overview of international, national, and state-related events in all important areas of life. MDR's programming will provide informational and educational services as well as advice and entertainment in accordance with the cultural mission of broadcasting. Programs will serve free individual and public formation of opinion [*freien individuellen und öffentlichen Meinungsbildung*]."[9] Public broadcasting thus not only informs an existing public; it literally is meant to form (*bilden*) publicity (*Öffentlichkeit*) through its work of informational and educational services.[10]

A second consideration is that this state-sponsored broadcast publicity spans both regional and national governmentalities. Public radio broadcasting in Germany began on a regional basis in the 1920s but was nationalized and monopolized by the Nazi leadership during the Third Reich. After the Second World War, the occupying Allied powers quickly dismantled what remained of Goebbels's Großdeutscher Rundfunk apparatus. Yet, wishing to maintain a strong public broadcasting system as a means of circulating anti-Nazi messages and values and seeking to alleviate their own fears about a resurgence of German nationalism, the western allies, led by the United States, reestablished a regional structure for German public broadcasting in their occupation zones. In 1950, the ARD[11] was formed in West Germany as a production consortium among the regional broadcasters (which currently number nine). East Germany meanwhile developed a centralized broadcasting system in keeping with Soviet media policy. In 1954, the ARD founded its first television channel, Das Erste, which restored public broadcasting to a national scale for the first time since the

1940s. However, 100 percent of the programming on Das Erste was (and is) derived from the regional broadcasters (proportional to the population of the area they serve) such that the regionalist logic of broadcasting remained intact.[12] German unification in 1990 saw a further extension of regionalism. Although there was a significant push among media professionals to maintain a single eastern German broadcaster to address the common experience of the German Democratic Republic (GDR), political authorities decided instead to create two regional broadcasters in eastern Germany, MDR and ORB (which served Brandenburg, and later fused with Berlin's public broadcaster to create a new organization, RBB).[13]

Despite the depth of its regionalism, supporting the ARD is undoubtedly a national political priority. It is currently the best-financed public broadcasting network anywhere in the world.[14] Funded largely by a nationwide tax applied to every household owning a radio receiver or television set, the ARD has a staff of over 23,000 and an annual operating budget of €6.3 billion, spending €1.3 billion more annually than what is usually considered the world's largest public broadcaster, the BBC.[15] MDR alone reported an operating budget of €649.1 million in 2009, of which €576.9 million came directly from the federally mandated receiver fees.[16] Comparatively, the United States' Corporation for Public Broadcasting (which serves a population thirty-five times as large as MDR's) received a congressional appropriation of just $400 million (€279 million) for the same year.

The third consideration is that public broadcasting in Germany continues to enjoy strong popular resonance. Despite growing competition from private broadcasters since the 1980s, ratings for both ARD television and radio remain quite high. In 2010, considering the two national public TV channels along with all "the thirds," the television channels of the regional public broadcasters, the ARD network had over a 43 percent market share, roughly equivalent to the combined market shares of the channels owned by Germany's two largest commercial television corporations, the RTL Group and ProSiebenSat.1 AG (23.0 percent and 20.3 percent, respectively).[17] ARD estimates that its radio programs are even more successful, with a total audience of 37.63 million and a reach of 51.1 percent of the population (as opposed to 30.77 million and 41.8 percent, respectively, for private broadcasters).

The relative robustness of German public broadcasting has inflected debates over the future of news mediation in rather distinct ways. For example, although the Internet is generally regarded as revolutionary force with the power to disrupt print and broadcast news organizations, one also hears concerns that public broadcasters will leverage their massive resources to colonize and control the online domain. As German public broadcasters completed their transitions to digital production in the second half of the 1990s (MDR radio, for example, converted from analog tape to full digital production in 1997 and 1998), commercial media companies, including both broadcasters and newspapers, began to lobby the German government relentlessly to prevent public broadcasters from developing new content services for the Internet. They argued that such services would unfairly disadvantage the private sector and create disincentives for private media companies to invest in developing new online information and entertainment services. "Essentially," a high-ranking administrator of another German public broadcaster confided to me in 2009, "the private publishers and broadcasters are terrified that the public broadcasters will run them out of the Internet. It's true we have advantages over them in terms of reputation and in not needing to make a profit. On the other hand, the fear often seems rather hysterical to me given the actual page view data. The *Privaten* (private companies) are simply trying to protect their market from more competition." I visited the online departments of four German public broadcasters in 2008 and 2009 and my interviewees unanimously expressed the hope that the *politische Beschränkung* (political constraint) of their online initiatives would be relaxed. One departmental director commented, "It's a very unsatisfying situation. All of us know that online is the future. And yet we are being restricted from taking full advantage of our online capabilities."

German public broadcasters' online initiatives are governed by an interstate broadcasting agreement, the Rundfunkstaatsvertrag (RStV). Much to the disappointment of my interviewees, the twelfth revision of the RStV, which took effect on June 1, 2009, renewed firm limits on public broadcasters' online activities. Diana H., the program director at mdr info, explained these limits to me as follows: "Basically, there is a long list of prohibitions and only a few things we are allowed to do. For example, anything that we have broadcast on TV or radio can be put on our Internet page. But only for seven days maximum. Afterward, everything must be erased. We are not even allowed to archive past broadcasts." The core principle of the RStV is that public broadcasters must restrict their online activities to *sendungsbezogene* (broadcast-related) content. Thus, for example, the text of a radio interview or a television clip could be placed on a public broadcaster's website for a week. But a public broadcaster's online department could not research and develop its own "unique content" and then publicize it for any length of time. In my research experience, the vast majority of MDR's Internet activity was indeed limited to the republicization of broadcast content. This is an interesting case of content imitation and automaticity driven not by technological (e.g., shovelware[18]) or praxiological (e.g., overwork) considerations so much as by institutional procedures, specifically by the neoliberal orientation of German (and EU) broadcasting policy to favor private competition over public service.[19]

Even given the restrictions of its online activities, mdr info is widely considered by its staff to be thriving. According to reception statistics, mdr info has never had such a large audience—362,000 listeners (4.4 percent reach[20]) in March 2011—which ranks it among the top three news radio channels in Germany. Many at mdr info felt that they owed their success to their 24/7 news model,[21] which was well suited to audience expectations for constant informational availability in the digital era. Indeed, as many journalists pointed out, mdr info was a truly "a child of the digital era." It was only the second public news radio channel founded in Germany[22] and began broadcasting news, traffic, and weather every fifteen minutes on January 1, 1992. Michael S., mdr info's first news director, found the fast-time character of the channel "exhilarating" after several years of working the GDR radio. But he also noted that the demands of processing and producing information, even in the early days, were extraordinary. By 1996, he calculated that his team was producing 245,640 news reports and 201,656 news features a year (averaging, in sum, 1,225 *Informationen* (pieces of information) a day, fifty-one per hour).

The year 1996 was also the first I visited mdr info as part of my earlier research project on the professional transition of former East German journalists to life and work in reunified Germany. I still recall something that Michael said to me in passing during that visit, "You know, Dominic, there's another transition going on here as well which you should think about, which is this whole transition to living in an information society. That is a large part of our mission here, to help people, and perhaps East Germans are a special case in this regard, come to terms with living in an information society."

Reimagining Professionalism for the Digital Era

I had the chance to speak with Michael about transitions again thirteen years later. In the interim, much had happened in the news industry, and it was clear that broadcast journalists were now also struggling to cope with "living in an information society," a society whose sheer informational density and dominant communicational trends like online, mobile, and social media seemed to be undermining the legitimacy of the unidirectional hub-and-spoke pattern of broadcast messaging. Michael and I sat in the café of MDR's radio production center in Halle, together with his successor as news chief of mdr info, Rudi B., ruminating on what all these new trends meant for public broadcasting and for news professionals. The praxiological and mediological coordinates of our conversation will, by now, be quite familiar.

> RB: It's always claimed in portraits of the impact of the Internet that people are now eternally seeking their own information out for themselves. But, I don't think the listeners want to do that. I think [*laughs*] I think a listener wants a pro to filter out [*ausfiltern*] what's the most important information for them. He doesn't want to be dropped into this ocean of information but rather to sit comfortably on the beach with a radio he can switch on from time to time and know that, in the ten minutes a day that he can sacrifice to the news, that the pros are going to be able to tell him what is going on.

MS: According a recent ARD study, there are basically two groups of media users. The one group is over twenty that want exactly what Rudi said, they want, regardless if it's a newspaper, radio, or TV, they want someone else to make this selection decision [*Auswahlsentscheidung*] for them. Then there is a second group, ages fourteen–nineteen, who are just entering the media landscape [*Medienlandschaft*], like my daughter, who like to find things for themselves on the Internet. She also reads a newspaper, of course, *Der Tagesspiegel*, the most boring newspaper in the world [*we all laugh*]. The study says that the next ten years will answer the question as to whether this generation will have the same relationship to media [*Medienverhalten*] when they are in their midtwenties when they have jobs, get married, perhaps have children, or whether it will change.

RB: But, if you want to know the truth, here is the thing that troubles me. The need for news journalists has, in my opinion, never been greater. The ocean of information is only getting bigger. But it's getting harder and harder to do this job. For example, when things are being marketed as these great sensations, as great medical advances or economic events, for example. And we sit here looking at these reports with our current capacities, and we can no longer decide whether something is important or not because we lack the technical understanding.

MS: Ach, Rudi, news journalists have been sharing that lack of self-esteem for eighty years [*laughs*]. You can read people saying the same thing as far back as the 1920s.

RB: Yes, but it *is* getting worse. For example, we've had a running daily debate over the swine flu [H1N1 virus] for quite a while now and we have not yet been able to determine whether this flu is something to be taken seriously or not—yes or no. We just don't know. We keep sending out bulletins about something that could be nothing but hype. Now, of course, you could say that it's not our job to determine what is dangerous and what isn't, maybe we should leave that to people themselves to make that judgment. But that's not what the listeners *want*. The listeners are only too happy to hand this judgment over to news journalists but we don't know enough to make an evaluation either.

DB: But why does it seem like it is more difficult *now* to separate hype from real news?

MS: There are two sides to it. On the one hand there has been a professionalization of the people who push their messages on to the market. There's been a decisive surge of professionalization [*Professionalisierungsschub*] there. In terms of packaging news so it sounds good. I just read a thesis about the connections between PR work, advertising, and the news agencies. It showed how PR people have increasingly learned how to package their messages for the news agencies so they will make *Meldungen* (news reports) out of them. Then, on the other side, when I look at how many young people are working in *Redaktionen* (editorial collectives) these days, at the private broadcasters especially, where some of them don't even have an Abitur,[23] I think that's the issue. Professionalization on the one side, deprofessionalization on the other.

RB: There are just so many more players these days. In the German market, you used to have the media, news agencies, organizations, and lobbyists. Now suddenly you have all these additional players. Suddenly anyone with a telephone or an Internet connection is profiling himself as a "content provider." T-Online, AOL, Yahoo, Google, they are all operating in the news business now too.

MS: And, many of the news agencies are beginning to give up that gatekeeper function. Some of them seem to have acquired the habit of simply resending anything that arrives in their office without much review or reflection. And, when you see the conditions under which those people have to work, you can hardly blame them. They have to deal with such an overflow of information, one can't expect that they can provide the same kind of filtering as before [*Rudi nods vigorously in agreement*].

DB: If the news agencies give up their gatekeeper role does that responsibility then become yours?

MS: [*smiling*] Well, we serve the public [*Wir dienen ja die Öffentlichkeit*].

RB: [*seriously*] Which is why the job has become that much more challenging.

I found "professionalization on the one side, deprofessionalization on the other" a remarkably elegant formulation. But two more fundamental insights crystallize in this conversation. The first is how centrally professionalism figures in journalists' diagnosis of both the challenge and solution of maintaining a positive form of *Öffentlichkeit* in the era of digital information. The second is how the skilled core of news professionalism is reimagined from, for example, reporting and generating original news and toward the filtration, selection, and gatekeeping of already existing content. The news director of another German public broadcaster put it similarly in an interview:

"The amount of information on the same topics is growing explosively. And that brings the journalist into a role that he perhaps did not have before, namely . . . to tell me what of this information is really important, what is believable, and what is trustworthy. Before it was more the role of the journalist to publish something that without his research would not have existed, but today the role is increasingly to evaluate the material that others are generating. And to organize it. For, in the end consumer is still the way he always was, with limited time and with limited competence."

Of course, the problem was that news journalists were often acutely aware of their own limitations of time and competence. As Rudi insisted, no news journalist, no matter how diligent and intelligent, could function as an expert gatekeeper in all matters. In my observations at mdr info, I saw that journalists were extraordinarily invested in honing their expert awareness of relevant news issues. They engaged other news media voraciously. At the same time, there were only so many minutes in each day. Priorities needed to be set and nonjournalistic experts had to be enrolled to ensure that mdr info could meet its public service mission.

Performing Publicity

In academic theory of publicity, it is not uncommon to emphasize the generative role of circulating discourse in the constitution of publics.[24] Mdr info took this principle a step farther. More so than in other *Redaktionen* profiled in this book, I found that mdr info treated internal evaluative discourse as essential to successful acts of informational externalization and circulation. In other words, the *Redaktion* emphasized that the quality of their labors of publicity depended on first circulating discourse elements (e.g., ideas, questions, statements) among journalists in an experimental fashion. Rudi was fond of telling me that *Der Kollege ist der erste Hörer* (a colleague is one's first listener) and Diana said that no broadcast could succeed without adequate time for exchange and critical reflection. Collegial discussion was deemed necessary to help determine both which stories were worth covering (the question of news relevance) and how selected stories would be framed and through which external, expert voices (the question of news strategy). Whereas editorial meetings at AP-DD and T-Online were shorter and tended to coordinate decisions already finalized elsewhere, mdr info's morning and midday conferences were typically longer (forty-five minutes and thirty minutes, respectively), more open-ended and decision-reaching.

Editorial meetings began with a rundown of potential *Themen* (stories, themes) by the *Chef vom Dienst* (CvD) followed by a few minutes of discussion of each of the major themes (conversations involving, most days, the program and news directors as well as other off-duty CvDs and representatives of other smaller departments like business, contact, planning, and sports). Certain topics such as classic breaking news events like fires, earthquakes, and accidents generally stimulated little sustained discussion of relevance or strategy. Moreover, it seemed quite true, as Rudi suggested, that journalists sensed the limits of their expertise in a variety of domains, including scientific and technological *Themen*. Such topics received less framing discussion and more consideration of what experts could add authoritatively and engagingly to them. "We're looking for a nice mix," Rudi explained over lunch one day, "of light issues and heavy ones, of domestic and foreign coverage, of politics and business themes. We look for balance and place a lot of value on it."

My observational experience was that given the programmatic significance of *Meinungsbildung* (formation of opinion) at MDR, political expertise was something of a lingua franca within mdr info.[25] Political topics invariably received the greatest attention and deliberation within the editorial meetings and as such occupied the heart of mdr info's labors of publicity. The following discussion took place during mdr info's morning editorial meeting four days after the election and conveys well how the *Redaktion* strategized how to cover the major political *Thema* of the day.

Diana H. (program director): So, this idea to do something in Berlin tomorrow, say more about that.

Bodo K. (CvD): I can imagine basically two variants, either focus on the dream couple, Merkel and Westerwelle,[26] and how they are balancing the competing pressures of the FDP and CSU or on how the SPD are licking their wounds on thin ice. And we look at those who are going to the lead the party in the future.

DH: But isn't this the same thing that we've been hearing?

BK: Eh, well, how would it be if we concentrated on the actual distribution of ministries between the CSU and FDP? The good feelings could be threatened if it comes to a dispute between the proud FDP and the CSU in Berlin. It could be the case that the crypt will have to be opened and someone supplied with another ministry. Just a suggestion. To shine a light in the direction of the government.

[*There's no immediate reaction and a long moment of silence follows; unseen sirens howl by outside the window.*]

DH: Should we return to the [coalition negotiation] issues we've already covered? Domestic security and data privacy?

Tobias D. (journalist): If we want to do that, then it would be better done on Monday, when the coalition negotiations will actually begin. Because we're going to have to do a *Vorbericht* (preliminary report) on the key issues under negotiation anyway.

BK: Well, to get a four-day break from this [story] wouldn't be a bad result [*everyone laughs*].

Michael K. (current affairs chief/CvD): Personally, I find this SPD story the more interesting one [*another long pause, interrupted only by the sound of BK clicking his pen*]

BK: It is said that the SPD lost, no later than Agenda 2010, their position as Germany's real *Sozialpartei* (welfare party). Their status as a populist party [*Volkspartei*] *ist quasi verschroedert worden* [has been sort of "Schrödered" away] [*a few chuckle appreciatively at the neologism* verschroedert]. Then we could ask the question, is it enough to put forward a fat man and a pleasant woman as the new faces of their politics or does the SPD not need, programmatically, a completely new beginning? And if it's a new program, what do they stand for? Nahles stands for something very different than Gabriel's network does.[27] Or something like that.

DH: Or, what I was just thinking, was to do how these networks originated, to offer a chronology of the whole thing. What these people were doing the past several years, how they were selected so to speak, how people in these positions honestly can wait years for their chance, and who's with them and what connections they made in this or that context [*pauses, laughs deprecatingly*] . . . a kind of chronology of events . . .

Kerstin H. (CvD): [*interrupting*] I'd be particularly interested in the personalities, in what they stand for, to connect also to the content of the politics. We've said something about this but I don't think we've pursued it very deeply. That is, what Ms. Nahles stands for and who is standing behind her and what Mr. Gabriel stands for and who is behind *him*. We've only said that he used to be a bit of an unloved child in the SPD but now is better liked. Good, that's three sentences but we haven't said more than that.

DH: No, no, we've said it since the beginning. They are both against Hartz IV, they are both against retirement at sixty-seven. They stand for very strong termination protection [*Kündigungsschutz*], all things that are typically considered left-wing in the SPD. I mean, we could do it again but . . .

KH: But, I mean, I mean, they are *in such a hurry*. With the defeat and with the party conference coming up and they are casting around hectically . . .

DH: Maybe we should do a portrait of Gabriel?

BK: Maybe, but something else on this question that Kerstin raised. The chronology here is one of pragmatic consolidation in the interest of survival. It's also a matter of careers. I mean, when the boat's taking water, everyone has a bucket in hand. But when that's over, the struggle starts again. Who's going to be at the helm, who's going to be the cook, the navigator, etc.

Rudi B. (news chief): But let's stick to the personages [Gabriel and Nahles], that is, that there will be those who will be left behind. To be in someone's network doesn't mean automatically that you will end up in a position of power.

MK: True, but I'd like to know how they plan to work together with [Frank-Walter] Steinmeier who really was the architect of Agenda 2010. I mean, do they *have to* work together with Steinmeier? And the second question of course is what role [Klaus] Wowereit has played in all this?[28]

[*General nods and murmurs of approval at the table at MK's idea. No one else seeks to modify this set of questions and JH, seemingly eager to reach a consensus, raises her palms, smiling.*]

JH: Good, but let's not overburden our colleagues in Berlin with this. So can I ask you, Tobias, to help Kerstin to develop a double portrait on Steinmeier and Wowereit for tomorrow?

TD: Happy to do so, you can count on us.

One gets a good sense of the intimacy and seriousness of political attention at mdr info in this conversation. Key figures in national politics enjoy not only recognition but familiarity ("a fat man," "an unloved child") and political machinations and alliances are a subject of interest and scrutiny. But note, in particular, the time and energy the *Redaktion* devotes to discussing contexts and angles and to formulating questions. In such moments, journalists explained to me, they were seeking to get inside the minds of their listeners and to imagine what questions they might already have about a developing political situation. Or, more in the traditional logic of journalistic authority, what questions the listeners *should* be asking themselves and what knowledge they needed to find answers. All of my MDR interlocutors shared this sentiment, which was well expressed by Hagen: "It's not sufficient to simply bombard people with raw facts when what they really need to form an opinion is the sum of facts plus orientation or context." The editorial meetings thus offered a space for testing informational prototypes. In the exchange above a possible feature on the CSU and FDP became a story on the SPD's need for a new platform, before becoming a portrait of the SPD's new leaders, before finally settling on how those new leaders would interact with other important figures in the party. Each iteration was given a trial performance by a CvD and trial reactions from the assembly. In this respect, the meetings' intimate intellectual labors also modeled the *Redaktion*'s connectivity and dialogue with its audience. Just as in MDR's charter, the meetings both anticipated the circulating discourse of *Öffentlichkeit* and called it into being through performance.

But intimacy, of course, also suggests a certain temporality. Editorial meetings could be so experimental and performative because they tended to focus on features (*Beiträge*) production as well as on review of previous programs. Planning and realizing original features necessitated a time horizon of twelve to eighteen hours to allow time for identifying the issues and key questions, arranging interviews, cutting the segments, and reviewing them for quality.[29] Given that features came in a number of genres (reports, background stories, press reviews, portraits, interviews) and covered an immense diversity of *Themen*, it was difficult to generalize about what constituted a good feature. But they typically sought to offer explanatory narratives rather than simply represent facts. Michael the CvD told me, "It's nice when a feature can tell a story, when it can connect to people. Which is tough with a topic like coalition negotiations when it's just facts, facts, facts." We then listened together to a portrait of a man reminiscing about a large demonstration in the former GDR town of Plauen twenty years later. "It's a nice portrait," Michael said, "I think we'll use it. There were some details that were very nice. His jeans jacket being three sizes too big for example. You took what you could get on the black market in those days. People will remember too."

Within the temporality of features production, time could be set aside for the discussion of background and context and for the imagination of storylines, affective reactions, questions, and answers. But features production was only part of mdr info's news practice. The frontline of managing fast-time newsflow occurred outside the editorial meetings, on another floor of the MDR radio complex, in mdr info's news department. The news department was primarily responsible for monitoring news agency feeds for breaking news and for producing a news report every fifteen minutes, twenty-four hours a day.

Perpetuum Mobile

Fast-time production seems a general condition of news journalism in the digital era. But, as we have seen in the other case studies, fast-time production appears with different accents and with subtle modulations of rhythm and flow. AP-DD operated mostly in a continuous breaking news model but with a variety of scales of advance planning that helped make breaking news more susceptible to administration. T-Online operated largely on a two-hour cycle of *drehen* (spinning) yet one that was punctuated by more frequent surveillance of web analytics and optimization techniques. mdr info's news department was governed by what journalists described as *viertelstundentakt* (quarter-hour time).

In a certain respect, quarter-hour time had an absoluteness to its structure that was unknown to the other *Redaktionen*. AP-DD sought always to put out its bulletins ahead of its competitors but, even on the treadmill, extra seconds could always be spared for a better formulation or for checking facts or spelling. At T-Online the situation was even more flexible—not a whole *Dreh* could be delayed, but individual stories could be and certainly were actualized at different rates without sacrificing the overall organizational commitment to refreshing content. As Hagen put it, gesturing to one of several vividly red digital time displays that were visible everywhere in the mdr info newsroom, ":00 is :00." There was no excuse or possibility for not having one's *nachrichten* in the hands of the news reader at :00, :15, :30, or :45. As another one of the *Redakteure* put it, mdr info news worked in "a constant state of countdown."

Here is the complete *Sendeschema* for mdr info, the breakdown of what a listener can expect to hear and when, every hour around the clock.

    xx.00   News/Weather/Traffic
    xx.06   Reports, Background, Interviews
    xx.13   Markets in Frankfurt, New York, Tokyo
    xx.15   Headline News/Weather/Traffic
    xx.17   Current Events, Regional News, Service, Culture
    xx.28   Complete Weather Forecast
    xx.29   Outlook for the Coming Half Hour
    xx.30   News/Weather/Traffic
    xx.36   Reports, Media Review, Opinion
    xx.40   Sports

xx.45   Headline News/Weather/Traffic
xx.47   Current Events, Regional News, Service, Culture
xx.58   Weather
xx.59   Outlook for the Coming Hour

Every hour, mdr info broadcasts thirty-three minutes of features, interviews, and regional news; sixteen minutes of news reports/weather/traffic; five minutes of sports; two minutes of markets; two minutes of detailed weather; and two minutes of overviews of the upcoming news. The schema was designed as an intricate mosaic of different forms of news that would, in the words of assistant news chief Marc H., "fully inform the listener who turns us on for a half hour twice a day, but not bore the listener who has the radio on in the background constantly."

The news reports structured the broadcast hour, dividing it into four fifteen-minute "Reports," R1, R2, R3, and R4, that, in the language of the office, were referred to more or less interchangeably with the :00, :15, :30, :45 *Achsen* (axes) of quarter-hour time. All four news reports were produced by the news department, who were located at one edge of the mdr info newsroom in two small clusters of three workspaces. Hagen explained to me, gesturing to their somewhat cramped work area, "We don't talk a lot about the great dreams of the digital era around here. The actors here are limited to filling the *Nachrichtenfläche* (news space) in the program." Pointing at the long queue of news stories on his content management system (CMS), he chuckled, "it's basically a *perpetuum mobile.*"

Normally, the longer news reports on the hour and half hour involved five or six *klassichen nachrichten* (classical news reports) six or seven sentences in length. The news reports at :15 and :45 offered five reports as well, but in the *Schlagzeile* (shorter headline) format of two sentences: a lead defining the core of the bulletin and a second *ergänzender Satz* (supplemental sentence) that helped to either round out or situate the lead. The division of these tasks changed throughout the day as the size of the news department varied. The department's full complement was five *Redakteure* between the hours of 10:00 a.m and 4:00 p.m., which was considered the period of highest news volume. Two of the journalists represented the *Kernteam* (core team), one of whom acted as shift supervisor and was responsible for the :00 report, while the second was responsible for the :30 report. A third *Redakteur* handled the headlines for :15 and :45. Two other *Redakteure* were known as the ZbVs (*Zur besonderer Verwendung,* for special assignment) and available for special assignments, including listening to interviews and other material of interest to the department, background research, factual confirmations, among other tasks. The sixth seat in the news department cluster was occupied by a journalist who wrote news reports for mdr sputnik, MDR's youth channel.[30]

The news department did not enjoy the luxury of leaving their stations for long editorial meetings to discuss *Themen* and strategize news coverage. Their own daily departmental conference could be as short as ten minutes. In addition to writing news reports in quarter-hour time, the news department had the principal responsibility of monitoring the *Agentureingang* (incoming news agency reports), a process that demanded here, as elsewhere, constant screenwork. Phone calls, e-mail messages, even checking competing news organizations' websites and video were relatively infrequent practices as compared with the other *Redaktionen* profiled in this book. By my calculations, well over 90 percent of mdr info's screenwork involved word processing or the *Agentureingang*. Yet the archipelago of individualized screenwork was given social substance by a more or less continuous reflexive discourse on what was occurring in the newsflow and what projects the news department was working on. Here again, we find publicity-in-action. Individuals would enter and exit the conversational flow, disappearing into feverish bouts of typing and editing only to return to react to a news agency report, to share an ironic observation with a colleague, to ask for clarification or information, to negotiate a division of labor, or to test a textual formulation for accuracy or acoustic elegance. Often times, the interlayered threads of reference became so complicated that it seemed to require, from an external perspective, an extraordinary degree of attentional multiplicity. For example, during the following exchange between Harold F. (*Kernteam*), Marike K. (headlines) and Olav S. (ZbV), none of them looked away from their screens as they discussed, in a little over a minute, the division of themes for the :45 and :00 and a provocative quote from the ongoing coalition negotiations in Thuringia.

HF: Marike, I'm just going to toss out Samoa, the Sumatran earthquake will stay—the dead and the experts saying this and that. And will that work for you?

MK: For the :45. I'll do Samoa.

HF: Yes, and then everything will be clearer and *this* [*waving a piece of paper in Olav's direction*] is something *Olav* can do now that there are more casualties in Samoa then previously thought.

OS: Oh good.

HF: Yes, there are more. Now, Matschie's[31] speech . . . [*calling up a dpa report on his screen*]

OS: My favorite part is the quote where Herr Matschie says about Bodo Ramelow,[32] "A red-red-green coalition would be like a five-year-long self-help group for Bodo Ramelow" [*HM and MK both snort with laughter*].

MK: Cruel.

HF: You have to wonder what he's thinking.

OS: Oh, I imagine it was just a little extra provocation against Herr Ramelow.

HF: Maybe, but he's positioning himself to become "Minister President." Shouldn't he be avoiding those kinds of personal vanities? Well, since he said it . . .

OS: It could be that . . .

HF: [*laughing*] No, no, listen, you don't need to get into Matschie's head.

Still, part of the joy of the work seemed precisely to be the opportunity to get into various public figures' heads. *Öffentlichkeit* meant a certain intimacy with political events and actors. There was obvious pleasure in sharing clever commentary and in dissecting current events, especially in sharing and refining their expertise of important political *Themen*. As befitting radio, mdr info had a lively oral culture. But the silent culture of textuality was equally dynamic. When a news agency report appeared that was judged worthy of incorporating into the program, the *Redakteure* worked quickly to confirm the report and to rework it textually for radio. This could take as long as a half hour or as little as five minutes for high-value breaking news. Once a *Thema* entered the rotation, it could stay as long as four hours, depending on the density of the news day. Even stories whose news information did not substantially change were rewritten continuously in order to keep their formulations fresh for radio. For example, on May 23, 2011, as part of the ongoing struggle to manage its debt crisis, the Greek government announced a plan to privatize several public services and holdings including shares in its telecommunications and postal services and several harbors and airports. Although the *nachrichten* were all based upon the same set of news agency reports, over the next several hours the headline changed several times before finally cycling out of the *Spitzenthemen* (top news)[33]:

Greece to sell state property in order to contain its mountain of debt (7:30 p.m., 8:30 p.m.)

Because of mounting debt, Greece will give up more of its state property (8:00 p.m., 9:00 p.m.)

In its fight against the threat of bankruptcy, the Greek government has announced a new savings program (9:30 p.m., 10:30 p.m.)

With restricted expenditure and privatization, Greece hopes to secure additional international financial aid (10:00 p.m.)

With a new savings program and the sale of state property, Greece hopes to avert the threat of bankruptcy (11:00 p.m.)

Composing headlines meant making key information modular, as this case reveals. Combining and recombining informational modules allowed for multiple permutations of the same story. The *Kernteam* would typically produce two different versions of a story for the :00 and :30 reports and then repeat these versions no more than twice in a story's lifecycle. Although such textual adjustments may seem superficial, inside the *Redaktion* they were considered vital for maintaining the attention and interest of the *Stammhörer* (regular listeners). Indeed, semantic precision was a constant touchstone of discussion in the news department. Not only did the *Redakteure* review each other's written *nachrichten* and suggest improvements, they raised and debated the meaning and *Aussagekraft* (expressive power) of specific formulations as well as those that appeared in agency reports and other news media. *Das klingt ja ein bisschen komisch* [that sounds a bit off] or *Das klingt schön* [that sounds good] belong to a class of similar evaluative phrases that occurred with great frequency.

At times, language was also crafted with the specific expectations and sensitivities of the audience in mind. During a news department meeting, Hagen raised the question of how they should formulate the description of one of the many events marking the 20th anniversary of marches and protests that occurred in East Germany in September and October 1989, as Communist Party rule in the GDR weakened and eventually collapsed.

> Hagen: Here too is something to discuss. A sensitive point regarding the formulation. Is it a *Kundgebung* [demonstration]? The "first large" one? I came up with the formulation "first mass *Kundgebung*" because every city claims "We had one on the 11th of September," "We had one already on the 1st of October" [*chuckles from the group*] and with such *Befindlichkeiten* (senses of belonging) . . .
>
> Marc: What we used on the :30, "One of the first," I think is best, because all these superlatives . . . Overnight four reports came in with superlatives like "first largest," stuff like that, but when you check into it, the basis for them is not clear. So in general I'm a bit suspicious of the superlatives.
>
> Harold: And "first" wouldn't be sufficient?
>
> Marc: No, that's nonsense—they weren't the first, you have to relativize the characterization . . .
>
> Rudi: Yes, of course [the demonstrations] originated in Leipzig . . .
>
> Hagen: These were additional . . .
>
> Rudi [*shrugging*]: We just have to fiddle our way through [*durchmogeln*] the formulation.

Such moments of discourse certainly involved the craft of perfecting the semantic dimension of representation. But there was again the process of illocutionary performance at work as well. The constant discussion of how certain formulations might "sound" and sound to certain people simulated the condition of oral publicity, modeling and invoking the larger listening audience on the basis of the more intimate community of discourse and debate in the *Redaktion*.

Publicity without Feedback

Journalists were also aware that their ability to simulate their audience and its *Öffentlichkeit* had its limits. It was difficult to forget, for example, that although their audience was growing in size, it was also narrowing demographically. The average age of mdr info listeners had just passed fifty in 2009. It was particularly straining for the *Redaktion* to imagine and model the voices and interests of a younger audience who seemed simply to be disengaging from broadcast publicity in favor of the lateral connectivities of the Internet and social media. Since the RStV drastically inhibited MDR from developing new online initiatives for its listeners, there seemed to be little that could be done to combat the narrowing of mdr info's radius of publicity. As practiced as the *Redakteure* were in performing *Öffentlichkeit* in microcosm, these performances were unsettled by the recognition that publicity in the digital era seemed overlaid with the expectation of some form of fast-time bidirectional exchange that mdr info was not, at least under current conditions, capable of providing.

I wondered whether journalists rued that they could not participate more actively in lateral communication with their audience and often found that they did, slightly. There was genuine and general disappointment in the *Redaktion* with the restrictions imposed on their online activity. Yet, I also found that many journalists associated online activity with an undermining of their professional authority, a professional authority they understood as essential for the operation of any positive *Öffentlichkeit*. Marc talked through the ambivalence of what he termed *Zweiwegkommunikation* (two-way communication) in a later interview:

> "Like everything else in the world there are two sides to this. On the one hand, I'd love to know what people are really interested in. We have a certain *Handwerkszeug* [craft tool], news criteria, and we think that's [*shrugs*] OK. But it doesn't quite add up. I can take my news criteria and write six news bulletins but whether those will actually have the effect I imagine, I have no idea. I could imagine perhaps a tool that people could use to click on in real-time about whether they are interested in something or not. And I wonder how many of our *Themen* would then simply disappear because people may not be interested in them although they are things that people *ought* to know. That is what I find dangerous about this two-way communication. It's true, we know far too little about our listeners; it's a common complaint, and there's ever more research and the findings are usually that people want news, weather, traffic—which is basically what we already know [*laughs*]. . . . There was this amusing study where they read a focus group the news and gave them all little buttons to push when they heard something they were interested in. This was right here in Saxony-Anhalt. So, first topic: 'In Saxony-Anhalt, the government

decided . . .' Good, buttons pressed, everyone was interested. Second topic: 'Chancellor Schröder . . .' And immediately all fingers [came] off the buttons [*laughs*] and they didn't click again for a while. Then came the weather and everyone clicked again. If I had some real-time feedback capacity like that for thousands of people, *maybe* I could use that for orientation [*drauf richten*]. But I can't do news on demand [*wunschnachrichten*]. If it's going to be two-way communication then it would have to be a truly *organized* form of two-way communication."

The flow of Marc's thinking turns the problem over and then inside out. At first, the absence of deeper knowledge of the listeners' interests is lamented. This was an absolutely sincere sentiment at mdr info, I believe. But then another sincere sentiment—the dangers and uncertain value of real-time contact with the anonymous mediatic mob—emerges. Finally, we arrive at the stipulation of a more organized, limited mode of two-way communication, one that surfaces and preserves the core principle of journalistic authority (to decide, ultimately, what has news value and what does not). *Wunschnachrichten*, the practice frequently attributed to aggregators and other online-only news organizations, were out of the question. This stipulation was invoked very frequently in conversations that concerned the social role of public broadcasting. Journalists commented, as Rudi did, that they dare not sacrifice their ability to exert a gravitational power over the ocean of information. The public could swim too far into the currents and drown. As an early analysis of mdr info concluded, "It cannot be the task of news radio to spread as much information as possible and thus to expand the information glut [*Informationsschwemme*] further. News radio instead must provide hourly and daily order to what [Neil] Postman has described as 'info-chaos.' By quickly and competently selecting and processing information that could be important for listeners, news radio should make it easier for listeners to orient themselves."[34]

But the *Redakteure* were uniformly aware that the art of providing orientation instead of glut was complexly attenuated to a changing media ecology and to the shifting values and attentions of fast-time globalized society. It all came down to professionalism. Marc again, this time very animated, thumping his palm on his desk:

"Listen, in principle anyone can make news now. I can set up an Internet page and copy/paste RSS feeds, an impossibility before [digital media] by the way, and then I'm in the game. That's why it's more important than ever for us to be professional today. Yes, there has always been time pressure but the quantity of incoming information is simply higher than it used to be. And then in addition there are all of the real-time sources. Live TV coverage is much more comprehensive than it used to be. Ten or fifteen years ago there weren't live press conferences in this country. There's more material. And in seconds on my computer I can call up an archive of past material for research. Crazy. The job has just become more complex. And the art of it is no longer selection [*Wählen*] but deselection [*Abwählen*]. I just saw a report in the *Frankfurter Rundschau* on the agreement on *Kindergeld*.[35] To simply send that back out? No problem. But *should* I? Is it really worth a report? To answer that question you need professional *Grundsätze* [principles]. But you also need life experience and experience in the news business since so many things repeat constantly, perhaps not exactly the same events, but themes, and you have to ask whether the informational value is there. The principles are simple: Is it new? Does it have value? But the judgments are complex. I feel I'm personally relatively open to new news trends. But people are increasingly complaining about the boulevardization of news in the last fifteen years. [*lowering his voice to a whisper*] But what *is* boulevardization? Values change in a society; what might have been something for the boulevard fifty years ago, say jazz music, is today something for the *Kultur* section. The question is not to judge something as boulevard or pure but to ask whether it is new or not and whether it has informational value. I have to hold on to these values, to be professional."

Marc's emphasis on holding to values may sound like ethical conservatism. His emphasis on organization and order may sound ethnotypically German, a matter of a cultural investment in administration. Indeed, the professionalist discourse I encountered at mdr info was surely inflected by the paternalism of German postwar statecraft, perhaps even at some level by the German (Protestant) conviction that *Ordnung muss sein*. But we have also heard the invocation of professionalism in the other case studies in this book. I think that this discourse signals above all a germinating reinvention and survival strategy for journalistic expertise in the era of digital information. In Marc's testimony, the praxiologies of professionalism trump the mediological specters of info-chaos, of the boulevard and its distractions, of overload and confusion. Vague and troubling forces are repurposed into objects of professional knowledge and intervention. In a nutshell, here is the logic of reinvention: in earlier models of journalistic expertise, the principal problem was how to inform the uninformed. Now, the contemporary iteration of expertise seeks to orient and focus the overinformed on those topics most relevant to them. Both iterations are, I would emphasize, entirely capable of channeling expert privilege and pastoralism on behalf of a public.

Region and Relevance

At mdr info, the public to be watched over and cared for was rarely defined in terms of age, gender, and political and social orientation and almost always in terms of region. Region identification was a complex issue because there was no compelling historical rationale for lumping Saxony, Saxony-Anhalt, and Thuringia together in a broadcast region. Each state was fiercely proud of its own regional and local traditions and contrasted them with the others. At the same time, the three states' common heritage in the GDR had been explicitly denied as the principle for regional publicity during the process of German unification, a process that I have described elsewhere as one of de facto colonization of the former GDR by the former FRG (Federal Republic of Germany).[36]

So, although regional significance (*regionale Bedeutung*) was continuously invoked in discussions of news relevance and national and international *Themen*, it was often unclear on what basis regional significance could be determined. One of my interlocutors told me that he and his colleagues liked to use the question, "Would this interest anyone in Leipzig or Magdeburg?" as a principle of news selectivity. But he admitted that the question was fairly rhetorical. Without a stabilizing discourse of the cultural unity of the broadcast region, in my experience, regionalism tended to default back to the common experience of the GDR. There was no sense in which the *Redakteure* sought to promote an "East German identity" through their work at mdr info but since most of the staff had grown up in the GDR, they were aware of shared East German experiences and senses of belonging that were really all that aligned Saxony, Saxony-Anhalt, and Thuringia as a meaningful regional cluster in the first place.

mdr info journalists also slyly identified the national German media as having a regional basis of its own in the former FRG. They pointed, for example, to the national media's repetitive signaling of eastern German differences. That signaling involved circulating overt stereotypes such as eastern Germans' allegedly greater attitudinal proclivities for, among other things, xenophobic intolerance and postcommunist nostalgia.[37] In other cases, the marked differences were more benign in their content but expressed an unmistakable understanding that eastern Germans still did not quite belong in the unified nation-state some twenty years after unification.[38] Harold, one of the more talkative *Redakteure*, rarely sought to suppress his pointed sense of irony when he would review the *Agentureingang* and encounter what he perceived as the exoticization or demonization of eastern Germany. It happened nearly every day. One morning it was, "I wonder how, twenty years after the *Wende*,[39] that someone would still think to award a special 'East German media prize.'" On another it was irritation at dpa's coverage of a bank failure that tied it to the bank's absorption of eastern German debt: "I see. It's all about the past. It's our fault."

In this respect, regionalism at mdr info stood in loose antithesis to what the journalists perceived as the dominant interests of the nation. It was not necessarily a negating antithesis. National political affairs received quite constant coverage (as did regional political affairs). And major international events and issues, topics for the national *Leitmedien* (lead media), also made frequent appearances, seemingly exempted by their informational importance from the "Would this interest anyone in Leipzig or Magdeburg?" litmus. More complicated and sometimes contentious discussions of regional relevance ensued from what might be glossed as "national debates" that lacked the hard news currency of events and factual information; for example, the polemics of publicity surrounding immigration.

During one morning editorial meeting, Kerstin tentatively suggested the idea for doing a feature on a recent appearance by Thilo Sarrazin, a German economist and pundit who made international headlines for his highly controversial statements and book about the failure of Muslim assimilation in Germany and elsewhere in Europe.[40] She recognized that Sarrazin's statements had recently received a great deal of press in Germany, "but what was interesting about his appearance last night is less what he himself said than the fact that the audience didn't criticize him but rather said here's someone who's telling the truth and it needs to be possible to talk about the truth in this country and . . . maybe that could be a *Thema*." Bodo picked up the concept enthusiastically but suggested interviewing an immigration economist whom he had heard speak and who was, unlike Sarrazin very level-headed [*sehr nüchtern*] and who could perhaps offer a concrete cost-benefit analysis of immigration. A divergence of options emerged. In essence, Kerstin was pitching a *Beitrag* (feature) on the limits of free speech in Germany whereas Bodo was arguing, in his own words, "to come at this rather overextended debate over Sarrazin from a new direction, with a foundation in facts rather than ideology."

Unfortunately, this led to an argument between Kerstin and Bodo over which was the better angle that enrolled Diana and Rudi as well. Diana seemed sympathetic to the idea of doing a fact-based piece but Rudi shook his head and said, "It would be a Herculean task to do a complete accounting of costs and benefits of immigration. There are too many variables. I don't believe there is a balance sheet upon which you could say Sarrazin is either right or wrong. I'd be afraid that it would just make the debate more sympathetic." After a few more minutes, no consensus or compromise could be reached. The conversation was entering into a zone of bad *Öffentlichkeit* and Diana reached for regional relevance as a failsafe for restarting conversational performativity in a more positive direction: "[*sighs*] I don't think this is something for us. When they do polls in the region, scarcely anyone knows who Sarrazin is. It's mostly a *Thema* in Berlin and perhaps in the culture pages of the national press. But I don't think the Saxon-Anhalters are very engaged in this debate. I mean [*raising her voice to overcome low level but rising dissent from the table*], I mean, in the end nothing really happened. Come, colleagues, let's move on."

Sound and Meaning

Beyond its regional particularities, another very obvious difference between mdr info and other kinds of news practice discussed in this book is that its products are (mostly) heard rather than read. I was interested from my first day at mdr info in understanding how the largely visual screenwork of news journalism intersected with the auditory basis of radio.

I was surprised to find that the auditory qualities of radio played a remarkably ancillary role in the production process. Given the demands of their screenwork, the news department did not actually listen to the mdr info broadcast, at least while they were in the office. The CvDs did listen to the broadcast and to a large quantity of possible *Beitrag* material besides but I noticed that they often listened to features at accelerated playback, as much as four times faster than normal speed, so that they could review features at a fraction of their actual length. Much sonic detail was lost at high speed—the tones and textures of voice and background sound, for example. Yet, this seemed unproblematic to the CvDs because informational content was their principal matter of concern.

At the same time, as noted above, mdr info journalists were quite concerned with how their news reports "sounded." The aesthetics of writing radio news was clearly attuned to the acoustics of reading aloud. And, yet, the journalists never actually read their reports out loud themselves. The final text of the news reports and headlines was always read silently by the *Kernteam* in double-spaced print format because this was the same textual interface that the news readers themselves used. One could argue, of course, that reading silently is itself an auditory as well as visual practice. Moreover, the written language of radio news was, in a more basic sense, already composed for hearing.

Once one of the newsreaders brought Hagen back the print copy of his *nachrichten* to point out a spelling error. Hagen chuckled at the missing "s" in the word *Bundesbürger* (citizen of Germany). I asked Hagen whether the news department routinely received feedback from the readers. He replied, "Sometimes the readers will tell us if something doesn't sound right to them." "But only the brave ones," his colleague Anke joked and they laughed. "Yes," Hagen confirmed, "they endure quite a lot." Then he paused and waved the paper in his hand. "It used to be the case that we wouldn't have cared so much about a spelling error, as long as the reader wouldn't stumble over it. But now the text is automatically posted to the Internet as well." He went on to explain that the automatic postings of *nachrichten* to the Internet had affected the way the *Redaktion* considered language.

"There is such a thing as radio language. When I build a *Meldung*, I start with the agency text but then translate the core of the report into shorter, declarative sentences, more active verbs, sometimes less wordy formulations. Radio should have an 'aha effect,' not leave a listener wondering what he just heard. In the old days, the key thing was that the text had to be *verständlich zu hören* [comprehensible to listen to]. Now, with the Internet, we are getting more requests that our pieces be formulated so that *die gut lesbar sind* [they are easy to read]. This is also a technical issue. In the old days, to make things easier for the readers we'd type in a series of arrows wherever we thought they might pause for emphasis. But those arrows didn't look good when the reports were posted on the Internet, so now we use color coding. These are just details, but they are details where the reality of the Internet affects us. Add all of these details together and they can be *belastend* [burdensome]. There are colleagues here who say, 'Hey, we do radio' and wonder why we should be worrying about how text looks on the page. But, okay, we're multimedial now and we can't get off a moving train."

Multimediality, the fact that mdr info was now publicizing visual as well as auditory news content, introduced new concerns into how *Redakteure* formulated their reports. At the level of sentence structure and word choice, multimediality could generate tensions between written and oral modes of expression. But these tensions were not frequently highlighted and it was Marc's impression that this was because mdr info did not work with *Originalton* [more colloquially known as *O-Ton*; literally, "original sound"] but instead with the performance of texts that were produced in house. Thus, the basis of all mdr info's content was ultimately written rather than oral. Even the features were based by and large on correspondent reports rather than on tape of original acoustic recordings. mdr sputnik news did use *O-Ton* and Marc, who also worked in their news department, felt that original sound could add value to news reporting. "I think hearing Chancellor Merkel's actual voice, for example, has informational value. Does she sound tired, does she sound elated? It adds something to a *Beitrag* beyond simply the words she used, which anyone could repeat."

When I pushed Marc to say more about the aesthetics of using original recordings in radio news, he shifted away from informational value to the ethics of editing tape.

"One important aesthetic question is how to maintain the natural patterns of speech. Politicians, for example, unfortunately speak always and incessantly with their voices raised [*sprechen leider heute alles und immerzu mit der Stimme oben*] which you can't cut out without losing their whole message. But the most important question is to be careful in cutting to make sure that the sentence maintains the speaker's meaning with as little distortion [*nicht zu sehr verfälscht*] as possible. It's fine to take out pauses for thought [*Gedenkpausen*] and breathing sounds [*Atmer*]. But you could hear a tape in which someone was thinking over something like 'I . . . never . . . read . . . much . . . Herta Müller' and in a second take those pauses out and make 'I never read much Herta Müller!' But then you've changed the meaning. And obviously you can never ever cut out a decisive word so that another meaning arises."

The preservation of original meaning, of informational content, remained a more dominant consideration than, as Marc put it, "acoustic elegance."

Quarter-Hour Time

The struggle to meet professional standards of acoustic elegance, informational accuracy, and news relevance was an issue that arose frequently in my interviews at mdr info. All the *Redakteure* addressed the psychic stress of operating in a perpetual countdown mode. Michael described how time itself tended to unravel the best intentions and efforts of professionalism. "You could probably measure this with mathematical precision. When the quarter hour advances, with each passing second another criterion drops away: beauty, sentence length, depth of research [*Schönheit, Satzlänge, Recherchetiefe*]. You reach the point where you must decide: Is it more important that what I am writing satisfies my categories or that I get the thing out?" According to Michael, the pressure to get the thing out always triumphed in the end.

Quarter-hour time was certainly a pressured mode of labor, and its temporal compression exerted a high degree of influence over the practice of judgment. Yet it was not simply a solvent of professional intentions. Its constantly evaporating moments also represented a temporality susceptible to craft intervention and structure filled with opportunities for professional performance. This tension was exquisitely evident in moments when the news department struggled to get high-value breaking news into the next axis. Let me give one extended example from the morning of October 6, 2009.

The *Redaktion* had known for weeks that the Nobel Prize in physics would be awarded that day and past experience had taught them that Nobel Prize announcements were usually made around 11:30 a.m., with a flurry of agency reports following a few minutes later. This meant that in the course of normal news planning, a slot was already being held in the 12:00 p.m. news report for the expected Nobel Prize announcement.

It was a slow news morning. All the *Redakteure* were already bored by the molasses-like pace of the coalition negotiations in Berlin and Thuringia and nothing else was pressing. Hagen, who along with Anke was working in the *Kernteam* that morning, said he was looking forward to the Nobel announcement. I asked whether this was a case of a *Pflichtmeldung*, news they were obliged to report on whether or not it met their news criteria. Hagen shook his head—no, the Nobel Prizes were not *Pflichtmeldungen*, although they were *planbares Wissen* [predictable knowledge] that they could prepare for in advance. "No, we're glad to do them. The prize is internationally recognized. And although with the scientists, the names usually mean nothing to people, the research can be interesting for them, especially if a German wins.

It's certainly better than what we have as a top story now. It will bring a certain vital-ization [*gewisse Belebung*] to the program. We'll have something to discuss and natu-rally a feature has been planned as well. Anyway, it will give the program a kick; it will shake things up a bit."

But at 11:00 a.m., an *Eilmeldung* (urgent news bulletin) arrived with the announce-ment that Deutsche Bahn would raise its ticket prices by 1.8 percent for 2010. Marike, who was working headlines, saw it first and said loudly, "Uh-oh, Bahn is raising prices. Ach, the pigs!" There was a short burst of conversation surrounding when to run the story: in the :15 headlines or in the :30 news report. Did the *Thema* deserve two sentences or six? The figure of 1.8 percent did not seem a very dramatic increase but it would affect the vast majority of their audience in some fashion. One of the ZbVs observed that the prices could not stay the same because of inflation. But Hagen reminded the others that the last time they had covered Bahn a couple of weeks be-forehand they had reported an expert's prediction that prices would stay the same or even go down because of lower energy costs. The deviation from the earlier expert prediction was newsworthy in itself. In the end, they agreed to run the *Thema* in the :15 headlines.

But the news value of the Bahn story seemed to grow over time, perhaps, ironi-cally, in part because of the discursive labor invested into it by the *Redaktion* to ana-lyze it. As Rudi said to me on another occasion, "If a story is interesting enough to provoke an argument among us, it could be that there's something there for the public [*Publikum*] as well." By 11:27 a.m., Hagen told me he thought it was *eine spannende Frage* (a suspenseful question) whether to do the Bahn or the Nobel Prize as the :00 lead story. "Bahn will still be fresh and is definitely consumer-oriented. And if the Nobel is again an American [*laughs*], who no one has heard of then . . . But I always find it very interesting to explain the research even if that's certainly easier to do on TV or on the Internet than it is on radio."

As 11:30 a.m. came and went without the Nobel announcement, one could feel the tension level rising in the department. Every second counted for the purposes of back-ground research and writing and these were now being stolen away from them by the Swedes and the news agencies. At 11:35 a.m., the beep-beep of another *Eilmeldung* produced a collective exhalation. But it was a false alarm, a report on a multiple car accident in Saxony; important regional news yes, but not top-story material. With each passing minute, the Bahn seemed to secure its top story position, because the likelihood of being able to produce a credible alternative disappeared. At 11:41 a.m., the CvD Kerstin made an unusual appearance in the news department to talk about what to do for the :00 axis. Only Anke appeared to still hold out hope that they could manage the Nobel Prize for the top of the hour.

Kerstin: What do you have planned for your :00?

Hagen: Bahn.

K: I'm wondering about the R1 axis, how I should put it together . . . If nothing's new, then Bahn.

Anke: Nobel Prize.

H: Bahn.

K [*to A*]: But only if it comes, right, it could come after twelve, no?

A: Yesterday it was 11:30.

K [*surprised*]: Hmm . . .

H: We're still waiting. To make a decision.

K: So, basically, either the Nobel Prize , , ,

H: Nah, unless it's a German. I'd doubt it.

K: But the price increase isn't so dramatic either . . .

Marike: But in view of lowered energy costs and a low inflation rate it is . . . And for midday it's the only new thing [*Neuigkeit*] . . . What else do we have, the Left Party?

K: Fine, with the Bahn we can do a feature. With the Nobel Prize too. If it all fits it will be a minor miracle. . . . Thanks, folks, I just wanted to get on the same page [*eine Einheit bilden*].

Kerstin left and everyone returned to work, typing away, with Hagen focused on his Bahn story. The tension level continued to rise, however, since it was obvious that under certain conditions (a German prize winner) it would still be optimal to do the Nobel Prize as the :00 lead.

At 11:50 a.m. Hagen checked the digital display on the wall and then shrugged his shoulders at me. His Bahn *Meldung* was all but complete.

Hagen [*smirking*]: The Nobel Prize for Physics will evidently not be awarded this year.

Anke: It's really peculiar that they don't have it out. Every day it's been 11:30 and today not even at 11:45.

H: I think that the time has been set at 11:30 for years now.

A: I thought so too.

H: Shall I ask the CvD to call Stockholm? [*to me*] That's a joke.

At 11:52 a.m. finally, *finally*, there was a beep-beep. A round of sighs of relief across the desks and Anke says, "Now!" The whole department immediately goes quiet as everyone processes the first agency report individually. Only Marike mutters, "English."

Thirty-one seconds after the first report, Hagen arrived at a new decision: "If I just do a short version, I can get it in as the lead." His keyboard begins clattering a second later. Other *Eilmeldungen* are beginning to arrive from other news agencies.

Hagen has seven minutes and eleven seconds before :00.

The most important information to convey in the first iteration of the story is not the details of the science and its implications but the national and institutional affiliations of the laureates. Yet the seeming simplicity of this information is defeated almost immediately by the complex émigré experience of one of the three 2009 physics laureates, Charles Kuen Kao: born in Shanghai; raised in Hong Kong when it was British territory; educated in the United Kingdom; professional work as a fiber optics specialist for the ITT corporation in the United Kingdom, United States, and in several European locations; academic affiliations in Hong Kong and the United Kingdom; joint British and American citizenship. The problem is that the news agencies have not agreed on how to capture Kao's life experience in the lexical efficiency demanded by fast-time news practice.

[6 mins., 35 secs.] Marike: OK, AP says China/Great Britain and two from the USA.

[6 mins., 29 secs.] Anke: So, he's British. What do we write? Born in China?

[6 mins., 27 secs.] Hagen: We'd better check . . .

Everyone is typing or checking other news venues for clues as to how to define Kao. With five minutes and fifteen seconds to go two additional *Eilmeldungen* arrive almost simultaneously; one is a corrected version from dpa.

[5 mins., 6 secs.] Anke: dpa is saying only China now.

[5 mins., 5 secs.] Marike [*reading*]: "imaging semiconductor circuit" . . . [*sighs*]

There's bustle and murmuring conversation around the whole news desk as everyone reacts to the breaking news. Behind me I hear someone near the RvD desk say, "We've really got to hurry."

[3 mins., 20 secs.] Another *Eilmeldung* arrives. Marike opens it immediately and laughs, "Now AFP says USA, Great Britain, and Canada!"

[3 mins., 19 secs.] Anke: Oh, noooooo.

[3 mins., 16 secs.] Hagen: And what about the Chinese guy?

[3 mins., 14 secs.] Marike: He's British.

[3 mins., 12 secs.] Hagen: You mean he's not really Chinese?

[3 mins., 11 secs.] Marike: Yes . . . no . . .

[3 mins., 10 secs.] Anke: Of Chinese ancestry.

[3 mins., 8 secs.] Marike: A Briton of Chinese ancestry or a Chinese working in Britain . . .

[3 mins., 4 secs.] Hagen: Then we should say Chinese, or?

[2 mins., 55 secs.] Marike: It's being marketed differently everywhere . . . that he works in Great Britain seems certain.

[2 mins., 46 secs.] Anke: Let's take a look . . . [*she opens up the* Wikipedia *entry for Kao*] Charles . . . Kao . . . He has a British mother . . .

[2 mins., 37 secs.] Marike: That makes sense, the Chinese seem to have a habit of using names that can also be understood in the west.

[2 mins., 31 secs.] Hagen: Really? . . . [*typing intensely*]

[1 min., 58 secs.] Anke [*triumphantly*]: OK, got it, Kao was *born* in Shanghai!

[1 min., 55 secs.] Marike: Then, of Chinese ancestry, just as it said.

Anke also discovers a few seconds later, much to our collective surprise, that Kao's *Wikipedia* entry already contains the sentence, "He won the Nobel Prize in 2009." Scarcely six minutes after the first *Eilmeldung*, *Wikipedia* has scooped the vast majority of news organizations. "Crazy," Anke says in obvious wonder.

[0 mins., 59 secs.] Hagen: I'm going to make it for the lead.

[0 min, 45 secs.] Hagen's desk printer hums into life and spits out a single piece of paper. Hagen reviews it very quickly.

[0 mins., 20 secs.] Satisfied, with a soft "yes" of accomplishment, Hagen propels his desk chair backward with both legs, swivels, and runs across the newsroom, dodging desks and colleagues, to hand the piece of paper to the newsreader who is lingering, somewhat anxiously, in front of the broadcast booth, with seventeen seconds before the red broadcast light goes on. Hagen gives him a brief word of explanation or perhaps encouragement.

[0 mins., 3 secs.] Hagen returns to his desk, sits down, and thumps the desk with his hand, obviously proud of his accomplishment. Still aglow, Hagen turns back to me. "Just a quick explanation, I decided for the Nobel Prize story, because [*pauses, not quite sure himself*], it was my sense of things [*weil ich das empfinde*]."

Having sat with him through the whole shift, the course of events did seem somehow self-explanatory. In a sense, the delay of the announcement had cathected the Nobel Prize story with even more attention and interest. The Bahn was a satisfactory replacement and an important story—but not a sensational one. When the Nobel announcement was made just within the window of time when it could be produced for the :00, the competitive desire to break the news surged. And, like watching a sports competition, I found myself strangely emotionally absorbed in someone else's performance struggle. Although the stakes seem objectively minor, those gathered there experienced a heroic moment of journalism, something worth running across a room and celebrating. A few minutes after the :00, Hagen showed me with satisfaction that mdr info had been one of only two ARD channels to have managed to get the Nobel Prize in their :00 report. Later in the day, Hagen mentioned his achievement again in a way that made me understand that these were the kinds of moments of praxiological success and achievement that lingered longer in memory, the thrills of challenging and defeating the countdown that offset the endless flow of quarter-hour time and the considerable tedium of normal screenwork. "It's part of the job," explained Hagen. "Sometimes you just have to say, okay, I've got five minutes and I can do this. It's just three or four sentences. You crack your spine and earn your pay."

News Gone Wild (Bluewater)

Many of the *Redakteure* at mdr info began their careers before the full digitalization of radio. But no one, I discovered, missed analog tape. Indeed no one could think of a single disadvantage to the digitalization of production that had taken place in the late 1990s. The closest was Harold who said there something slightly satisfying about pushing a start button and watching a tape begin to spin. "But beyond that, there's no comparison. With tape, you cut the original and it's gone. With digital, you can play with the recording as much as you like and still preserve the original in case you want to start over." Yet the *Redakteure* were also very aware that as the digitalization of production helped multiply efficiencies and outputs across the entire news industry, a denser informational environment ensued. They also recognized that with informational density came, inevitably, higher workloads for information filtering and higher, faster expectations for production. And with a greater volume of work came more stress, and perhaps even more anxiety dreams.

Of all the *Redakteure* at mdr info, Marc seemed the one most interested in how a digital *Medienumfeld* (media environment) was affecting how journalists practiced their craft. The problem seemed, frankly, both to fascinate and to trouble him. During our first interview in September, Marc expanded on the connection between digitalization and what he described as a "homogenization" of news content.

> "Today we work in a constant state of comparability. Before digitalization we were encapsulated [*abgekapselt*]. I mean, we could listen to other radio stations but it was relatively difficult. So I sat relatively shut off in my own little world of news. I got material from the news agencies, I received material from the reporters, and that was, so to speak, everything. And, I could watch the *Tagesschau*[41] at 8:00 p.m. and could compare myself to that but that was just one program. I can't prove this but I suspect that this comparability has influenced how we select *nachrichten*. The fact that I can go online and immediately see what other media are doing. I think that the regional broadcasters had more local color before. Now with [other news radio stations like] Inforadio, with B5, with SWR, the coverage is more or less the same

although each of us maybe seek to add a certain regional inflection. . . . News *Themen* are more homogenous today then they used to be."

Following on our earlier conversations, I asked Marc if, in addition to new technical and institutional capacities for monitoring of competitors and peer stations, that the organization of news production and circulation had made a difference as well.

"I do think that the agencies are contributing to this phenomenon. Ultimately, it's a question of quantity. If one agency or all the agencies go after a *Thema*, and not just with a single *Meldung* but with continuing coverage, that event will somehow gain more weight. If I'm facing the continuous pressure [*Dauerdruck*] of six agencies updating a story on an hourly basis then I'd probably be more inclined to put it into my own *nachrichten*. And with the agencies I do think there's this very negative tendency that information becomes news very quickly, information that wouldn't have been considered newsworthy before. Because there is this enormous competitive pressure among them: who can get it out first. It's one of those things that if I have the time to stand back, I can ask why are we doing this. But if I'm sitting there in the middle of it, like they are, being bombarded by flashing red *Eilmeldungen*, with breaking news scrolling on n-tv, with *Spiegel Online* headlines, and who knows what else, then I am drawn into this competitive struggle, into this media hype too. And it's the case that more information is being circulated these days that is simply not news."

Marc then paused thoughtfully before asking, "Have you heard about Bluewater?" I had not, but Marc took a file out of his desk that contained a series of clippings and printouts related to an event that had generated much media attention and discussion in Germany a few weeks before.

Bluewater was a cleverly designed PR hoax by a German film director Jan Henrik Stahlberg seeking to promote his film *Short Cut to Hollywood*, a satirical comedy about three middle-aged Germans seeking fame and fortune in the United States by manipulating American media's thirst for spectacle. Although Stahlberg's film was mostly panned in Germany and ignored elsewhere, his hoax promises to have a longer afterlife. Around 9:00 a.m. on September 10, 2009, someone alleging to be a native German cameraman employed by a local television broadcaster in southern California began calling *Redaktionen* across Germany alerting them to breaking news of a suicide bombing in a small town in California called Bluewater. The cameraman told the German journalists that there was already video material on his station KVPK-7's website. A KVPK-7 website did exist that contained breaking news video material and a report in which a news anchor described eye-witness reports of three "Arab-looking" men storming into a restaurant with explosive belts just before two explosions were heard.

Bluewater is a fictitious place and the KVPK-7 website was designed by Stahlberg and his collaborators to look like the site of an authentic American local TV station.

The video material was footage from a scene in his film in which the three protagonists had pulled a similar stunt to gain media attention. Stahlberg and his colleagues
also set up a fake City of Bluewater website to "prove" the city's existence and local
police and fire department phone numbers which contained authentic California area
codes but which had been set up to reroute, via Skype, to an apartment in Berlin
where inquiries could be answered by one of Stahlberg's team. Additionally, the KVPK-
7 site offered fake Twitter reports from alleged eyewitnesses, which could be indepen-
dently "confirmed" by looking at the Twitter feeds.

The brilliance of the hoax was that there appeared to be several independent
sources (a local TV station, government officials, and independent eye-witnesses) that,
in combination, could confirm the event had occurred. This seemed an adequate
source base for a news report, especially given that the event had taken place at night,
when major U.S. media could be expected to react more slowly. Indeed, the promise
of an inside scoop on a breaking news event, which, had it been true, would certainly
have been covered across the world, proved too tempting to pass up. No doubt much
to Stahlberg's delight, his hoax hooked the biggest prize of all, Germany's leading
news agency, dpa, which sent out the following *Meldung* at 9:39 a.m. on September 10,
local time.

> Los Angeles (dpa)—In the small town of Bluewater, California, local broadcaster
> vpk-tv is reporting a suicide bombing. The station is reporting that two explosions
> occurred in a restaurant and that police responded and evacuated the restaurant.
> Whether there were injuries remains unclear. The restaurant did not appear to be
> destroyed in the first released images. The perpetrators have been described by the
> station as of Arab descent.

With dpa's imprimatur, other *Redaktionen* quickly fell in line. Within minutes
Bluewater was picked up as breaking news by other German *Leitmedien*, including
the news TV channel n24 and the online editions of the *Süddeutsche Zeitung, Die Zeit,
Die Welt, Berliner Morgenpost*, as well as many other online news sites. Three other
dpa *Meldungen* appeared over the next hour and a half, including the seemingly improbable information from KVPK-TV that the three bombers survived the assault
and were members of a Berlin-based rap group called the Berlin Boys 666 who had
bombed the restaurant in order to promote a new album. Marc deadpanned, "You
have to wonder what dpa was thinking. Rapping suicide bombers? Really?" dpa did
apparently become increasingly concerned as the day went on that none of the American *Leitmedien* had picked up the story, especially since the alleged bombing had
occurred in such close proximity to September 11. At 1:44 p.m., dpa finally retracted
the story. Forty minutes later, a competing news agency, ddp, broke the news that the
Bluewater story was Stahlberg's hoax.

Bluewater was a major embarrassment for dpa and one that prompted dpa's assistant editor in chief, Wolfgang Büchner, to issue a rare public apology to their clients. Büchner also posted a statement, "Six Lessons from Bluewater," on dpa's intranet, which was leaked and discussed elsewhere in the German media as well. Lesson One was, "In our rivalry with our competitors, accuracy must always take precedence over speed."

The lesson Marc learned from Bluewater was different: the agencies were increasingly vulnerable to disinformation. "It's both a question of their overload and a question of this incredible competition they have with each other to be first." As Rudi had noted as well, "We just can't trust them to be gatekeepers in the same way as before."

This was not to say that Marc or his colleagues doubted the value and performance of the news agencies entirely. Indeed, I recall Marc's fist-pumping excitement when dpa picked up a *Meldung* he had sent out on the Thuringian coalition negotiations. Recognition from dpa remained a gold standard of excellence in German news journalism even after Bluewater. But Marc felt that the hoax proved that a certain frantic impulsiveness was infiltrating even the most stately and secure estates of news journalism. Rudi was of the same opinion. "Die Sitten verwildern sich" (the customs are going wild), he liked to say of the news industry as a whole. Being first was coming to be more important than being right; *Themen* were being given coverage too soon and with too little reflection; there was an odd tendency to hype stories like swine flu where the substance was not even clear. Rudi laid most of the blame on the expanding volume of information and the overloads and time pressure that accompanied it. But, of course, inadequate training and focus of journalists themselves were also to blame.

There was just the one solution. Michael reminded me, with firm conviction, "There are strategies against the time pressure, and the decisive criterion to my mind is professionalization. A well-trained news journalist with a firm system of values [*festes Wertesystem*] and firm sense of news value will be able to manage *nachrichten*, even under these conditions." Professionalism offered if not a cure to the wilding of the news industry then at least the courage to deploy expert practice in that industry's defense. Michael seemed more convinced than the others that the praxiological powers of professionalism were adequate to counteract the rising tides of digital information. No one predicted a triumph of humanity over water. And yet, the levies needed to hold.

Months earlier, Michael had described to me a visit to the AP-DD bureau in Frankfurt at the invitation of our mutual friend Paul. "I couldn't believe it when I saw what was going on at that work station, Dominic. Four screens! Insanity!" I had to smile. Somehow, in Michael's recollection, the density of interfaces at the *Slotinsel* (slot island) had grown from three to four. Having served as news director at mdr info for nearly a decade, I knew that Michael was not easily intimidated. He had literally spent years in quarter-hour time. And yet mediological phantoms proliferated even in his memory. Then it was Michael's turn to produce an impish grin: "Four screens. I wouldn't want to spend a single hour of my life in that chair."

Which brings us back to our ethnographic alpha and omega: screenwork. In chapter 4, I offer five more general reflections on news journalism under the influence of what I term "digital liberalism." These reflections are built upon the three case studies and engage other scholarship. My intent and hope is to offer a more transparticular portrait of the key conditions and dynamics of contemporary news journalism as well as a sense of how its current *Zwischenformen* might evolve in the future.

Chapter 4

The News Informatic

Five Reflections on News Journalism and Digital Liberalism

In a changing society, and especially after the Industrial Revolution, problems of social perspective and social orientation became more acute. New relations between men, between men and things, were being intensely experienced, and in this area, especially, the traditional institutions of church and school, or of settled community and persisting family, had very little to say. . . . An increased awareness of mobility and change, not just as abstractions but as lived experiences, led to a major redefinition, in practice and then in theory of the function and process of social communication. . . . The press for political and economic information; the photograph for community, family and personal life; the motion picture for curiosity and entertainment; telegraphy and telephony for business information and some important personal messages. It was within this complex of specialized forms that broadcasting arrived.

We have now become used to a situation in which broadcasting is a major social institution, about which there is always controversy but which, in its familiar form, seems to have been predestined by the technology. This predestination, however, when closely examined, proves to be no more than a set of particular social decisions, in particular circumstances, which were then so widely if imperfectly ratified that it is now difficult to see them as decisions rather than as (retrospectively) inevitable results.

—Raymond Williams, *Television: Technology and Cultural Form*

Radial Messaging, Lateral Messaging

This author grew up in a world where broadcasting represented the dominant model of newsmaking and news circulation—a model that seemed destined to endure indefinitely. A few decades later, very little seems durable about the broadcast model of news, except perhaps its process of diminishment. Indeed, we live in a media environment today in which the model of broadcasting that Raymond Williams described so elegantly and accurately in his 1974 study, *Television*, seems increasingly quaint. Over the past thirty years, broadcasting has not only experienced a pluralization of national and transnational production centers (e.g., cable and satellite broadcasting). But those centers have also been both augmented and undermined by a plethora of new media technologies, institutions, and habits oriented toward communication between small numbers of highly mobile and increasingly active producer-receivers. The messaging radii and hierarchies typical of classical broadcasting appear, more often than not, to be yielding their authority to peer-to-peer meshes of communication, whether in the form of the proliferating vibrant micropublics of "social media" like Facebook and Twitter or in the global ubiquity of mobile telephony. And, just as Williams might have predicted, this situation "seems to have been predestined by the technology." Any Web 2.0 evangelist, or for that matter, journalistic account of new media, would assure us that the galactic computational linkages composing the Internet were themselves the doom of broadcasting monopolies of informational circulation and the catalyst for an irresistible sprawl of grassroots co-messaging.

Yet, the endurance of such tales of inevitability is precisely why we must remain mindful of Williams's method of analysis. Williams illustrated how the industrialization of European society generated social dynamics (rapid urbanization and intensified translocal migration, for example) that shifted scales, speeds, and pathways of social interaction in ways that invited if not necessitated innovation in social communication. Scientific and engineering work on the application of electricity to communication proceeded in a domain partly, but only partly, insulated from military, political, and commercial interests and decision making. Some innovations, facsimile reproduction for example, were technologically possible centuries before there was any obvious public purpose or institutional demand for them. Thus, certain inventions were forgotten, only to be rediscovered later under more immediate pressure or optimal conditions. Other inventions, like telegraphy, developed specialized military and commercial applications long before becoming more widespread instruments of communicational relations and publicity. As Williams puts it, "particular social decisions" were made regarding development, institutionalization, and commercialization at all phases of technical emergence; decisions that refracted the actancy of technology through the agency of human purposes and understandings.[1] Williams would be the first to admit the revolutionary power of electronic mediation; but he believed that no portfolio of technologies and effects emerged exactly as it was intended to, nor as it pleased.

Indeed, Williams argues his case against the technological determination of social communication so efficiently and persuasively that one would think that particular argument to be settled once and for all. But it has not been settled and never will be. As I have discussed at length elsewhere, media theory is riven by different ontologies and by different perceptions of causality.[2] Moreover, I am doubtful that formalist and technologically deterministic theories of mediation will ever disappear, if for no other reason than that they are elegantly straightforward and secure ways of marking the phenomenological limits of human agency in the dizzying flows of social mediation. The inverse of the proposition that media are little more than passive instruments and conduits for the achievement of human purposes is the idea that media are technological or environmental forces that shape and determine our purposes in ways we are unaware of. Which evokes a figure like Marshall McLuhan, a media analyst no less subtle and provocative in certain respects than Williams but one whose fundamental(ist) commitment to the causality of medium dooms him to serve as a foil to Williams's historical materialist and institutionalist sensibilities.[3] The debate between methods of media analysis is not epistemologically trivial but its encampments are relatively predictable. Rather than touring the trenches of competing theories, I will skip ahead to a multiattentional[4] portrait of the situation in which news journalism finds itself today.

For this task, Williams's historical analysis offers two conclusions that remain insightful and helpful points of departure. The first is that the history of electronic mediation exposes an oscillation between a potentiality for point-to-point, often two-way messaging and a capacity for hub-spoke, less often two-way, messaging. I suggest that we term the former the *lateral potentiality* of electronic communication and the latter the *radial potentiality* (figure 4.1). Williams notes that the institutionalization of lateral messaging actually predated radial messaging in the development of broadcasting: "A technology of specific messages to specific persons was complemented, but only relatively late, by a technology of varied messages to a general public."[5] We live today at a time when the proportional significance of lateral messaging is once again ascendant. Indeed, one suspects that, had he lived to analyze them, Williams would marvel at the way in which many of the signature technologies of digital communication today (like social media, blogs, wikis, and SMS text messaging) incorporate unique fusions of lateral and radial messaging potentials and have the ability to address dynamic

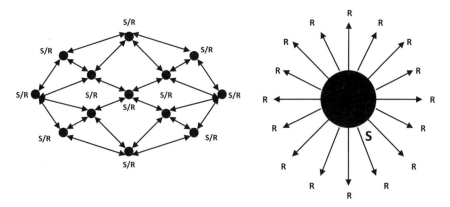

4.1 Lateral versus radial

networks of mobile senders and receivers, even to constitute relatively spontaneous, interactive micropublics that span continents and time zones.

But the many marvels of digital media would not obviate the implications of Williams's second conclusion: that broadcasting in the twentieth century never resolved an intrinsic tension between centralized, institutionalized production and mobilized, isolated reception. In Williams's model, broadcasting developed slowly but purposefully to overcome the challenge of social communication (particularly political and market communication) in the face of a broader dynamic that he terms "mobile privatisation," the increasing mobility and isolated domesticity of modern European social experience.[6] Broadcasting, whether in the service of commercial or governmental interest, needed to operate at scales, speeds, and with informational density unprecedented in the history of communication in order to make its messaging radii intersect with actors who were seemingly less securely positioned and yet more shielded from centralized authority than ever before. Yet, these new scales, speeds, and density also needed to be financed and controlled. Licensing fees and advertising revenues became the most common techniques developed in western nations in the twentieth century. But these were solutions that in turn required some level of consent from an audience who remained largely disengaged from the production process of broadcasting and who thus represented a site of potential resistance. Williams views the development of twentieth-century broadcasting as a struggle to assert new commercial and governmental hegemonies, but broadcasting's considerable social power and many communicational successes were continuously challenged by the relative fixity of its productive organization and by the relative monology of its radial messaging.

I am quite certain that Williams would not have believed for a moment that what I am terming "classical broadcasting" was doomed to eventual failure any more than he believed it was inevitable it had arisen in the first place. Yet the development of the Internet through new alliances of scientific and military aspiration helped, alongside the emergence of cellular telephony, to create the communicational infrastructure for a revolutionary intensification of lateral messaging that has deeply impacted institutions and habits of social communication across the world. Williams would likely view the popularization of the Internet and mass mobile telephony as new responses to mobile privatization through these institutions' capacity to provide new communicational linkages among a social field of ever-more itinerant, decontextualized, and isolated actors. But he would also appreciate how quickly and radically these new arrangements and practices of social communication have upset the delicate political economy of their forebears. The wedge between production and reception has been driven deeper. The easy reproducibility and global reach of digital news texts and images, for example, has deeply undermined their value and status as commodities. Yet, the production of original news content remains localized and costly. Mid-twentieth-century financial instruments such as licensing and advertising have thus far proven inadequate to manage what appears to be the increasing unhinging of centralized news production/circulation/reception from mobilized news reception/circulation/production. Thus, the "business model," as it is commonly termed, of newsmaking is in ruins, a condition that is accelerating the erosion of the institutions of mid-twentieth-century broadcast news. Meanwhile, the lateral revolution advances and the radial institutions that not only anchored a certain understanding of "news" but also liberal-democratic conceptions of political publicity seem increasingly aged, indeed "gerontocratic,"[7] and incapable of renewal. The future appears bleak to many, exhilarating to a few, and uncertain to all.

It is difficult to avoid normative judgments about the state of news today, especially when one is as personally invested as I have become in news and its practitioners. But, I seek to avoid the premise that what we are facing is a "news crisis" and that this crisis is an obvious effect of a set of known and predictably causal commercial and technical forces. Without diminishing a critical analysis of power in mediation, the brilliance of Williams's method is his ability to develop a historically attentive schematization of the sometimes co-elaborative but also often contradictory forces involved in the institutionalization of electronic mediation. Williams's equivalently serious and nondogmatic approach to the problem of causality is precisely what, in my view, enabled him to predict the next thirty-five years of televisual media development (from the rise of paranational media conglomerates to flat-screen television monitors) with such uncanny accuracy and to foresee if not exactly the Internet then at least the struggle toward "universal accessibility" of electronic communication and information sharing.[8] His attention to the multiple causalities threaded through every institution is also what allowed him to stay alert to signs of alternative media futures in a moment of corporate media dominance he described rather optimistically as a "short and successful counter-revolution."

My opening argument is thus not the obviousness of crisis and decline but rather simply that a rebalancing between radial and lateral messaging has impacted every site and aspect of (northern[9]) news production, circulation, and reception over the past fifteen years. These impacts have rendered epistemic distinctions between terms like "production" and "reception"—radialist categories at their core—increasingly hazy. Although the financial and monetary implications of the lateral revolution have been dramatic and duly attention-getting, they still represent only one salient dimension of the current situation. In the remainder of the chapter, I offer five more-specific reflections on the state of news journalism today, reflections that are based primarily on the three case studies in this book but that are also cross-informed by other scholarship on contemporary news journalism and by my fifteen years of talking to journalists in Germany and the United States about the shifting conditions of their craft.

First Reflection: The news journalist is increasingly a sedentary screenworker

This is the premise with which I began this book. But even had I not, I believe it would be the unavoidable conclusion of the ethnographic studies. Thorsten Quandt's remarkable study of five German newsrooms offers corroboration. On average, Quandt found that journalists spent 32.1 percent of their time on screen-based search-related activities, 21.5 percent of their time on screen-based text production, 14.9 percent of their time on communication via media, and only 1.8 percent of their time "Moving/walking around."[10] With computerization, the popularization of the Internet, and the institutionalization of web browsers, search engines, and desktop content managing systems, screenwork has emerged as the dominant operational activity of newsmaking. The contemporary news journalist is therefore predominantly a screenworker. Foreign correspondents, investigative journalists, and beat reporters have not disappeared from popular images of journalism, but they no longer represent, strictly speaking, actual norms of practice in northern[11] news journalism. And while roaming truth-seekers still do exist in journalism, they too, like the rest of us "information professionals," are spending more of their time engaging screens.

Screenwork first emerged as an aspect of newsmaking in the 1970s and 1980s, driven by organizational initiatives in news media and elsewhere in western corporate culture to harness personal computers and office-based digital information systems to generate new production efficiencies. In the news industry, computerization was originally viewed as a means of improving word-processing speed and reducing labor costs through the automation of composition and some copyediting work.[12] But in the process of institutionalization, computers rapidly became involved in every aspect of news production from marketing to layout to archiving, creating new opportunities for automating tasks previously accomplished directly by humans and for concentrating remaining production tasks in the hands of fewer newsworkers. Veteran journalists who could recall work life before computerization frequently related to me how much larger the support staff had been, how much more time they now spent at their desks, and how their individual workloads had increased.

Of course, journalism has always had its sedentary side. Typewriting, for example, also involved seated production; phone use before the era of mobile telephony likewise. The crucial difference between previous forms of "sedentary journalism"[13] and its contemporary variant is how screenwork currently channels an unprecedented number of key journalistic tasks (e.g., word processing, text editing, archival research, breaking news monitoring, surveillance of the competition, and intraoffice communication and coordination) through a single interface with a normally fixed location. Although, as we have seen in the ethnographic studies, other media like conversation and telephony persist and play important roles in the life of newsmaking, screens have come to represent the constant focus of professional life, the one relatively concentrated nexus through which an abundance of exchanges of labor, language, and knowledge pass. When journalists describe their work today in terms of information filtration, management, even curation, we can see how professional self-understanding is being shaped by screenwork's own "curation" of epistemic flows, flows whose multiplicity and interchangeability give experiential substance to abstract, generic categories like "information" and "content."

The implications of the centrality of screenwork to contemporary journalism are, however, by no means obvious and inevitable. As Williams argued, there is always the matter of decisions made and institutionalized. In this respect, the evident locational fixity of screenwork could change were laptop or tablet interfaces rather than desktop interfaces made organizational priorities. I witnessed no office use of laptops or tablets in my three studies in Germany but the effort at AP-DD to co-locate the three slot desks on the slot island was notable for its attempt to reduce isolation and to enhance communication across the desks.

Similarly, the informational operations and architecture of the Internet can be viewed as technological black boxes from the point of view of a newsroom. But the achievement of fast-time screen-based monitoring of a variety of information channels depends critically upon specialized content management software, like newsLINE IV, which in turn has been developed to respond to organizational priorities, especially the prioritization of breaking news coverage. In professional and organizational environments that support mottos such as "get it first but get it right," the surveillance of competing news organizations becomes a matter of establishing hierarchies of value. The fact that journalists devote so much of their time to monitoring what other *Leitmedien* (lead media) are doing certainly has to be understood in the context of the fast-time informational density of the Internet. But it also has to be understood in the context of organizational priorities that define the significance of that fast-time density, especially in the context of the competitive orientation of the news industry more generally. As we saw with mdr info, this competitive orientation impacted even powerful noncommercial German broadcasters as they perceived news agencies retreating from their traditional gatekeeper function with regard to news value.

Screenwork does not obviously lead to news automation or imitation, although this is a common accusation. It is powerfully tempting to link the word-processing functionality of copy/paste and the ubiquity of shovelware with the echoing of verbatim or nearly verbatim text throughout the news industry. Yet, once again, shovelware is no neutral technical innovation but rather a software response to particular organizational demands and decisions. Further causal variables include how avidly a news organization or a specific managing editor privileges speed of recirculation over novelty and how the size of a news staff relative to its workload may or may not encourage journalists to draw upon already existing text to meet production expectations. Even in the supposed empire of textual imitation, T-Online, we found that the organizational importance of copy/paste and shovelware was tempered by a variety of textual strategies for innovating "found text." Rather than a single act of reproduction, imitation at T-Online meant a compositional continuum in which text assemblages of new and gathered material typically grew iteratively around a core news agency text that was often erased in the process.

None of these observations prevent us from discussing the implications of screenwork in news journalism today. They simply remind us that it is not the screens and their various embedded (hardware) and enhanced (software) technical features that are the only causal factors at issue. In my third reflection below, I discuss what I feel to be the most salient implications of the current regime of screenwork for northern news journalism. In other words, what the current experience and practice of screenwork may itself be *causing*. However, it is important first to attend more closely to the broader political and social dynamics that intersect with the practical, organizational, professional, and technological dimensions of screenwork just described.

Second Reflection: The life informatic is also the life late liberal

Although seemingly an unremarkable technical interface, screenwork also might be viewed to incorporate and elaborate the political ontology of late liberalism. This rather dramatic-sounding proposition requires some further background. Since its consolidation in nineteenth-century European intellectual culture, liberalism has appeared in many forms and many voices.[14] It is, in my view, an intrinsically plural and ceaselessly mutating political discourse. But, across its plurality, liberalism nevertheless has featured certain core premises, the most important of which is its valorization of individual freedom, the celebration of seemingly autonomous and self-generative individuality that Beth Povinelli has aptly termed "autological."[15] Liberalism's most fundamental epistemic operation is to foreground the experiential fact that to some extent we can always believe ourselves to be unrelated beings, encountering the world "out there" through individualized senses, ideas, and bodies that are to a significant degree self-sovereign. Translating inchoate experiential understandings of biotic autonomy into the more certain and transindividual languages of political ontology, liberalism grows a worldview that promotes individuality as the most natural state and positive disposition of humanity. Social relations exist, of course—liberalism cannot deny them—but liberalism typically maintains that meaningful, positive social relations are familial and at most communitarian. Like Margaret Thatcher, liberalism is ultimately skeptical that something like "Society" actually exists as a meaningful reference for politics. Once beyond families and communities, liberalism offers us zones of exchange (in other words, markets), a discourse on rights, and political institutions for the remediation of incommensurable interests and differences (in other words, pluralism). Above all, individual rights are sacrosanct, including an individual's right to free expression, to pursue freedom even to the point of dominating other lesser individuals, to own and to amass individual property, and to dispose of that property as he or she sees fit.[16]

Comparatively, liberalism's twin[17] in modern European social philosophy, socialism, tends to valorize the phenomenological experience of interindividual relatedness, the recognition that no matter how much we might wish to believe human life is an island of selfhood, experience constantly reminds us not just of the archipelago of other selves but that our selfhood is in every way constituted through and contingent upon interaction with other selves and with transindividual societal institutions. Of course individuality exists—socialism would never deny it—but individuality is never held to be sovereign; rather it is, like Émile Durkheim's famous proposition "man is double,"[18] treated as the biological medium of a set of social forces or relations. In its more dramatic variants—twentieth-century communism, for example—the needs and interests of selves are entirely degraded relative to the interests of Society (and its political caretakers). More often, individualism is simply overtly or covertly moralized as a negative force of self-interest that undermines communitarian investment. Although often deemed opposite in their philosophies, the relationship between liberalism and socialism can also be viewed as one of mutual entitlement. Each crystallizes its political ontology around an experiential pole of modern sociality: autonomy (for liberalism) and relatedness (for socialism). Liberalism acknowledges relatedness but valorizes autonomy; socialism valorizes relatedness but acknowledges autonomy.

Given its experiential core, all modes of liberalism, to a greater or lesser extent, seek to diminish those aspects of experience that seem to compromise or to correct individual freedom and autonomy. What I term here "late liberalism" refers to the modes of western political liberalism that arose in the wake of global decolonization, beginning with the disruption and dissolution of European colonial authority in the 1950s and 1960s and culminating in the oil shocks and currency destabilization of the 1970s.[19] The collapse and partial resurrection (through international finance, development, and new military interventions) of western imperialism in the latter half of the twentieth century is a story that is overall too complex for these pages.[20] The relevant point is that for the first time in several centuries, western political hegemony was seriously challenged, a fact that tore at the fabric of its political fantasies of (eternal) global governance. But one cannot say that western fantasy has been humbled in the process. Accelerated by the defeat of European state socialism in 1989–1991, western liberalism has become ever more zealous in its mission to naturalize and globalize autology.[21] Late liberalism has developed a softer, "progressive" variant, the weakening bloodline of Keynesian welfarism that seeks to harness the forces of the market and the genius of individuals to sustain national communities. The spectacularly unsuccessful effort to institutionalize a global market in rights to carbon emission is a paradigmatic example of contemporary social liberalism in action. Yet, the more dominant and viral variant of late liberalism is what has become known, to its critics, as "neoliberalism."[22] Neoliberalism is normally recognized for its ontological investment in markets and commerce as the basis of all social action. But neoliberalism is also ruthlessly autological, seeking to suppress interindividual relatedness and reciprocal obligation under the pursuit and satisfaction of individual wills and desires.

Neoliberal political imaginaries assume entrepreneurial and consumer subjects who are able to circulate effortlessly in zones of transaction.[23] However selective and fantasy-laden these imaginaries may be, the personalized interfaces and lateral and mobile messaging capabilities of digital media enhance their experiential grounding and conceptual intuitiveness. Yet, we still do not fully understand the relationship between the innovation and diffusion of digital information and communication technology since the 1980s and the global proliferation and legitimation of neoliberal political-economic theory and policy during the same period. The historical co-occurrence is certainly striking. But few analysts of either neoliberalism or digital media have sought seriously to tease out the causal relations, if any, between the two.

To be more precise, a number of scholars[24] have connected the proliferation of digital information and communication technology to the formation and acceleration of post-1980s globalization, especially in terms of their enhancement of fast-time transnational communication and coordination in sectors such as finance. But few have examined whether there is, at root, some codeterminate dynamic between neoliberalism and digital media. Paula Chakravarty and Dan Schiller are a refreshing exception and make a convincing case that what they term "digital capitalism" has played a key structural role in the consolidation of neoliberalism globally, first as a showpiece of neoliberal intervention to open new markets for a growing "information society," second by helping to establish the fast-time transnational information networks required for finance capital to overwhelm the regulatory structures of nation-states, and third by offering powerful new communicational means ranging from microblogging to satellite and cable television for translating the neoliberal worldview into doxic truth.[25] By contrast, celebrated critics of neoliberalism such as Gérard Duménil and Dominique Lévy tend to interpret digital information technology as at best a subsidiary factor in the consolidation of neoliberal theory and policy.[26] Critics of commercial broadcast media such as Noam Chomsky and Robert W. McChesney have meanwhile analyzed at length the naturalization of neoliberal worldviews in the genres and narratives of news and entertainment.[27] But, interestingly, the Internet and social media are rarely seen as instruments of neoliberal domination. They tend to be recognized for an at least partial capacity to resurrect participatory democracy in the face of neoliberal propaganda.[28] If anything, critics of commercial mainstream media continue to view digital media as a potentially antineoliberal locus of hope in the struggle over information.

The relative disinterest in exploring the relationship between digital media and neoliberalism reflects a tendency to see the former as a politically neutral technology and the latter strictly as a matter of discourse or at best ideology. What I think we need to better understand is the phenomenological juncture between digital media and neoliberalism, the way in which the spread of lateral, mobile media interfaces and institutions might help to make autological discourse more experientially intuitive and epistemically compelling. And, likewise, the way in which a broader socialization to late liberal subjectivity might encourage the popularization of media interfaces such as mobile data devices and immersive gaming that promise and to some degree confer the experience of an idealized form of autological freedom. Natasha Dow Schüll's work on digital gambling shows how newer gaming platforms "accommodate players' demand for isolation by protecting them against the intrusion of incoming signals."[29] But beyond disengagement, the ultimate objective of such interfaces seems the erasure of body/machine interface into a phenomenological zone of pure absorption. This zone is at once deeply autological in that it permits no interindividual awareness and exchange and yet also disruptive of the classical liberal autology of rational individuality, as I discuss at greater length in the epilogue. Liberalism, we recall, mutates. A more familiar example is how common spaces of middle-class sociability in the Global North (bars, cafés, clubs, restaurants, for example) are increasingly notable for co-locating people who are paying more of their attention to their mobile data devices (smartphones, tablets, laptops) and less of their attention to each other. We need to understand the implications of such widespread apparent distractedness upon relations and knowledge.

The ethnographic studies in this book offer no final word on the juncture of liberalism and digital information but they do offer concrete and provocative points of departure to inspire further investigation. In the case of T-Online, for example, it was particularly evident how the use of digital media both presupposed and helped to reinforce late liberal political imaginaries. Digital information technology, particularly web analytics, was designed to measure, in aggregate, the individual actions of a cryptoliberal public of unassociated "unique users." At the same time, the organizational and editorial decision to institutionalize web analytics as a decisive consideration in selecting *Themen* (stories, themes) helped naturalize the idea of an intrinsic link between news value and consumer preference. As difficult as it proved to be for journalists to read user intention into the hieroglyphics of analytics data, the feedback capacity of digital information offered the promise of understanding consumer desire, thus aligning the project of news journalism very closely with that of the advertisers who bought space on t-online.de on the basis of similar analytics data. At mdr info, and AP-DD as well, we saw how the importance of screenwork emphasized the importance of an individual journalist's absorptive engagement with diverse, fast-moving data streams and de-emphasized the importance of other kinds of interactions (as well as bodily movement). I think it is fair to say that screenwork both assumes a certain kind of entrepreneurial professional subject (one searching far and wide for relevant information, skillfully juggling multiple tasks) and helps to naturalize that subjectivity through an attention-dominating visual interface that positions offscreen-based interactions as distractions to the individual engagement of a world of data.

To return to Williams, interfaces like screens and mobile telephones can operate both as symptoms and agents of mobilization and privatization. They can create phenomenological conditions of communicational interface under which autological subjectivity can thrive. But they can only do so given particular modes of institutionalization and conditions of usage.[30] I do not wish to overstate the impact of media interfaces on the constitution of late liberal subjectivity. Yet when so much work and nonwork time is spent engaging these interfaces, it would be wrong to trivialize their impact either.[31] I also do not wish to suggest that screenwork is somehow making us "less social." A better gloss would be to say that screenwork is making us "differently social."[32] My point is really that the mode of social subjectivity linked to twentieth-century Keynesian publics and broadcast interfaces appears to be evaporating (as broadcasting itself transforms) and that new modes of sociality are emerging that seem more amenable to autology. Perhaps this is because the lateral revolution positions actors as individualized mediating micronodes rather than as passive targets of (collective) broadcast communications. My provisional diagnosis, based upon the research for this book, is that techno-institutional processes such as computerization and digital information and politico-institutional discourses of late liberalism have coevolved, at times reinforcing and naturalizing each other, promoting novel bundles of epistemics and ethics that deserve to be termed "digital liberalism." The life informatic of contemporary news journalism must also be viewed as a life late liberal, so much so that it seems increasingly difficult to distinguish between them.

Third Reflection: The phenomenology of screenwork contributes to imitation in contemporary news and likewise to feelings of increasing automaticity

Pablo Boczkowski, a fellow scholar of news journalism in the digital era, elegantly summarizes the current condition of the news industry: "The paradox is the remarkable increase in the amount of news available and a perplexing decrease in the diversity of its content."[33] Boczkowski further notes that neither journalists nor consumers tend to be satisfied with this state of affairs but both confess to feeling powerless to change it. Likewise, at all three nodes of German newsmaking analyzed in this book, journalists both recognized and criticized a rising trend of imitation in news media. Some saw imitation as an effect of the increasing reliance of other news organizations on news agency feeds for basic news coverage. Others attributed greater homogenization of themes and texts to interorganizational surveillance under fast-time conditions of decision making. Still others recognized the ability of new technical features such as copy/paste functionalities to enable highly efficient processes of republication. Boczkowski is unconvinced, and rightly so in my judgment, by the argument that news imitation is a predictable effect of technological causes. And, yet, identifying the right balance of causalities is no simple task.

On the one hand, the elephant in the corner is clearly the impact of finance and investment culture upon publicly traded commercial news organizations. The German news industry has been better cushioned from this impact through the combination of a robust public broadcasting sector, a more loyal news audience,[34] and overall less exposure to financial markets. In the United States, by contrast, even when newspapers have remained profitable, institutional investors (like investment banks) have depressed their valuation as assets because such investors have little faith in the long-term profitability of print media.[35] This has led to a perverse situation repeated at newspapers across the United States where still highly profitable news organizations have been forced to cut staff and output to please an investment culture seeking short-term profit. Institutional investors' cannibalization of U.S. newspapers is an Aesop-worthy parable of strangling the goose laying the golden egg. It has generated crisis conditions where less self-interested investment practices would have given news organizations more time to adapt to the ecology of digital information. Instead, we find many news organizations, especially newspapers, now starving themselves to the point of extinction or irrelevance, and then lamenting that everything was predestined by the technology.[36]

Staff reductions have almost inevitably led to a contraction of the quantity and quality of news content generated by newspapers, which remain, along with news agencies and broadcasters, the principal sources of original news reporting. The sale of AP-DD to ddp in 2009 is instructive of how the crisis affecting print journalism has been passed on to news agencies as well. Newspapers still represent the majority of the client base and revenue stream for news agencies in both Germany and the United States. But subscription levels have dropped as newspapers have cut their budgets through the fat and into the bone.[37] No one from AP spoke to me on the record about the decision to sell their second-largest European bureau to a competitor, but two theories circulated in Germany. The first was that AP so desperately needed the cash from the sale to support their U.S. operations that they were willing to sacrifice a profitable and highly distinguished subsidiary. The second was that AP viewed the German news agency market as too competitive to avoid mergers in an era of declining client subscriptions. So, rather than invest more deeply in Germany through acquisitions, AP opted to pull out of the market altogether. In either case, the net result was a further reduction in the quantity (and, in all probability, quality) of original news content in the German language.

One way of accounting for Boczkowski's paradox is to say that because there are fewer and fewer authorized newsmakers operating today, they are capable of producing less original content. But that content circulates ever more widely as other news organizations attempt to provide the same levels of output with fewer resources invested in original news. This was Friedrich's diagnosis in chapter 1—that more and more news agency material was being utilized, often verbatim or thinly edited, to cover widening gaps in client news organizations' coverage. The case of T-Online shows that entire news organizations are now built around reprocessing news material generated elsewhere.

But other large animals lurk in other corners too. It is difficult not to find technological arguments for content homogenization at least partially persuasive. It would certainly be difficult to imagine the same scales and speeds of news imitation without copy/paste functionality, without shovelware and content management software, and without the fast-time newsfeeds permitted by digital information systems. Part of what enables imitative practice is the relative ease and efficiency with which it can be accomplished given the desktop, screen-centered instrumentarium now available to any digitally networked newsmaker. Even if we ultimately reject a monocausal argument of technological determination, we should recognize the extent to which the information and communication technology institutionalized at western news organizations makes it increasingly simple to locate news text, reproduce it, and repurpose it, all in a matter of seconds. The invention and availability of desktop editing software has opened up new conditions of possibility for creation that subvert straightforward distinctions between originality and imitation. As noted in chapter 2, I remain unconvinced, for example, that T-Online practiced a purely imitative mode of news journalism although it would be impossible to describe it as original news journalism either. A better approach would be to lift an analogy from digital music and consider T-Online's model as a kind of "news mashup." And, far from isolated, T-Online's textual practices are becoming more representative of newsmaking across other media.

I would highlight the phenomenology of screenwork as another, relatively unexplored, dimension of news imitation. It would only be a slight overstatement to say that journalistic awareness of a news story always begins on a screen. It is meanwhile simply factual to say that the evaluation, production, and circulation of news text always involves screenwork. What we learn from the three case studies is that screenwork's promise of universal informational access and connectivity is textured by attentions and inattentions clustering around habitual patterns of monitoring, rapid judgments concerning news value, and intense bouts of word processing and messaging. The attentional density and dynamism of screenwork generates an experiential horizon unto itself, one that can be (and perhaps necessarily is) cut off for significant lengths of time from offscreen engagements. Recall that journalists spoke to each other frequently in order to help coordinate their evaluational work. But as often as not their eyes never left their screens while speaking since the attentional demands of what was occurring on-screen were perceived to be too important to direct full attention elsewhere. In this state of rapidly rotating half-attentiveness, if a story, a *Thema*, was not already available through some channel on journalists' screens, then its chances of being recognized as newsworthy diminished drastically. Conversely, if a *Thema* was multiplied across different browser windows and newsfeeds, its visual presence routinely translated into the perception of greater news value. Marc highlighted this phenomenon in chapter 3. And, when the normal intensity of screenwork was heightened by breaking news conditions, as we saw for example with the Nobel Prize announcement at mdr info, a journalist's capacity to attend to offscreen events and circumstances was further disabled.

Does a deep on-screen focus guarantee textual or thematic imitation? By no means. But combined with organizational imperatives to remain up-to-the-moment with newsflow, screenwork certainly creates ripe attentional conditions for following the thematic and even textual decisions made by other news media. In this respect, we should view the phenomenological experience of screenwork as contributing directly to the "artificial *Aktualität* (timeliness)" that worried Isidora in chapter 1, a phenomenon we know more commonly as "herd mentality" or "echo effects" in news media. Cases like Bluewater[38] (in chapter 3) show that it is increasing easy to hoax not just one news organization but the entire herd with the help of a compelling visual interface and a patina of authority. Routine practices of monitoring and imitation accomplish the rest. Nevertheless, the crucial factor, in my view, remains phenomenological. News journalists typically work today in a state that combines myriad informational distractions, roving attention, and professional and organizational demands for fast-time judgment. Under these conditions, a tendency toward imitation might be viewed not as a matter of expediency, nor of unimaginativeness, but rather as an attempt to move safely through the dizzying blur of informational possibilities competing for news presence. If one were to occasionally doubt one's capacity to maintain *Überblick* (overview) of the news scene, as all the journalists I interacted with did, those anxieties could be soothed by deferring to the authority of respected *Leitmedien*. The fact that *Themen* are very often established and harmonized through interorganizational cues suggests a widespread impulse toward finding shelter—breakwaters against the ceaseless waves of new information—an impulse that is apparently just as essential to professional newsmaking as its competitive impulse toward novelty.

How news journalists narrate their work today confirms this point. In all three ethnographic studies, we repeatedly heard an oscillation between praxiological and mediological convictions. On the one hand, journalists felt a secure sense of productive agency over whatever they were working on at that moment. On the other, they were acutely aware of environmental conditions of fast-time flow, informational abundance, and technical automaticity that they felt relatively powerlessly to counteract. The balance between praxiological and mediological awareness varied by person, by task, by moment. Many journalists insisted that they felt their powerlessness increasing. In chapter 3, Michael S. notably reminded us that journalists have been voicing mediological anxieties for decades. He is certainly correct that the struggle between spirit and system, between agency and automaticity, in human social knowledge is a very old one indeed.[39] But there are also many signs in this book and elsewhere that suggest that news journalists may be correct to feel that their work is becoming more treadmill than craft.

Among that evidence is the dominance of screenwork itself, which, under current conditions at least, miniaturizes the space of agentive labor and makes it both more fixed and more virtual.[40] To the observer, the screenworker is sitting in a chair, staring at a screen, clicking and typing. This is not the beat reporter interviewing eyewitnesses on the street, let alone the helmeted foreign correspondent traveling into a war zone. And, yet, the phenomenology of news screenwork is nothing if not constant action. So many channels and stories compete for one's attention; the inputs must be watched constantly even as one must also continue word processing, editing, spellchecking to guarantee a steady flow of output as well. It is a delicate and constant struggle for balance, but a struggle that is reenacted daily in the same desk space, in the same corporeal posture, through much the same routines. A day's screenwork can be exhilarating or boring, but even on the best occasions one leaves work feeling exhausted from coping with so much flow. The feeling of being an isolated user, adrift in a vast ocean of information, also belongs to this phenomenology. Screenwork confronts one constantly with the mediological truth of the existence of massive networks and torrential flows of messaging that are sublime objects of wonder, barely susceptible to our agency.

Fourth Reflection: The rebalancing of radial and lateral potentialities of electronic mediation over the past two decades has unsettled the regimes of publicity and journalistic authority that developed in mid-twentieth century

Journalism spent much of the twentieth century persuading itself that its domain of professional expertise and authority was the discovery, articulation, and radial messaging of publicly relevant information. Journalism largely yielded its nineteenth-century habits of political advocacy and persuasion in favor of a modernist professional ambition to incorporate the expertise necessary to "tell citizens what they needed to know." Even in national journalistic traditions, like Germany's, that maintain strong traditions of political and hermeneutic editorialism, the professionalization of journalism led to a firm association of journalistic activity with an objective domain of opinion-free facts to which journalists had special access through their investigative research and networks of (expert) sources.[41] The rise of the professional principle of journalistic objectivity also involved securing a model, both theoretical and practical, of publicity in which an audience of citizens exercised ceaseless demand for new messages about facts-in-the-world (information) that they were incapable of provisioning for themselves. The postwar regime of modernist developmentalism[42] no doubt strongly supported and cemented these core elements of the model of journalism as a monopoly expertise in public information. And, mid-twentieth-century broadcasting correlatively strengthened the facticity of all other domains of modernist scientifico-technical expertise through its enabling of the radial dissemination of centralized expertise and authority and through its relative disabling of responses from the nonexpert peripheries.

Yet this rather cozy arrangement of journalistic professionalism was blindsided by the rapid incursion of lateral messaging into its seemingly secure broadcast spheres in the 1980s and 1990s. The blindsiding exceeded the dominant broadcast domains of radio and television because a radialist self-understanding of journalism had become generalized across news media. It is clear, at least retrospectively, that print and news agency journalism, which remain the most significant areas of journalistic reportage and news composition today, had very much come to model their news publicity upon radial broadcast publicity. News agencies viewed themselves as wholesalers of raw news to radial news clients. Newspapers and news magazines meanwhile had come to depend upon large, secure, mostly passive readerships for their financing and reputation. News journalists across media embraced the authority to define publicly relevant information. In my interviews with news journalists in the United States, I consistently heard critical commentary about the "arrogance" of journalists before the Internet, a sentiment that was often allied to thinly veiled longing for a less contingent and compromised power of professional expertise.

Over the past twenty-five years, across the world, from the Global South to the Global North, radial journalistic authority has been challenged by the expansion of lateral messaging. But the degree of challenge has varied from nation to nation. American journalism has been among the most strongly impacted through the conjuncture of the relatively widespread availability and use of digital information and communication technology for lateral messaging, the aforementioned financial crisis, and the nearly absolute political and cultural hegemony of late liberalism. The final point is critical. "Establishment journalism" is widely criticized by both progressive liberals and neoliberals for its informational economies of scale, for its inattentiveness to issues held to be vital, for its unresponsive radial monology, and for its hidden ideologies. Debates over the desirability and efficacy of "citizen journalism" have proved to be a flashpoint for such concerns and have generated peculiar alliances between corporate media managers seeking citizen (e.g., cost-free) content and lateralist revolutionaries seeking to explode radial news publics into networks of co-informing citizens.[43] Since the United States represents something of an epicenter of digital liberalism globally, it makes sense that the authoritative relationship between newsmaker and newsuser has been most dramatically unsettled there.

In Germany meanwhile, radial journalistic authority remains at least somewhat more secure, buoyed by a more diverse political culture, more stable financial models, and by the stronger hierarchical relations of expertise characteristic of state welfarism and supported in no small part through public broadcasting and public education. In my interviews with German journalists, I found them much more prone to trivialize the threat posed by lateral media than U.S. journalists were. Citizen journalism and blogging, as we heard in the case studies, were familiar concepts but treated with almost universal disdain for their value as news media. Both AP-DD and mdr info seemed relatively insulated from the vicissitudes of lateral messaging external to the *Redaktion*. AP-DD continued to operate comfortably in a radial mode, even as it began reimagining its client base to include end users as well as news organizations. mdr info journalists meanwhile expressed their feeling that citizens needed their expertise to select and curate information on their behalf. It was striking that even at T-Online journalists stressed their capacity to operate as a "classical *Redaktion*" in the interest of serving what they envisioned as classical national publicity (*Öffentlichkeit*). Indeed, we recall that they saw the Internet as a unique and powerful instrument for *strengthening* national publicity and the radial authority of news journalism rather than as a force that would undermine them.

At the same time, T-Online gave us glimpses of the broader destabilization of ra-dial publicity in the era of digital liberalism. The screen and Internet interfaces shared by journalists and audience alike, and the clicks and web analytics that brought them into direct association, helped generate "the user" as a spectral presence in the news-room. Users' interests and motivations were a matter of constant professional concern even if those interests and motivations could only ultimately be guessed at. But in a news organization whose operating revenue depended on click performance, as T-Online's did, not guessing was unthinkable; user preferences had to be accommo-dated in terms of journalistic decision making, even on a minute-to-minute basis. If the expectations and institutions of radial publicity shielded journalistic authority and expertise from a passive field of messaging targets, then the lateral and bidirectional messaging capacities of the Internet can, particularly in association with neoliberal commercial models of citizenship, weaken that shielding. We should not underesti-mate the residual institutional power of classical broadcast relations in contemporary news media. Online news mediation, for example, remains dominated by news orga-nizations with roots in broadcasting and print.[44] Although some of those news orga-nizations accommodate consumer preferences directly in thematic selection, others eschew the potential for bidirectional communication. However, even in a country where professional news journalism and the authority of radial messaging remain relatively robust, the ethnography of newsmaking offers signals of the transformative impact of digital liberalism. And, as more Germans seek their news through online sources and mobile devices, those impacts are likely to deepen.

Fifth Reflection: The medium of news continues to matter in an era of screenwork and multimedia diversity; institutions and habits of newsmaking even more so

My reflections on screenwork to this point might be interpreted as taking the position that the practice of news journalism is now essentially the same whether it takes place in a newspaper, on radio, for television, online, or at a news agency. This is a subtle question. On the one hand, it is fair to say that the predominance of screenwork (and its allied software practices) across news media has helped generate new forms of equivalence in newsmaking. Importantly, these equivalences have multiplied *within* news organizations as well as *between* them. For example, if being a news agency slot-ter meant, once upon a time, a set of practices involving monitoring a teleprinter, pa-per, pencils, and transacting assignments with colleagues within easy reach, then that taskscape has, aside from the occasional printer still soldiering on, by and large become condensed into the purview of screenwork. Moreover, although slotters still hold distinct editorial and decision-making authority, many of their practices, for example fast-time monitoring, text-editing and word-processing, are now tasks in which nearly all journalists engage on a routine basis. Indeed, there is a sense in which the slotter and her multiple screens simply reflect a more elaborate and intensified variant of the modes of routine journalistic screenwork that we also encountered at T-Online and mdr info.

In addition to a certain on-screen convergence of taskscapes, we should also consider the broader environment of news messaging that lies just beyond the surfaces of the screens, the environment that long before the advent of the Internet, McLuhan presciently described as the "world-pool of electronic information movement."[45] The constant attention paid by all news journalists today to the currents, flows, and eddies in that pool also creates a form of equivalence, even when journalists are watching different reflections cast by different ripples in different depths of water. Few journalists can afford to ignore the news tides circling the earth driven by the gravitational power of the news agencies and other global *Leitmedien*. For McLuhan, the medium of electronic information was *the* message of the contemporary, "unraveling the entire fabric of our society"[46] but also creating the possibility of new forms of instantaneous connectedness. Using a narrower conceptualization of medium, Nicholas Negroponte inverted McLuhan's dictum, arguing that "the medium is not the message in a digital world. It is an embodiment of it."[47] Negroponte's point is that digital information could message flexibly and laterally across multiple media, a fact that eroded the distinctiveness of assemblages of stimulus, information, practice, materials, and technology called things like "radio" and "print" in radialist language. Had Negroponte perhaps taken McLuhan's use of medium more in the spirit it was intended, he would have understood that they were in complete agreement. McLuhan's point was that the source of transformational power lies in digital information itself because *it* is the medium of electronic media, the continuum of so many messages.

But to complement these observations, the ethnographic studies reveal that medium, in its everyday radialist sense, does continue to matter in news journalism, just as it continues to matter how an organization's news operations are being financed and what organizational and professional priorities have been established for newsmaking (breaking news as opposed to commentaries or features, political news versus entertainment coverage, for example). Although it might be generally true to say that news journalism operates in a fast-time temporality, we encountered a great variety of different rhythms and speeds of newsmaking in the ethnography, both among and within news organizations. AP-DD, for example, could probably lay claim to the greatest emphasis upon breaking news. But at the same time it was the news organization that engaged most actively in long-term planning. Likewise, the different lengths and priorities of editorial meetings in the three ethnographic cases reflected qualitatively different practices of determining news value and strategizing news coverage. At mdr info the performance of publicity reflected not only the financial advantages of German public broadcasting but also its mission to generate positive *Öffentlichkeit*. Although there is no doubt that screenwork reflects a major zone of overlap in news practice, it has not made news journalism homogeneous across organizations or media.

The best evidence that medium continues to matter in news journalism is that journalists who have cross-media experience avow that it does. Recall Jürgen's discussion in chapter 2 of how, in comparison to newspaper journalism, he felt in online journalism as though he could never "switch off." Or, Michael S.'s observation in chapter 3 that he could not imagine spending a single hour of his life in the AP-DD slot. There are powerful arguments circulating today that news organizations of the future will shed their carapaces of monomediality and deliver news content instead across a multiplicity of different channels to a multiplicity of different mobile reception devices. To quote one of my American interviewees, the Internet strategy director of a public radio broadcaster, "If we can reconceptualize our newsroom as a mini-wire service feeding out to different platforms, then we're going to be much better off in the long run." Looking at the online portal of any major news organization, one sees that this reconceptualization process already has considerable momentum behind it at most western news organizations: Radio broadcasters like mdr info have begun to offer text and video, newspapers offer video and audio clips, news agencies offer news and interactive graphics directly to end users. Moreover, multiplatform circulation has accelerated dramatically in the past few years with the increasing market dominance of smartphones and the arrival of tablets that are capable of providing new points of mobile access to news messaging and, it is desperately hoped, new revenue streams. But the important questions of what portfolio of channels future news organizations will cultivate and how end users will come to seek news content are steps removed from newsmaking as informational practice. For the kinds of routines and practices described in this book, organizational priorities, professional norms, and the even more diverse field of individual habits are more immediately consequential. Suffice it to say that newsmaking still supports a significant degree of diversity in its modes of professional agency.

Newsmaking and Newsflow Tomorrow

All five reflections beg the question: What happens next? The German and American journalists with whom I spoke during the research for this book shared many concerns about the state of news media today. To be more specific, they did not seem overly concerned with the enduring relevance of news since they viewed news as, by definition, relevant public information and could not imagine a future society in which there would be no need for information or for specialists in managing it. But they did wonder how the institutions of the news industry would have to be reinvented in order for the craft of newsmaking to survive, let alone thrive, in what I have termed the "digital liberal" era.

As an avid news user and news researcher, I have spent many hours wondering the same thing. The signs often look grim, from the downsizing and boulevardization of newspapers to the increasingly carnivalesque character of television. Much in the spirit of Williams's concluding forecast on the future of television, let me offer five brief predictions about how newsmaking will persist and reimagine itself in the years to come. Some are more fantastic, some more controversial, than others. All were informed by the conversations about the future of news that are the substance of this book.

1. *The search for a new "business model" for news will prove to be quixotic.* The problem of financing news media will never be "solved" because, as Williams has taught us, the problem ultimately lies in a structural tension between centralized messaging and mobilized reception. Nevertheless, more effective responses to the structural tension will be developed. As the Internet is further subjected to the logic of private property enclosure,[48] new techniques and compromises will be developed to guarantee more secure means of commodifying and monetizing digital texts and images. We already know that there will be never be a perfect regime of digital commodification given the relative ease with which digital texts and images can be reproduced and circulated. The digital commodity is like a bag full of fog as compared with the bounded, thing-like, use-valuable commodities imagined by classical political economy. As we have seen, the fast-time reproduction and recirculation of digital news content has driven its exchange value perilously low relative to its use value. But with improved techniques of enclosure, the bag will seem less leaky and its contents more substantial over time. These techniques will not be singular—some will be driven by commercial advertising (including embedded advertising that no longer can be easily disabled), some will involve licensing and pay-per-view fees (including tiered paywall schemes like the New York Times Company's experiment to allow some open access but to charge regular and heavy news users a premium[49]), and some will involve nonprofit and grassroots support structures. I prefer to be optimistic that newsmaking, even quality newsmaking, will persist in this new ecology. But it may become increasingly isolated and limited in its messaging. One fears particularly for the future of public affairs and investigative journalism as compared with business and entertainment/sports journalism, the two domains of news journalism strongly aligned with neoliberalism. For the time being, in the country where a news industry crisis seems most dire, the United States, there seems little popular will to sever radial messaging from late liberal ideology and the "capitalist realism"[50] that offers little recognition of news as a public good whose utility exceeds considerations of price and profit. This is

unsurprising since neoliberalism seeks to dissolve public institutions into private commodities wherever it can and public affairs-oriented news journalism is no exception. Yet, as the German case shows us, there are alternatives even in countries dominated by late liberal politics. In Germany, a stronger public broadcasting sector has helped stabilize public affairs journalism in a time of rapid technical transition (and of neoliberalization of media policies in the European Union).[51]

2. *Imitation and content homogenization will entrench, and we can expect to see a continuing contraction of original newsmaking at radial centers.* The sad truth is that the aforementioned decline in the exchange value of original news content has created a treadmill effect. Original news content has less value (in purely capitalist terms) which incentivizes disinvestment in news-producing staff, which in turn intensifies imitation in news output, making news content seem even less valuable than before. The treadmill effect will be difficult to disrupt where the dominant institutional apparatus of newsmaking remains vulnerable to the neoliberal edicts to increase profitability and shareholder value at all costs. For this reason, we can expect even more "infotainment" and other cheaply produced, market-friendly fare in the near future. But imitation will likely also stimulate new organizational strategies of innovation in specialized niche markets. Heavy emphasis on local news ("hyperlocalization") is one such strategy; focusing on specific kinds of news or on news analysis is another; augmenting a shrinking field of correspondents with cross-national news partnerships or larger networks of independent news providers (e.g., stringers) is yet another. Commercial news organizations across the world are acutely aware that monetizing their news content depends upon their ability to differentiate their output from the domain of breaking news content widely available via news agencies. In other words, now that AP and Reuters newsfeeds are freely and directly available to end users via news aggregators like Google News as well as via smartphone and tablet applications, why would those users pay to receive the same content reposted through a client news organization? Yet, understanding the value of distinctive high-quality content is not the same as understanding how to organize and finance its production and circulation. Many news organizations will move away from breaking news coverage and toward news analysis, where distinctive interpretive voices and background research more easily differentiate coverage across organizations. As news agencies themselves contract, one suspects that there will be new breaking news coverage opportunities available as well. But to take advantage of those opportunities, news organizations will have to show a willingness to gamble on remaining invested in "making news."

3. *Nonprofit and low-profit newsmaking is the future.* As much as they are desired, the mass captive audiences characteristic of mid-twentieth-century broadcast publicity will not return. The pluralization and lateralization of social communication in the past quarter century has generated new conditions of receptivity that are denser

and at once more various, dialogical, uncommitted, and distracted than in the decades that preceded them. Newsusers more rarely identify with specific broadcast publics and personalities than in the past and where strong loyalty exists—for example, with Fox News or Pacifica Radio—audiences are typically far smaller than before the explosion of cable and satellite broadcasting. Combined with the vulnerability of digital commodities, wherever profits are sought in connection with newsmaking, lower rates of return should be expected. It is no secret that advertising revenue is already migrating away from news content and toward what advertisers view to be safer bets for capturing user attention like search engines, social media, and entertainment programming. News can and will remain a profitable enterprise in the late liberal Global North, but its profits will be diluted in ways that will eventually resist even the therapy of media monopolization (a process that has been underway for decades[52] and that has led to the deep entanglement of news organizations in fickle finance markets). In Germany, media monopolization has been hindered by merger laws.[53] Comparatively higher rates of taxation, less institutional investment, more state financing of news and better user solidarity[54] have also historically normalized lower rates of profitability for news organizations. So I expect the transition toward low-profit newsmaking to be less of an irritant there than in the United States. Yet, in the United States, it is also encouraging to see the beginnings of a movement toward non- and low-profit news cooperatives (such as ProPublica, California Watch, Texas Tribune, and Chicago News Cooperative) focusing on public affairs and investigative journalism and usually financed through a combination of foundational support, donations, and client fees. Whether these new ventures will prove sustainable and impactful is one question. ProPublica, for example, won a Pulitzer Prize for national reporting in 2011, the first online news organization ever to do so. Whether news cooperatives will be able to inoculate news journalism against fears of deprofessionalization is another. But the cooperative model is surely more likely to stabilize an unraveling sense of professional journalistic authority than talk of a transition to citizen journalism. Non- and low-profit news organizations are typically committed to filling gaps in news coverage that have appeared with the massive contraction of reporting staffs over the past decade. For this reason alone, we should all advocate for the establishment of non- and low-profit news ventures, support the ones that exist, and invent them ourselves if necessary.

4. *News organizations and newsmakers will develop new institutions and practices that incorporate the particular strengths of lateral and mobile media.* To return to Barbie Zelizer's observation that much newsmaking today takes place outside of newsrooms, as it becomes possible to perform more and more journalistic (and, importantly, organizational) tasks through mobile data devices, it will become possible to imagine the spatial-organizational model of newsmaking dominated by cubicled screenworkers as

a thing of the past. News organizations, including mdr info, are already experimenting with "backpack journalism" models in which a solitary journalist ("SoJo") reports, records, edits (usually on a laptop), and then transmits stories back to a home office.[55] These models are highly likely to become more popular since they reduce labor and equipment costs. The crucial question will be whether it will be possible to monitor and evaluate newsfeeds and to perform other kinds of routine tasks on a mobile basis as well. Could a slotter working from a mobile device handle monitoring, task distribution, and routine communication with other members of the *Redaktion* who would themselves be word processing and searching archives and online sources via their mobile devices? Could effective editorial conferences be held via mobile video- or teleconferencing? If such questions could be answered affirmatively, it would allow for news organizations to literally turn their production model inside out. Monitoring could be integrated with reporting, word processing with video- and audio recording of live events. News organizations would be able to operate with a much smaller core staff and less expensive office footprint and consist mostly of an interconnected network of newsgatherers and newsmanagers operating constantly "in the field," as it were, blending original content provision with the management of competing newsfeeds. This would amount to a mobile privatization of newsmaking itself, a shedding of the office carapace in favor of new flow-friendly arrangements of production. Although this miniature portrait sounds rather improbable from the perspective of contemporary news institutions and practices, it responds to the current pressure upon news journalism to reduce costs (but not in the ultimately self-defeating manner of reducing labor costs) while maintaining high levels of original news output. I strongly suspect that adaptations of the SoJo model will, in time, become increasingly normative at news organizations and spread to other editorial and managerial functions as well. Although I am suspicious of the political implications of naturalizing autology (e.g., the argument that somehow the SoJo model would guarantee better, more responsive and flexible journalism—there are, in my view, no such guarantees), if we assume the uninterrupted hegemony of late liberal ideology, a mobilized newsmaking model might be the best professional compromise available for supplying a rich stream of high-quality newsmaking on a low- or nonprofit basis. It might even undermine the tendency toward imitation. Screenwork would endure, but the phenomenology of mobilized screenwork could be a different life informatic entirely. The solitary journalist is perhaps as much an autological subject as the sedentary journalist, but he is at least more mobile, and hopefully more able to engage off-screen storylines and informational sources.

5. *Radial messaging will slowly reequilibrate itself with the lateral revolution.* When I tried to create a visual representation of how radial messaging would adapt itself to the lateral revolution, I found that I had re-created an uncanny replica of a figure in

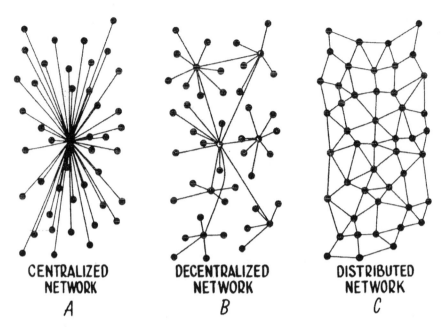

CENTRALIZED   DECENTRALIZED   DISTRIBUTED
NETWORK   NETWORK   NETWORK
A   B   C

4.2 Paul Baran's "Beating the Vulnerability Problem"

Paul Baran's 1967 paper for the RAND corporation, "Some Remarks on Digital Distributed Communications Networks,"[56] which explored how digital communications
networks could improve the security and survivability of military communications.
Baran's work was very influential for the development of the military's Internet precursor ARPANET in the late 1960s.[57] Baran's figure contains three diagrams, labeled
"centralized network," "decentralized network," and "distributed network" respectively and was titled "Beating the Vulnerability Problem" (see figure 4.2). The third
diagram, the distributed network, became the model for ARPANET architecture,
and Baran helped develop the technique of packet switching that enabled multiple
users to move digital data efficiently across shared networks by maximizing the flex-
ibility of channel use. Baran's distributed network schema elegantly facilitates lateral
messaging on a potentially infinite scale, a capacity that proved marvelously attractive as
the World Wide Web and e-mail were popularized in the 1990s. It would be very easy
to end the story there and to predict that radial messaging, as epitomized perhaps by
Baran's "centralized network" diagram, is doomed to diminish slowly and perhaps
eventually disappear as more and more modes of social communication—including the
radial epicenters of television and radio—come to be accessed through the distributed

digital networks of Internet and post-Internet communication. But such a prediction would ignore Williams's observation that the radial and lateral messaging capacities of electronic mediation are not alternatives, but rather represent a continuum between monodirectional and multidirectional (and between referentially specific and general) communication within which a full spectrum of different proportional relationships between radiality and laterality exist. In this sense, radiality will certainly endure even if radial messaging may not experience the same nodal strength and purity of signal that it enjoyed during the golden ages of terrestrially broadcast radio and television. The noise of lateral messaging now saturates social communication and looks to remain that way for the foreseeable digital liberal future. That said, look again at Baran's "decentralized network" diagram. This looks to me precisely how news organizations are now seeking to leverage the multiplicity of potential communicational channels in order to reach laterally engaged and distracted users. A central production point sends content to several different translation points where it is adapted for transmission in the hope of constituting several different overlapping radial (micro) publics. Some users may access a news organization's content across multiple channels, others across only one. But the adaptation of radial messaging into this more "decentralized" (better: pluricentric) model creates a more fine-grained meshwork of contact points than existed in the centralized (and presumably monomedial) models of the past. And, it will allow radial messaging to coexist in less obvious opposition to lateral messaging. Radial messaging will also certainly become more tolerant of bidirectionality than in the past. But it was interesting to note in our case studies that German journalists continue to resist the bidirectional overtures of lateral messaging as being too time-consuming and irrelevant to incorporate within their newsmaking. In thinking about the future of radial messaging, we should not forget that radial messaging was intimately involved in the constitution of twentieth-century regimes of professional expertise and authority. In other words, if "news journalism" is to endure as a distinctive jurisdiction within and vocation among the information professions, then it will have to continue to find ways to distinguish its messaging above and beyond the "mob" of lateral conversation. But since the radial megaphones of its past are becoming disabled, news journalists will have to avail themselves of more modest amplifiers and learn to use them with greater oratorical power, informational efficacy, and persuasive skill. This is the core challenge for newsmaking to persist as craft in an era of informational flow.

Epilogue
Informatic Unconscious

On the Evolution of Digital Reason in Anthropology

Thus the age of anxiety and of electric media is also the age of the unconscious and of apathy. But it is strikingly the age of consciousness of the unconscious, in addition.
—Marshall McLuhan, *Understanding Media*

Unconscious Electric

As promised at the outset, readers interested solely in the story lines of news journalism today could stop here. These final sections of *The Life Informatic* cycle back to the meta-anthropological concerns outlined in the prologue, and especially to the question of how studying the impacts of digital information and communication in contemporary news journalism brings into focus a parallel legacy of digital mediation and digital thinking in anthropology. Throughout the book, we have encountered praxiological and mediological certainties echoing among news journalists. And we have explored how the rapid fluctuation of praxiological and mediological understandings is sensible, even necessary, given the phenomenology of intellectual professional life in the era of digital information. I have hinted at a parallel rise of mediological certainties in anthropology and the human sciences but it is now time to reflect on that rise more substantively. This epilogue is thus motivated by a desire to better understand how practices and ecologies of digital information have impacted anthropological expertise and understandings over the past several decades.

To grasp our contemporary epistemic conditions, we need to look farther back into the origins of digital information. My core argument is that although digital media and digital culture reflect relatively new objects of anthropological research, there is a much deeper history of digital reason in anthropology and the human sciences. This epilogue schematizes that history and explores its implications for contemporary anthropological research and knowledge, including not least the analytical framing of this study.

But first, what is "digital reason"? If "digital information and communication" typically refers to those media invented and institutionalized alongside and after the industrialization of electronic computation, then I would suggest that we understand as "digital reason" the companion modes of understanding that have been shaped by experiential encounters with institutions, environments, and practical engagements of electronic computation. This reason has its manifest dimension: all the talk in public culture, so dense and various, about how digital information and communication has transformed and is transforming our world, our institutions, our relations, our values, our aspirations, and indeed, our modes of thought. As Charlie Gere writes, "To speak of the digital is to call up, metonymically, the whole panoply of virtual simulacra, instantaneous communication, ubiquitous media and global connectivity that constitutes much of our contemporary experience."[1] Anthropology and the human sciences have shared in this talk[2] and have thus contributed to the work of constituting digital mediation as a stable and thing-like domain with predictable causes and effects.[3] But digital reason has a latent dimension as well, a dimension that is epistemically consequential without, in many instances, having any obvious or immediate relationship to digital mediation. It is this more "unconscious" dimension of digital reason that interests me here. And, much as Sigmund Freud grappled with his *Unbewusste* (unconscious), to reconstruct this story we will have to think in terms of displacements, resistances, and symptom formations. I am interested in exploring how digital thinking has seeped into the foundations of epistemic activity in anthropology and the human sciences, indeed in discovering the ways that it has informed entire theoretical paradigms and analytical styles without disclosing its true intuitive basis.

Although this process will eventually reveal itself to be ideological rather than "unconscious"[4] in the traditional psychoanalytic sense, I begin with Freud's terminology to illustrate in more detail the exact ideological effect I have in mind. Before electronic computation was invented and industrialized with its mass impact upon knowledge (in the form, as we shall shortly see, of a new computational epistemology of "information"), there was electricity, indeed even "electric reason." As David Nye puts it in his marvelous study of the institutionalization of electricity in the United States in the late nineteenth and early twentieth centuries, "Like the computer in more recent times, electricity and electrical machinery provided persuasive images for the progress of society, the operation of the mind, the nature of the body. . . . Electricity was not merely one more commodity; rather it played a central role in the creation of a twentieth-century sensibility."[5] In addition to the many instances of electric sensibility circulating in late nineteenth- and early twentieth-century popular and public culture, electricity had a rich life of manifestations and latencies in academic culture and scholarship. An excellent example is Freud's conceptual work on the psychical apparatus and its normal and pathological modes of operation.

Working restlessly in the interstices of neurology, psychology, and clinical practice in the last decade of the nineteenth century, Freud became deeply interested in schematizing flows and states of energy within the psychical apparatus. Indeed, it is not an overstatement to say that Freud's model of the psychical apparatus was designed specifically to explain energy flows and states. In a very fertile yet tormented period of thinking and research between 1894 and 1899, Freud established the core elements of his model of the psyche (including, notably, the concepts of unconscious, preconscious, resistance, cathexis, transference), all of which will be familiar to anyone with even a cursory knowledge of the later phases of Freudian metapsychology and psychoanalysis. Yet this conceptual cluster first took shape in the context of Freud's effort to understand the energic operation of neuronal systems in his last great and unfinished work of neurology, the *Entwurf einer Psychologie* (1895).[6] The parallels between that effort and Freud's investigation of the energic interrelationship of what he termed the "psi-systems" (including unconscious, preconscious, consciousness, and perceptual systems) in the metapsychological chapter of the work that cemented his international reputation, *die Traumdeutung* (1899)[7] are obvious. Both works articulated a model of psychic operation as a largely homeostatic energy system managing exogenous and endogenous stimuli to maintain a tolerable load of excitation. In both variants, the crucial interrelationship of "primary process" and "secondary process" is defined in terms of energy flows.

In the *Entwurf*, Freud defines primary process as an organism's effort to maximally reduce excitation (excitation catalyzed presumably by internal drives for needs-satisfaction such as hunger and sexuality) and secondary process as the capacity of behavioral conditioning to maintain states of excitation for environmentally approved reasons (a capacity to endure endogenous and exogenous stimulation, experienced by the organism as pain or stress, deferring the pleasure of release through calculation, forward planning, or, simply, discipline). Although Freud had little neurophysiological knowledge to work with in developing this model besides images of the shape of neurons, he has been celebrated in the past few decades for uncanny insights into brain structure and operation that anticipated later advances in neurology.[8] However, feeling it a speculative failure, Freud almost immediately distanced himself from the *Entwurf*, (re)turning as it were from brain to mind and beginning a long embrace with psychology that paved the way to psychoanalysis.

In the *Traumdeutung*, Freud shifts media, abandoning the excitation of neuronal tissue and offering instead a more abstract conception of stimulus and energy flow. Nonetheless, primary process continues to represent the psychic apparatus's effort to reduce excitation. But now this is explained as matter of the charging (by what will later become Freud's id and drives) of memories into hallucinatory identifications. The psychic apparatus strains, irrationally to its core, to repeat past acts of needs-satisfaction, reducing pains of want through the pleasures of imaginary discharge. Yet, this process is interrupted by the secondary process of social-environmental conditioning that seeks to channel the search for pleasure instead through the intricacies of language and custom. The fact that the secondary process must continuously seek to repress and to deflect the primary process creates a fundamentally entropic condition in the psychic apparatus. In instances of psychosis, neurosis, and dreaming, Freud believed, we can see how the weakening of secondary defense mechanisms allows the energy flows of the primary process to more directly influence the systems of consciousness and perception (in the form of hallucinatory imagination) and/or the motor apparatus (in the form of any non-normative behavior ranging from nervous tics to full-blown sociopathy).

Indeed, in so many respects, Freud's early struggle to define the dynamics of intra-psychic energy flow shaped the course of his later work. For example, Freud's early thinking about how charges could carry across neurons led to a variety of later iterations of his cathexis theory. His speculations about how the axonal-dendritic structure of neurons would shape patterns of energy flow led to, among other things, the theory of overdetermination and the "supercharging" of particular ideas. Freud's application of the first law of thermodynamics (that the total energy of an isolated system remains constant) to his model of the psychical apparatus became the kernel of his later theories of neurosis insofar as those theories also took homeostatic systematicity as the model state of psychic operation, with endogenous and exogenous modes of stimulation providing a constant danger of systemic overload (and underload).

In the *Entwurf*, Freud described his energy form simply as "quantity" (*Quantität*) and theorized that the basic action of neurons involved putting this quantity into motion through discharge. But were Freud's psychic energy system, its flows, and quanta electrical in nature? This was never clear, least of all to Freud himself. Electricity was certainly in the air, so to speak. The first electric power company had begun operating in Vienna only a few years before in 1889 and the first electric trams began running in 1897, with all the public cultural fascination with electricity and artificial illumination seen elsewhere in the world.[9] Additionally, we know that Freud was aware of the electrophysiological research accomplished decades earlier by Emil du Bois-Reymond and Eduard Pflüger that showed that organic tissue both could and did carry electrical charges.[10] Terms related to electrical research such as *Energie* (energy), *System* (system) and *Ladung/Entladung* (charge/discharge) appear with frequency in both texts, but Freud stops short of claiming that what he is describing a form of endopsychic electrical current traversing a neurological or psychological circuitry. Freud was troubled, notably, by the absence of later scientific research that showed how charge could carry between neurons. Or perhaps he simply felt that it was too speculative to name psychical energy as a form of electricity. As Mark Germine summarizes in his insightful discussion of Freud's concept of energy in the *Entwurf*, "In Freud's model there is no circuit, as in computers, to bring about the flow of Freud's current. Yet, his 'quantity' could be blocked in its path and could build up to the point of finding some other path of discharge. This energy somehow accumulates in the brain, as if in a capacitor, which, however, does not behave like a capacitor, but more like a complex computer programmed with Freud's new psychological theories."[11]

We could take this ambiguity as a sign of poor concept work on Freud's part. But I would prefer to see it as a form of displacement, as a symptom itself of the latent epistemic influence of electricity in the human sciences at the turn of the twentieth century. Endopsychic electricity may well have been the force that Freud was striving to understand. But even if it was not, electricity offered Freud a *method of understanding*. Electrical energy charges, flows, and systematicity became key analytic analogies for Freud as he designed his metapsychological schema. Perhaps Freud's electrical symptomology is especially visible because of his own adjacency to laboratory and clinical science, the former having had established electricity as a vigorous domain of research and theory in the late nineteenth century. Or perhaps it was a matter of the newly electrified urban social environment in which Freud composed his model of the mind. Neither seems to me a trivial influence. In any event, the Freudian unconscious (indeed the whole of his model of psychic apparatus and operation) was, as it turns out, an exercise in electric thinking, an observation that we owe, not incidentally, to a later, more manifestly electrical philosopher, Marshall McLuhan. We have been thinking electrically in the human sciences for longer than we realized. But I am not arguing that "we" all have been thinking electrically in the same way nor that every theoretical current in the human sciences since the late nineteenth century has been impacted by electricity. This would be a gross oversimplification of the complexly subdivided and specialized attentions of concept work in the human sciences. My claim is more modest: that electric sensibilities belong to an ensemble of conceptual techniques of the twentieth-century human sciences and that strands of electric reason can be found in unlikely places with unintended consequences.

But this is only the preamble to the story I wish to tell. As Nye argues, the precondition of the development of what he terms the "electrical sublime" was the advancement of the industrialization and institutionalization of electrification. Electrification still leaves us a long way from understanding how digital information has impacted anthropological knowledge, let alone from understanding the origins of what Vincent Mosco has termed, not without criticism, the "digital sublime" more generally.[12] The most important intermediating developments were the industrialization and institutionalization of electronic computation and the rise of cybernetic and informatic theory, developments to which I now turn.

From Mechanized Computation to Digital Thinking

The mechanization of computation predated, of course, the application of electricity. Analog computers date to antiquity. Wilhelm Schickard and Blaise Pascal developed mechanized clocks and calculators in the first half of the seventeenth century. Joseph Marie Jacquard's 1801 invention of a loom that used punch cards to encode design data inspired the visionary work of Charles Babbage, Federico Luigi and Ada Lovelace on a steam-powered programmable "analytical engine" that was conceived as early as the 1820s if not completed experimentally until the late twentieth century.[13] The Jacquardian punch card also inspired the first true tabulation machine patented by Herman Hollerith in 1889 and put to almost immediate biopolitical use in the processing of the 1890 U.S. Census data. The Hollerith tabulator was something of a transitional device—an electrified tabulator fed by punch card data. But its success in reducing the processing time for census data from eight years to one earned it terrific publicity. Mechanized computation quickly became a growth industry. Iterations and imitations of Hollerith's tabulator were rapidly applied to the management of a variety of forms of governmental and organizational data, turning the term "computer," at first a description for a kind of human labor, increasingly into the description of a mechanical device for data management. Hollerith's Tabulating Machine Company merged with three other companies to form the Computing Tabulating Recording Corporation (CTR) in 1911. Data processing became a powerful industry unto itself before the First World War. CTR was producing two million punch cards per day by 1914 and renamed International Business Machines Corporation (IBM) in 1924. Companies like IBM and Remington Rand propelled further advances in electromechanical tabulation and recording technology in the 1920s and 1930s, creating industry standards (such as the IBM 80-column card, with each column representing a single digit or character) that endured as forms of data management until well into the 1970s.[14]

The industrialization and institutionalization of electromechanical computation thus date to the first decades of the twentieth century. Yet, tabulators were limited in the kinds of mathematical operations they could perform. Designed originally for addition, tabulators were not capable of subtraction, multiplication, and division operations until the early 1930s. Parallel experiments began, as early as 1928 with Harold Hazen and Vannevar Bush's work at MIT, on electromechanical "differential analysers,"[15] computational machines that could calculate logarithms and exponentiation, solve differential equations, and thus address more complicated mathematical problems expressing dynamic systems. These experiments produced the first electrified analog computers that were capable of solving equations with multiple variables and differential data. Bridges could be designed, gunnery systems could be controlled, tides could be analyzed and predicted. The governmental and military utility of electromechanical computation was immediately recognized and the further development of more sophisticated computers became a major area of government-sponsored research in North America and Europe in the 1930s.[16]

Some computational devices remained analog, meaning that they utilized hydraulic, mechanical, and electric components to create an electrical experimental system that directly modeled a physical phenomenon under investigation. This allowed differential analyzers, like other earlier analog computers such as slide rules, the advantage of measuring signals efficiently and continuously. The chief disadvantage of analyzers and other electromechanical analog computers was that they were somewhat inflexible in their operation, often being designed and built to solve only a particular set of problems then having to be rebuilt to accommodate new data and variables. Another significant disadvantage was that they tended to suffer from imprecision that was linked directly to the analogical capacities of electrical force to model other physical systems.

For solving some kinds of problems, especially those that involved relatively fast-time data from constant sources (again, gunnery systems were exemplary), analog computers operated tolerably well in terms of efficiency and accuracy. For this reason, some analog computers would endure for decades in their specialized operations.[17] However, even as larger and more sophisticated analog computer designs emerged in the second half of the 1930s, scientists and engineers continued to pursue more efficient, accurate, and multipurpose modes of computation. This pursuit was led by the theoretical work of figures such as Alan Turing and Claude Shannon, each of whom applied new levels of mathematical formalization and specificity to processes of computation and information management. Turing theorized and schematized the first stored-program computer in 1936. Shannon, while working on Bush's differential analyzer at MIT the same year, sought to rationalize its ad hoc circuit structure. Shannon applied the dualist schemata of Boolean algebra to the analyzer's analog switching circuits, creating the theoretical basis for new digital computation architecture.[18] "Digital" here meant a mode of computation that modeled external systems and processes not directly but rather by first converting signal data into Boolean binary digits of 0/1, a conversion that could be accomplished electrically by modulating voltage levels. Both Turing and Shannon were drawn into governmental research programs during the Second World War that sought to leverage the potentials of computation, both analog and digital, for military purposes, especially for improving gunnery systems and for cryptography.

The Second World War proved to be the crucible of a new regime, both theoretical and operational, of digital information. Wartime cryptographic research contributed directly to what Shannon termed "mathematical theory of communication,"[19] what would become more generally known as "information theory."[20] Shannon (and many others) saw the chief advantage of digital computation as its ability to "smooth data" by reducing what they deemed to be the imprecision associated with continuous signals. The idea was that the discrete (0/1) categories of digital information rendered minor deviations in analog signal levels irrelevant. Once excised from a continuous spectrum of signal, information could be made either true, that is, relevant to the communication, or false. Truly relevant signal (e.g., the new definition of "information"[21]) would be sharpened as a result. Shannon viewed the formalization of conditions of relevance as having no necessary impact upon signal content; it would simply streamline the organization of information transfer. As he put it, "Frequently the messages have meaning; that is they refer to or are correlated according to some system with certain physical or conceptual entities. These semantic aspects of communication are irrelevant to the engineering problem."[22]

The epistemic innovation of Shannon's information theory was to relieve communication of semantics. Information theory instantiated a content/form divide in communication and declared only the latter a relevant design problem. Much like the binary switches of digital circuitry, information theory depends foundationally on a binary gendering of relevance that relegates certain features (like semantic and indexical features) of the "continuous spectrum" of communication and knowledge to the status of noisy background distraction. In this respect, information theory seems intrinsically formalist. But it is important to note that the formalism evolved from a practical engineering problem and was intimately connected to the experiential horizon of computational engineering. Its formalist epistemology was not accidental, nor in all likelihood intentionally strategic (as though Shannon somehow meant to popularize formalist epistemology with his theory). No, I think it is better to consider Shannon's information theory like Freud's metapsychology as an ideological transposition, that is, as an epistemic procedure that converts immediate practical intuitions into more general truth conditions (see below). Information theory, at least in origins, was a computational ideology shaped by practices, challenges, and interfaces of computer design and usage.

The cultural significance of information theory multiplied greatly in the decades that followed as Shannon's digital coding paved the way for a new phase in the industrialization of computation and communication. Shannon had predicted correctly that the simplification and standardization of "information" greatly improved the efficiency of computational data transfer and management. The first digital programmable computers, also direct fruits of wartime research, appeared in the 1940s and were able to perform thousands of simple mathematical operations per second. This massive advance in computational power was also owed to the replacement of electromechanical wires and relays with early electronic (e.g., active electrical component) vacuum tubes, diodes, and capacitors. The "electronics revolution" of the 1950s, particularly the invention and institutionalization of the transistor and integrated circuit technology, offered the operational basis for logarithmic gains in processing power that in turn laid a foundation for the development of mainframe computers, computer networks, and personal computers in the 1960s and 1970s.[23] Even though the first digital electronic computers were massive and reserved mostly for military and scientific purposes, by the early 1950s commercial models were available and, much like electric illumination sixty years previously, increasingly visible to public awareness. *Time* magazine reacted to the public unveiling of what is often considered the first modern computer (ENIAC) in 1946 with a mix of appreciation and irony, labeling it "the latest and greatest mechanical brain—a series of dials, 18,000 tubes and cabinets, occupying an entire room."[24] Six years later, in a watershed publicity gambit, a Remington Rand UNIVAC I computer was made part of CBS news television's live coverage of the 1952 U.S. presidential election. Drawing upon early poll data, the UNIVAC I predicted the election outcome within 1 percent of the final tally.[25] UNIVAC I's impressive performance stimulated public admiration and anxiety about the growing intellectual powers of the "mechanical brains." Similar performances by UNIVAC I and its siblings over the next few years helped broaden popular awareness of research and engineering that had been hitherto cloaked in military, industrial, and academic institutions.

Early Symptoms of Digital Reason in American Anthropology

The late 1940s and early 1950s also marked the period in which the first signs of digital reason become visible in anthropological knowledge (as elsewhere in the human sciences). With the spread of both specialized forms of expertise derived from computation (e.g., information theory) and popular representations of computers, it would be impossible to know exactly when or how discursive or experiential contact with digital electronic computation first began to influence the epistemic work of anthropology. Rather than searching for a few brilliant brokers of digital understanding, I would prefer to think about "contact" in terms of a multiplicity of contact points strewn across a slowly changing epistemic environment. In Freud's view, any true symptom is overdetermined, a creature of multiple influences. During the 1940s and 1950s, digital thinking began to flow into the epistemic groundwater of anthropological expertise as electronic computation became more and more phenomenologically present in the lifeworld and "epistemic ecology" of the postwar period more generally.[26]

Still, there were certainly watershed events and brilliant brokers worthy of mention. The most significant of these seems to me the Macy Foundation Conferences of 1946–1953[27] in which two very influential anthropologists of the postwar period, Gregory Bateson and Margaret Mead, came into conversation with several legendary and soon-to-be-legendary figures in the development of applied information science such as Heinz von Foerster, Warren McCulloch, John von Neumann, Norbert Wiener, and, indeed, Shannon himself. Organized as an experimental venture in communication and collaboration between the sciences (especially biology, engineering, mathematics, neurology, and physiology) and social sciences (anthropology, psychology, and sociology), the conference participants sensed a theoretical revolution in the making, a revolution that was glossed by Wiener as "cybernetics" in 1947, and which received almost immediate scientific and public attention.

The central themes of the Macy Conferences (as their original title, "Circular Causal and Feedback Mechanisms in Biological and Social Systems" suggested) were feedback, control, and circularity in the communication and behavior of "complex systems."[28] The conferences began with discussions of feedback, homeostasis, and regulation in natural and social systems and developed into debates over information and communication.[29] As Bateson also later recalled, "In the early days of cybernetics, we used to argue about whether the brain is, on the whole, an analogic or digital mechanism. That argument has since disappeared with the realization that the description of the brain has to start from the all-or-nothing characteristic of the neuron. At least in a vast majority of instances, the neuron either fires or does not fire; and if this were the end of the story, the system would be purely digital and binary. But it is possible to make systems out of digital neurons that will have the appearance of being analogic systems."[30] Bateson's comment reveals that the conferences had absorbed contemporary debates within computer engineering about the relative capabilities and merits of analog and digital computation and extended them to new domains. This is perhaps unsurprising given that most of the major figures on the sciences side of Macy had been involved with military computation projects.[31] Conference convener McCulloch had produced a wartime paper exploring Turing's paradigm in the context of neural activity.[32] Von Neumann's work on the Manhattan Project had necessitated vast amounts of computation and brought him into contact with the ENIAC design team. Von Neumann had even developed his own design for a digital electronic computer capable of running flexible programs in 1945. Wiener had worked as an applied mathematician on automatic gunnery projects, which had brought him into early contact with information theory as well. In 1940 he had written a memo to Vannevar Bush, then chair of the National Defense Research Committee, proposing to build a model digital computer.[33] On the social sciences side, Bateson had worked for the CIA's precursor, the Office of Strategic Services, during the war designing radio disinformation campaigns and doing intelligence analysis in Burma and Thailand.[34]

I interpret the mission of the Macy Conferences as an effort to test whether the new epistemic lenses ground in the ultimate experience of wartime digital electronic computation were capable of peripheral and distant vision.[35] This mission may have been intentional, a deliberate strategy to mobilize theoretical knowledge from its home base in computer engineering and applied mathematics and to enroll new allies and spokespersons on the path toward paradigmatic dominance.[36] But it is just as possible that what seems in retrospect to be deliberate and strategic was not experienced that way at the time. The participants may have been carried forward by their investment in new methods of knowing whose hermeneutic and explanatory power they wished to communicate and explore. This is still a conversion process but not necessarily a conspiratorial or even pragmatic one. It is quite possible, in other words, that some of the Macy participants had spent so much time engaged in their specialized projects of digital computation that they had simply come to apprehend the world through that practical lens. And, that others, like Bateson and Mead, were able to intuit the emerging presence of digital computation in scientific knowledge more generally.[37]

In any event, what is incontrovertible is that cybernetics, like subsequent iterations of systems theory,[38] transposed thermodynamic, electric, and computational principles and designs into models of intelligence, language, behavior, society, even life. As cybernetics' neologist Wiener explained, blending computational and thermodynamic idioms, cybernetics was interested in how organizational order was produced through recursive systemic feedback—feedback which countered an overall environmental tendency toward entropy or noise:[39] "Thus the nervous system and the automatic machine are fundamentally alike in that they are devices which make decisions on the basis of decisions they have made in the past. . . . The synapse in the living organism corresponds to the switching device in the machine . . . . The machine, like the living organism, is . . . a device which locally and temporarily seems to resist the general tendency toward entropy. By its ability to make decisions, it can produce around it a zone of organization in a world whose general tendency is to run down."[40] Wiener's cybernetic theory clearly operates within the categories of computational epistemology but it also permits those categories to spread out into the world to define social organization and also to reach within into the brain to define neural organization. Cybernetics thus allows computational epistemology to universalize itself, to strive toward becoming computational ontology.[41] Wiener's exposition of cybernetics helps us understand why, despite their varying disciplinary backgrounds, research interests, and frequent conceptual disagreements, the Macy participants tended to agree about a fundamental *systematicity* of their objects of reflection and about the role that *recursive feedback operations* played in shaping behavior. Systematicity mediated conceptually between thermodynamic principles and the computationalists' design experience of a closed electrical circuitry.[42] Feedback meanwhile captured the important emphasis of early electronic computation on processing environmental signals, managing data, and adjusting behavior accordingly, whether in a digital or analog mode. Together these concepts merged into the model of adaptive systematicity that centered the cybernetic imagination.

As we have seen with Freud, cybernetics did not invent the centering of electric schemata as a mode of understanding human behavior. But, as one of the more influential global intellectual currents (like psychoanalysis too[43]) of the 1950s and 1960s, cybernetics surely helped to cement and popularize electric-computational schemata as apt terms for engaging and explaining various dimensions of human life, whether biological, organizational, or societal. It would be convenient to view the Macy Conferences as the portal through which digital thinking entered anthropology. But, interestingly, the immediate impact of cybernetics and information theory upon anthropology was rather limited.[44]

This was particularly true in the United States. Reading the American Anthropological Association's flagship journal *American Anthropologist* from the 1930s through the 1950s one encounters a discipline in remarkable transition from Boasian orthodoxy and a strong Native North American research focus toward an expanding and subspecializing range of theoretical, geographic, and topical interlocution in the postwar period. Digital thinking appears only erratically, however. This is perhaps sensible given the relative remoteness of anthropological research sites and communication practices from the metropoles of computational industry during the period.[45] For example, a concept like "system" was certainly analytically plausible in 1930s American anthropology (and earlier), but it was normally limited to the organization of kin and linguistic classification (e.g., "kinship system" was the most frequent use of the term) and it always imputed a more or less static model of closed organization[46] rather than the adaptive, environmentally sensitive systematicity theorized by cybernetics. The homeostatic, or as Clifford Geertz was to label it, "functionalist"[47] conceptualization of systematicity remained normative in American anthropology well into 1950s and 1960s, gradually expanding its range of reference beyond kinship to assert other modes of social systematicity as well (e.g., "political systems," "value systems," "economic systems").[48]

This is not to say that computational epistemology had no presence. Indeed, one can find traces of methodological incorporations of computational procedures dating back to the early 1930s, especially Harold Driver's and Alfred Kroeber's experiments in the statistical analysis of culture trait diffusion.[49] Such early experiments would later inform much more ambitious projects like George Peter Murdock's Cross-Cultural Survey at Yale University[50] that certainly echoed the computational aspirations circulating more widely in the sciences, industry, and government. But the Boasian network remained generally skeptical of what they viewed as a return to Tylorian scientism. Clyde Kluckhohn did identify statistics as a new research trend in 1939 and wrote with perceptive subtlety on the emerging politics of method in anthropology that would crystallize the polarizations between "qualitative" and "quantitative" methodology that have typified the social sciences ever since.[51] Still, two years after Kluckhohn's essay, Alexander Goldenweiser's evaluation of "recent trends in American anthropology" resists recognizing quantitative method, instead remaining comfortably within traditional Boasian coordinates.[52] Betty J. Meggers's 1946 review of recent trends in American ethnology lists "psychology," "acculturation," and "community studies" as the dominant new trends in cultural anthropology, with only a passing reference to Murdock's work at Yale.[53]

But there were other irruptions. Leslie White's 1943 paper on "Energy and the Evolution of Culture" and his various skirmishes with the Boasian establishment can certainly be seen as influenced to some degree by electric and thermodynamic thinking, particularly in White's theorization of a "social system" in which "energy is harnessed and put to work."[54] Then, the first direct reference to cybernetics in *American Anthropologist* arrived courtesy of Claude Lévi-Strauss.[55] His 1951 article, "Language and Social Laws," is an exemplary early statement of the mission of structural (here "metastructural") anthropology to achieve a deeper level of anthropological understanding, passing from the "superficial" level of observed behaviors and spoken language through to the "structural modalities" of "universal laws which regulate the unconscious activity of the mind."[56] and thus which, given Lévi-Strauss's rationalist and semiological assumptions, generate the actions of individuals and groups.

Lévi-Strauss seems thoroughly enchanted by the promise of electronic computation to achieve this mission. The essay opens, "In a recent work, whose importance from the point of view of the future of the social sciences can hardly be overestimated, Wiener poses, and re-solves in the negative, the question of a possible extension to the social sciences of the mathematical methods of prediction which have made possible the construction of the great modern electronic machines."[57] Wiener had noted the challenges the social sciences faced in terms of objective distance from the phenomena under investigation and the relative paucity of reliable data for analysis. But, Lévi-Strauss argues, we "find in language a social phenomenon which manifests both independence of the object and long statistical runs; which would seem to indicate that language is a phenomenon fully qualified to satisfy the demands of mathematicians for the type of analysis Wiener suggests."[58] Invoking Roman Jakobson,[59] Lévi-Strauss further claims the existence of a phonemic unconscious ("fundamental and objective realities consisting of systems of relations which are the products of unconscious thought processes") has now been irrefutably proven. But given the obvious difficulties of mapping and analyzing unconscious modalities of thought through the medium of "superficial" behaviors, Lévi-Strauss turns to computational power to advance the anthropological science of language: "If all of these modalities could be analyzed by our machine, established mathematical methods would permit it to construct the 'metastructure' of the language, which would in certain complex cases be so intricate as to make it difficult, if not impossible, to achieve on the basis of purely empirical investigation."[60]

Structural anthropology, articulated more or less synchronously with the codification of early cybernetics, represents the first obvious rooting of digital reason in anthropology. It very clearly reflects the ambition to import computational designs and practices into the human sciences. Why digital thinking found traction in this anthropological movement is partly a question of intellectual environment and circumstance. The Second World War had brought structural linguistics to New York where it encountered information theory in-the-making and discovered an alliance of interests.[61] After the war, Lévi-Strauss brought those experiences back with him to Europe as he formulated the principles of structural anthropology.[62] Then, in Paris, there was more circumstance. Wiener's manifesto *Cybernetics* was actually first contracted and published in Paris, receiving much critical acclaim in France in 1948, the year before Lévi-Strauss's own legendary work, *Les Structures élémentaires de la parenté*, was published.[63] And, it was also partly experiential: Lévi-Strauss's famous eschewal of field research after his return to Paris in favor of "armchair" data processing surely made computational epistemology more intuitively compelling for him (or vice-versa).[64] Yet, however richly it drew upon information theory, structuralism never approached Shannon's computational formalism; it was a different intellectual practice and one that incorporated other lines of intuition as well. Likewise, as structural anthropology took shape, computation became a more complex (and remote) object of desire for Lévi-Strauss.

But none of this directly affected the very chilly reception that structural anthropology received in the United States in the early 1950s, at least in the center of disciplinary power and communication that was the *American Anthropologist*. Omar Moore and David Olmsted responded in 1953 that, "Prof. Lévi-Strauss is likely to be disappointed if he believes that linguists will be able to work effectively with his various formulations, since they are either ambiguous or so perilously close to being meaningless that it is difficult to discover his position."[65] However, Moore and Olmsted concluded their rather devastating dissection by clarifying that they did not wish to reject in principle "the use of mathematico-deductive techniques in the study of social science problems, or the use of sequence-controlled calculators."[66] Ever so subtly, the computationalist bathwater was preserved in the hope that it would attract a better baby.

The Informatic Unconscious of Anthropological Culture Theory

In 1961, eight years after the end of the Macy Conferences, Mead cited the case of cybernetics as a quintessential example of anthropology's "failure to make appropriate cross-disciplinary relationships [that] has reacted unfavorably upon our own central communication among ourselves and upon our capacity for orderly growth."[67] She noted the analytical power of cybernetics: "within which it is possible to discuss details of the central nervous system, or the behavior of a variety of life forms within an ecological setting, or a mother weaning her child." And yet, Mead concluded, although "Anthropologists participated in the initial formulations and a few anthropologists have used the family of models that come from information and communication theory . . . the use of such models has not penetrated the central core of the discipline."[68]

At one level, Mead was certainly correct—there was scant evidence in the major journals and conferences that information theory or cybernetics had had a major impact on mainstream American anthropology in 1961. Yet, it would seem that anthropology, or rather more importantly, anthropologists, had become saturated enough with digital talk and digital thinking (public as well as academic) that a major symptomal outbreak was ready to occur. Indeed, as though responding to Mead from beyond the grave, the very next issue of *American Anthropologist* featured the posthumous publication of Kluckhohn's last essay, "Notes on Some Anthropological Aspects of Communication."[69] Kluckhohn frames his approach to language in terms of Charles Hockett's cybernetically inflected communication theory.[70] He also clearly takes the mission of structural linguistics seriously as he seeks to compare and synthesize certain insights from structuralist and Whorfian approaches to language. Although Kluckhohn was always one of the more heterodox Boasians, clearly a tipping point had been reached. Over the next decade, direct appropriations, engagements, and criticism of cybernetics and information theory began to appear with relative frequency in *American Anthropologist*, in more and less seminal variations.[71]

The early 1960s is the period in which we can speak of an informatic unconscious forming in American anthropology. New trends in culture theory, whether in its structuralist (e.g., Lévi-Strauss) or interpretivist (e.g., Geertz) variants, uniformly revealed the influence of digital thinking. Yet, no matter how much anthropologists cathected either computation itself or computational epistemology in their desire to capture or secure new informational and analytical powers, there were also frequent instances of resistance and rejection. Thus, my gloss of the "unconscious" character of anthropology's relationship to digital reason. Freud's "unconscious" was, we recall, marked by the juncture of desire and resistance, of charge and blockage. And, anthropology's accommodation of digital reason certainly did not come without struggle.

Lévi-Strauss's *La Pensée Sauvage* (*The Savage Mind*, 1966a) is an excellent example. As noted above, Lévi-Strauss had earlier demonstrated a great sense of conviction in the possibility of computational machines to advance anthropological science. Indeed, other scholars have argued that the entire post-Jakobsonian structuralist movement in the human sciences can be viewed as part of the rising influence of digital thinking upon European intellectual cultures, particularly in terms of the rigorous binary distinctions of code from content. [72] As one might expect then, serious computationalist overtures remain in *Pensée Sauvage*, particularly in discussion of the "classification of classifications" and in the Boolean lattice structure of the "totemic operator," which Lévi-Strauss describes as a "programme, reserved for the ethnology of a future century."[73] Elsewhere, however, he backtracks to mathematical set theory for the crucial analogies for his distinction between magical and scientific operations in human knowledge. [74] Then Lévi-Strauss backs further away from computational epistemology in his distinction of conceptually determined practice from good Marxian praxis and the "undoubted primacy of infrastructures."[75] But Marxian praxiology is likewise an accommodation to the time and place of Parisian intellectual culture in the 1950s and 1960s. And, there is little doubt that computation and information theory hovers in the wings of *Penseé Sauvage*. At one point, Lévi-Strauss wonders whether punch-card computation will be able to definitively prove the "system of transformations" in Australian aboriginal classification. In the last pages of the book, after his deconstruction of Jean-Paul Sartre's dialectical philosophy, Lévi-Strauss cites information theory as the highest advance of scientific reason yet one which could not have arisen without the intervening epistemic work of the savage mind, "For a theory of information to be able to be evolved it was undoubtedly essential to have discovered that the universe of information is part of an aspect of the natural world. But the validity of the passage from the laws of nature to those of information once demonstrated, implies the validity of the reverse passage—that which for millennia has allowed men to approach the laws of nature by way of information."[76]

Lévi-Strauss contextualizes the work of the savage mind in terms of information theory and it might be possible on this basis to reimagine his project in the book as a kind of epistemological genealogy of information theory. But this does not seem the right interpretation to me. There is something restless, uncommitted, slightly anxious about these marginal appearances of digital thinking. They seem to be epistemic tics. Lévi-Strauss is not, or no longer, willing to give himself over entirely.[77] In *Pensée Sauvage*, the growing presence of information theory in the human sciences is no longer an umambiguously positive matter for Lévi-Strauss. In the simple act of historicizing information theory as he does, we find the desire for computational powers merged with resistance to accepting information theory as ontology.

In Geertz's culture theory, the ambivalence is even more obvious. If one's only encounter with Geertz was his well-known 1967 critique of Lévi-Strauss, "The Cerebral Savage," one would come away with the sense of a principled rejection of all things cybernetic and informationalist. The essay contains a variety of devastating remarks but the following stands out: "What a journey to the heart of darkness could not produce, an immersion in structural linguistics, communication theory, cybernetics, and mathematical logic can. Out of the disappointed romanticism of *Tristes Tropiques* arose the exultant sciencism of Lévi-Strauss' other major work, *La Pensée Sauvage*."[78] Geertz's critique of cybernetic "sciencism" seems a premonition of his impatient dismissal of information theory in his epochal 1973 article, "Thick Description," which deserves, as much as any one text,[79] to be considered the epitomizing statement of American anthropological culture theory of the period. Geertz writes there, in conclusion, "Nor, on the other hand, have I been impressed with claims that structural linguistics, computer engineering, or some other advanced form of thought is going to enable us to understand men without knowing them."[80]

Yet, Geertz arrived at his manifesto for an "interpretive anthropology" through earlier work, still clearly influenced by Talcott Parsons's systems theory,[81] on "the evolution of mind." Writing in 1962, Geertz wants to resuscitate the anthropological analysis of the emergence and distinctiveness of human intelligence despite his recognition that past efforts in this direction have been deeply problematic, "Burdened in the past by almost all the classic anthropological fallacies – ethnocentrism, an overconcern with human uniqueness, imaginatively reconstructed history, a superorganic concept of culture, a priori stages of evolutionary change – the whole search for the origins of human mentality has tended to fall into disrepute, or at any rate to be neglected. But legitimate questions – and how man came to have his mind is a legitimate question – are not invalidated by misconceived answers."[82] Strikingly, and not unlike his later opponent Lévi-Strauss, Geertz's article takes a strong informationalist turn and he concludes, "In sum, human intellection, in the specific sense of directive reasoning, depends upon the manipulation of certain kinds of cultural resources in such a manner as to produce (discover, select) environmental stimuli needed – for whatever purpose – by the organism; it is a search for information." The concept of "cultural resources" becomes for Geertz something like a computational and analytic program for the mind to organize this information "because of the high degree of generality of information intrinsically available to the organism from genetic sources."[83]

Geertz develops this image further in his 1964 essay on ideology where we learn that "Culture patterns – religious, philosophical, aesthetic, scientific, ideological – are 'programs'; they provide a template or blueprint for the organization of social and psychological processes, much as genetic systems provide such a template for the organization of organic processes." Again, Geertz argues that culture is orientational "software." Humanity needs cultural information processing because of the emptiness of our genetic behavioral programming ("the reason such symbolic templates are necessary is that, as has often been remarked, human behavior is inherently extremely plastic").[84] And, finally, in 1966, only a year before the publication of "The Cerebral Savage," Geertz produces his most unambiguous cybernetic symptom, "The Impact of the Concept of Culture on the Concept of Man." In that article Geertz argues for how culture theory can help the human sciences to achieve "a more exact image of man":

> I want to propose two ideas. The first of these is that culture is best seen not as complexes of concrete behavior patterns – customs, usages, traditions, habit clusters – as has, by and large, been the case up to now, but as a set of control mechanisms – plans, recipes, rules, instructions (what computer engineers call "programs") – for the governing of behavior. The second idea is that man is precisely the animal most desperately dependent upon such extra-genetic, outside-the-skin control mechanisms, such cultural programs, for ordering his behavior.[85]

It is worth remarking that all three of these essays appear in the seminal essay collection, *The Interpretation of Cultures*, sunken beneath the call to interpretive anthropology. My point is not to cast doubt on Geertz's hermeneutic convictions or later, postcybernetic lines of thinking. It is rather that we should recognize that digital reason played a central role in the shaping of Geertz's culture theory. But, as with Lévi-Strauss, it was a line of thinking that was also eventually repressed, its epistemic charges deflected elsewhere. I do not think that Lévi-Strauss and Geertz were singular in this respect. The mid to late 1960s represented something of a high tide for popular cybernetics (further buoyed by the arrival of new electric celebrities like McLuhan). Yet the number of committed cyberneticists and information theoreticians in anthropology was never very many by comparison to the ranks of those who engaged the codes of digital reason in a more restricted way, perhaps flirting with cybernetic or information theoretical concepts or analytics before moving their attentions elsewhere.[86] Culture theory mainstreamed digital reason in anthropological knowledge but, true to its origins, in cryptological fashion. Even at the height of its intuitive popularity and institutional power, culture theory never exerted absolute hegemony in anthropological knowledge. But it did become powerfully identified, both inside and outside of the discipline, with the core of anthropological expertise and authority in the 1970s and 1980s.

Informatic Preconscious Today

Allow me to flash forward to the conditions of anthropological knowing today. I have sought to schematize these conditions in the prologue and, rather than reiterating them here, I will simply note several crucial intervening events of the 1980s, 1990s, and 2000s. These are the invention and institutionalization of: personal computers, the Internet, browsers and search engines, mobile communication devices, social media, Wi-Fi, and cloud computing. Alongside these inventions and institutions has come, most importantly of all, a massive expansion of expert commentary and public discourse concerning a "digital revolution" and its alleged transformation of every aspect of human life. Just as these technologies, institutions, and discourses have impacted the practice of news journalism, they have similarly impacted the practice of anthropology in ways that anthropologists have only very recently started to discuss in detail.[87]

Culture theory meanwhile seems to have lost a great deal of its charm and disciplinary power among academic anthropologists. But it is not because culture theory incorporated digital reason that it has lost its innovative edge. If anything, culture theory seems analytically outmoded because its mode of digital thinking is too indebted to an earlier phenomenology of electronic computation and digital information, one that was forged, as we have seen, in an era of "mechanical brains," electric circuits, and gunnery systems. That phenomenology predates the experience of data processors like personal computers, communication devices like smartphones, and informational environments like the Internet and Wi-Fi. It is difficult now to think in terms of bounded information systems, either adaptive or homeostatic, because we move, as the news journalists do, in seemingly boundless currents and "clouds" of information. Developments in mobile media have guaranteed that our informational "systems," such as they are, intersect and overlap with each other continuously. Like Arjun Appadurai's concept of "scapes,"[88] we sense complexity and motion but no longer the presence of a clear position outside of digital information that would justify thinking in terms of bounded systems. Our interfaces like screens are also always already within the digital-mobile environment. Put another way, our informatic sensibilities are now also ecological—"the system" has been overwhelmed by and absorbed into "the environment." As another theorist of energic flow, Gilles Deleuze, once put it, "the system is leaking all over the place"; its limits are now "constantly displaced."[89]

For this same reason, I think it is becoming increasingly difficult to speak of an informatic unconscious. Resistance, of course, remains. But it is softened by the phenomenology of digital information we encountered in the ethnographic studies. This is obviously not everyone's phenomenology, but it seems to me increasingly true of northern professional intellectuals in general, a class to which anthropologists by and large also belong. Under the experiential conditions of constant participation in processes of digital information and communication, it seems inevitable to me that digital intuitions would sharpen into digital certainties. This is for no other reason than the fact that digital reason finds its home, as we saw with the origins of information theory, in practical environments of electronic mediation. Thus it is unsurprising that theory in the human sciences remains deeply informed by digital thinking whether in the form of the still-lingering fascination with the legacies and legatees of French (post)structuralism and German systems theory, with the emergence of actor-network theories and a variety of other posthumanist experiments, or with the digital liberal codes of neopragmatism. Our workshops, our tools, our homes, our relations all share deeply in the life informatic.

Thus, our "memory systems," as Freud would say, those archives of past experiences which the secondary process consults to regulate behavior, are filled with digital data. This takes us from the domain of the unconscious into the domain Freud would have properly termed "preconscious," meaning that our systems of consciousness can now potentially engage digital reason without undue excitation. Digital thinking has become, in other words, accessible to the normative. Well, perhaps we are not quite there. Digital reason still produces friction in anthropology as elsewhere in the world. Praxiological understandings—attention to what human beings make and do—remain robust in anthropology, for example, just as we have seen that they do among news journalists. Yet, mediology has meanwhile become all the rage in the human sciences. A friend of mine wondered to me a few years ago, not without irritation, "Why is everyone going Deleuzian today?" I have had my own symptomal wondering about a seeming copy/paste mentality regarding Foucauldian theory in contemporary anthropological analysis. But such complaints obscure the fact that there is no conspiracy or fall from grace to be discovered here. What has happened is that as anthropological practice (like research practice and intellectual culture elsewhere in the human sciences) has come to be increasingly saturated with digital mediation, it has grown into the intuitive space already occupied by figures like Deleuze and Foucault, who struggled to think through digital ecologies before they were normatively accessible (thus granting these figures, in retrospect, the fateful position of revolutionary anticipation).

Deleuze and Foucault are so symptomal of contemporary theory in the human sciences that this point demands further elaboration. As James Faubion, Luciana Parisi, and Tiziana Terranova have all argued quite persuasively, Foucault and Deleuze were no cyberneticians in the Wienerian sense.[90] Indeed, they should more properly be viewed as post- or paracybernetic analysts whose thinking brushed against the grain of homeostatic-adaptive (first wave) and autopoietic (second wave) cybernetic models, seeking critical perspective on disciplinary schemes of thermodynamic-systemic enclosure and even on the emergence of "post-disciplinary power" that "operates in a space of flows, a liquid, turbulent space which it rules by way of modulation and optimization."[91]

But they were digital thinkers. That is to say, despite their critical engagement with cybernetic systematicities, Foucault and Deleuze are mediological theorists of the first order, thinkers of middles, flows, and of the relations between forces.

Deleuze, more radically than Foucault even, made energy and force into an ontology that backstopped his entire philosophical project. As with Freud, we might ask, is this force really electricity? But this is, I think, the wrong question. The right question would be: Would it really have been possible for Deleuze's sense of energy and intensity or for Foucault's sense of power *not* to have absorbed the nascent circuits and connectivities of computer information around it? We must be cautious, because there is no smoking gun, no secret moment of revelation to be found. The absorption process would have been gradual and banal. But, other contemporary mediologists, especially McLuhan, had already made the connection explicit. For McLuhan, it was impossible to think any longer outside the servomechanisms of electronic computation and the cool participatory flows of multisensory electronic experience. His language was thus electric, his writing an amplifier. Indeed in *Anti-Oedipus*, Deleuze and Félix Guattari ruminate briefly on McLuhan's electric language as a medium of deterritorialized and decoded flows, and on the computer as "a machine for instantaneous and generalized decoding."[92]

Late in Deleuze's career, his investment in digital reason becomes more explicit (recalling that digital reason need not be binaristic in a strict computationalist sense, only informatically absorptive of a given electronic environment). Take Deleuze's own postscript for example, the famous one that schematizes "societies of control."[93] Deleuze defines the condition of control in computational-informationalist terms: "The numerical language of control is made of codes that mark access to information, or reject it. We no longer find ourselves dealing with the mass/individual pair. Individuals have become '*dividuals*,' and masses, samples, data, markets, or '*banks*.'" Elsewhere, he writes, "The disciplinary man was a discontinuous producer of energy, but the man of control is undulatory, in orbit, in a continuous network. Everywhere *surfing* has already replaced the older *sports*." Deleuze's formulation was quite prescient given that the first web browser, WorldWideWeb, was released only a few months after the publication of his essay in 1990. He articulates the society of control at a moment when the Internet revolution is gathering; he smells something in the air. I am reminded of a brilliant moment at the end of Natasha Dow Schüll's article on digital gambling, where she writes, "Strategies of modern discipline such as fragmentation, regimentation, and discontinuity are not abandoned; instead they are sped up to a point where they function on a register of interactivity, adaptability, choice, modulation, flow, and continuity (Deleuze 1992); shock is absorbed." In good academic practice, Schüll invokes Deleuze in citational support of her analysis, but suppose that this too is a feedback loop, an echo chamber. Suppose that Deleuzian theory is already registering a phenomenology of intensified flow of digital information and seeking to articulate its affects and impacts?

Indeed, one way of understanding the "post" in "poststructuralism" is that it is precisely the difference of seeking to think digitally beyond the bounded systematicities of early cybernetics and toward digital orbits, hyperlinks, networks, environments. We find procedures, operators, codes, nodes, energies leaking everywhere out of closed circuitry. As Foucault put it, "Le pouvoir est partout; ce n'est pas qu'il englobe tout, c'est qu'il vient de partout."[94] This is political philosophy for the era of digital ecology, a sign, I believe, of the impact of an intensifying environment of electronic mediation and a summoning of academic mediology.[95] Other means of comprehending the world remain and will remain, but digital reason deserves to be treated as a gravitational force across the human sciences; it is increasingly difficult not to recognize it as such.

Informatic Conscious (Digital Ideologies)

The purpose of this chapter has been to surface an electric-computational-digital inheritance in anthropological thinking, to lever it out of the inky unconscious depths and into the light of discourse. Why? Is it my hope to offer the patient a talking cure? By no means. This exercise simply demonstrates my commitment to the ethics of anthropological reflexivity.[96] And, my sense that if anthropological reflexivity is to remain a worthwhile occupation then it should commit itself to analyzing the basis of our concepts, methods, and representations: that is, the things we choose to research and represent, the methods we use to compose knowledge, and the claims we make for the significance of our analytic work. I have harvested these traces of digital reason like driftwood on the shores of anthropological history in the hopes that a bonfire here will cast flickers of light and shadow on our conceptual conditions today. This is not a critique of digital reason so much as it is an effort to open a conversation on how digital mediation has impacted and is impacting anthropological knowledge today.

This conversation demands, I believe, a better understanding of how digital reason can be gaining presence at the same time that other modes of understanding the world remain too. Attentions, and the modes of knowing they anchor, rarely become extinct. We have to be able to explain the coexistence of different modes of apprehending the world like the praxiological and mediological understandings we encountered in the ethnographic studies.

I will begin with the concept of "ideology" which is the origin point of the sociology of knowledge and thus as good a point of departure as any. The problem with ideology in my view is that it remains, as a concept, too often restricted to meaning "false consciousness." I will not dispute that Marx himself and many later Marxians have deployed the term in that way. But that use of the term is not nearly delicate enough for the epistemic problem at hand. Notably, with *Ideologie* Marx meant not just the deformations of class consciousness and not just the "taken for granted" assumptions structuring knowledge.[97] *Ideologie* represented also, at a very basic level, a shielding of knowledge against its relational, situational contingencies in order to create the stable ontic field of forces and forms requisite for all further action (and thought). In the section of the *Grundrisse* termed "The Method of Political Economy,"[98] Marx was interested in how Adam Smith was able to generate his labor theory of value at the precise moment that he did, and Marx reasoned that this great revolution in political economic theory had everything to do with the fact that institutions of industrial wage labor were leveling out the practical distinctions between different kinds of productive activity in Smith's lifeworld.[99] As modes of labor became more interchangeable with one another and more monetarized, it became possible for Smith to intuit the homogenization of labor and to articulate universal theoretical categories of Labor and Value that took little heed of qualitative distinctions between different modes of productive activity. Theoretical truth (the labor theory of value) thus reflected an emergent social truth (the industrial interchangeability and monetary interconvertibility of wage labor).

Of course, Smith did not himself perceive this ideological mediation of his theoretical work. He did not recognize the environmental, historical transformation of productive activity that allowed him to think of labor as Labor. Good bourgeois imperial presentist that he was, Smith felt Labor was a transhistorical, universal fact-as-it-was. Yet, this was no personal failure of "false consciousness" on Smith's part. He was simply experiencing a process of ideological conversion, the *camera obscura* that, in Marx's dialectical mode of understanding, renders the particular and immediate into the transparticular and abstract. Ideology's principal operation therefore is to mark the domain of "the real" that exists beyond contingencies like history and mediation. Put another way, there is no knowledge without ideology since who thinks or acts outside of some intuition of "the real"?[100] Marx's analysis suggests that ideas emerge at the level of material relations defined by specific social and historical configurations of productive activity. But these ideas are then transformed, through the *camera obscura* of ideological refraction, from contingent relational judgments into absolute universalist judgments. Practical intuition becomes truth through ideology.

But here we reach the limits of Marx's theory of knowledge and the problem is the singularity of ideological effects. The *camera obscura* has but one aperture and but one epistemic transformation to offer. To understand a multiplicity of ideological effects, we need a different analytical instrument. Rather than the analogy of a *camera obscura*, we need to think about ideology as operating like an optometrist's phoropter (see figure 5.1).

The phoropter is an adaptive seeing machine containing a series of differentially refractive lenses that when correctly selected and sequenced guarantees a subjective experience of clear, precise vision. We can imagine that the lenses of the ideological phoropter are likewise multiple, the curvature of each being continuously ground and reground by different aspects of our activities and experience. Needless to say, no two

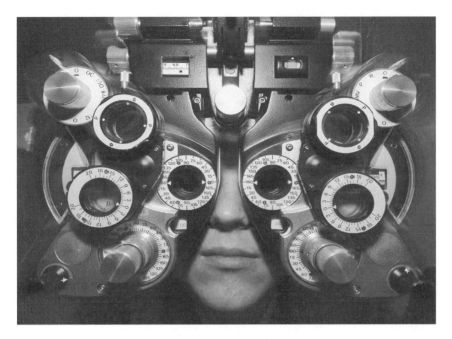

5.1 A phoropter

subjects achieve clear sight through the same sequence and selection of lenses. Yet, in all cases, multiple ideological refractions together produce a subjective experience of factual clarity and truthfulness that feeds into our many ontological and epistemological judgments about the world, its things, forms, relations, forces, and creatures.

Digital mediation contributes a powerful set or subset of phoroptical lenses, at least for those of us for whom practices and ecologies of digital information and mobile communication are matters of routine experience. But, as far as anthropology is concerned, we do not really understand how these practical and ecological intuitions have affected and continue to affect our professional practice. In other words, I believe that we need to reflect on how our research imagination, our research designs and methods, and our modes of analyzing and representing the world around us are adjusting to new informational and communicational circumstances. In the ethnographic chapters of this book we encountered news journalists struggling to maintain their expertise in assigning news value against the imitative currents of informatic flow. Has digital mediation not made our own expertise and authority vulnerable as well? Are we really unfamiliar with the exigencies of fast-time intellectual practice and with mounting demands of data processing? Do we not also sail oceans of digital information and wonder about our capacity to chart our own courses? Can we not also recognize how digital liberalism threatens to unravel our professional and organizational institutions?[101] In cybernetic terms, like the news journalists, we struggle to find and control signal with all the background noise. And perhaps this is all the more complicated for us since our anthropological craft has long been committed to finding the unexpected, often subversive, signals emanating from ways of life and understanding other than our own. A deep analysis of anthropological practice and knowledge in the digital era was not my project here; but this project has convinced me that such analysis should be an absolute priority for anthropological reflexivity.

Yet, its claims must be proportional. It would be perverse to assume that digitality is the only condition influencing our knowledge. We also need to maintain our analytical attentions elsewhere, to identify how digital lenses enhance, interact, or interfere with all the other lens configurations that contribute to our senses of the real. And, needless to say, we also need to be skeptical of such hopelessly visualist analogies, especially when it comes to recognizing those ideological contributions deriving from knowledges of affect, hearing, touch, and taste. This is why I term my analytical method, on display here, "multiattentional."[102] It is a method that is also, I strongly suspect, another experiment in digital reason, a kind of ecological phenomenology adapted to the receding systematicities and singularities of digital understanding today.[103]

Thus, I conclude here, like Freud in *Die Traumdeutung* ruminating on his own dreams and hoping to offer them in the court of scientific evidence. In such a situation, one has to choose between anxiety (maintaining an irritating energic overload) and laughter (the pleasure of momentary release). I will choose the latter. It is not unamusing to be caught, like Freud and his electric reason, performing the very epistemic effects I am seeking to analyze, in this case trying to think digitally about digital thinking. But such is this life informatic. Depending on your preferred analogy, we are reverberating with echo effects, infused by digital vapors, swimming with the informatic currents. Since Freud, we have known that symptoms are signs of life and that, much like the circularities of digital information, they are bound to happen again.

NOTES

Prologue

1. On the implications of the anthropological study of "cultures of expertise" see Holmes and Marcus 2005, 2008; Boyer 2008; Powell and Schwegler 2008.

2. See, e.g., Asad 1973; Behar and Gordon 1996; Bourdieu 1988; Clifford and Marcus 1986; Faubion and Marcus 2009; Hannerz 1998; Herzfeld 1997; Hymes 1969; Jackson 1998; Marcus and Fischer 1986; Rabinow 2003.

3. Jamieson and Cappella 2009.

4. There is a large and growing literature written by professionals and scholars that is devoted to defining and explaining a contemporary crisis of news and news journalism (Cortell 2010 and Fuller 2010 are good examples). The crisis is usually connected to the rise of the Internet, a concomitant information explosion, and the financialization of news organizations (see, e.g., Almiron 2010; Henry 2007; O'Shea 2011; Slayden and Whillock 1999). The impact of the news crisis is typically linked to a crisis of democratic institutions more generally (see, e.g., McChesney and Pickard 2011; Sunstein 2009). Although the condition of crisis is often described in universal terms, its clear locus is U.S. news and news journalism (McChesney 2010). In this respect, crisis literature shares a root system with criticism of media ownership consolidation and political conservatism dating back to the 1980s (see, e.g., Bagdikian 1983; Herman and Chomsky 1988). Although there is much to admire and to agree with in this literature, I try to avoid settling into a moral language of crisis and decline to describe the transformation of news today. For one thing, this was not typically the language preferred by my interlocutors in German news media, which is not to say that they did not find much worthy of criticism in contemporary news journalism. As I discuss at greater length in chapter 4, there are many reasons to be concerned about the future of news in western liberal democracy. But we are also dealing with emergent technological, institutional, and practical arrangements that have not yet settled. My argument is that news journalism is not condemned to any particular future; even in the U.S., it remains very susceptible to further transformation.

5. See, for example, Jay Rosen's seminal post "The People Formerly Known as the Audience" (http://archive.pressthink.org/2006/06/27/ppl_frmr.html).

6. Wulff et al. 2008.

7. Waters 2004.

8. See Chris Kelty's highly insightful discussion of the demise of the digital academic publisher, Rice University Press: http://savageminds.org/2010/08/31/how-not-to-run-a-university-press-or-how-sausage-is-made/.

9. See, e.g., McGuigan and Russell 2008; Jackson 2011; Monbiot 2011.

10. As reported in the *Economist* in May 2011 (http://www.economist.com/node/18744177).

11. Princeton University's new open access policy represents one response to this question (http://www.cs.princeton.edu/~appel/open-access-report.pdf).

12. Faubion and Marcus 2009; Gupta and Ferguson 1997; Kulick and Wilson 1995; Sanjek 1990.

13. The essays in Faubion and Marcus 2009 as well as Kelty et al. 2008 are notable exceptions and confirm my sense that the increasingly normative character of digital information practices appears to be triggering greater reflection on the implications of those practices for anthropological research and communication more generally.

14. See Boellstorff's (2008) theoretical discussion of virtuality and the advantages and disadvantages of virtual research; also, on the methodology of online research, see Hine 2000; Kozinets 2010; Miller and Slater 2000; Sade-Beck 2004; Williams 2007; Wilson and Peterson 2002.

15. Hannerz (2004) has discussed this kinship at length and with great insight.

16. See Mosco 2005 for a critical summary of such thinking.

17. See Boyer 2005.

18. See Steinbuch 1957.

19. Indeed, as scholars of science and technology studies have long taught us, the opposition is ultimately fruitless since the automaticities of technology are dependent upon the "embedded agency" of scientists and engineers who create experimental environments, designs, and prototypes. They are also dependent upon other social actors (bureaucrats, entrepreneurs, end users, for example) who put designs into practice and circulation. Technologies are social institutions as much as they are powerful material forces. This is a line of inquiry normally judged to extend from Mertonian social theory (Merton 1957) to research and concept work in science and technology studies, particularly in veins like SSK (sociology of scientific knowledge; Barnes et al. 1996) and ANT (actor-network theory; Latour 2005). A few (of many) excellent and relevant historical and sociological case studies are Collins 1990; Johns 1998; Knorr-Cetina 1991; Law 2002; Mackenzie 2006; Pinch and Trocco 2002; Rheinberger 1997; Shapin 1994.

Introduction

1. Larsson 2005, 2006, 2007.

2. In an early out-of-character interview (Rabin 2006) with another faux news organization, *The Onion*, Colbert commented, "Truthiness is tearing apart our country, and I don't mean the argument over who came up with the word. I don't know whether it's a new thing, but it's certainly a current thing, in that it doesn't seem to matter what facts are. It used to be, everyone was entitled to their own opinion, but not their own facts. But that's not the case anymore. Facts matter not at all. Perception is everything" (http://www.avclub.com/articles/stephen-colbert,13970/).

3. Glimpses and portraits of these transformations abound. See, for example, Baisnée and Marchetti 2006; Bird 2010; Boczkowski 2005, 2009, 2010; Boczkowski and de Santos 2007; Deuze 2007; Domingo 2008; Hannerz 2004; Klinenberg 2005; Paterson and Domingo 2008; Zelizer 2009.

4. Zelizer 2004: 14.

5. Baisnée and Marchetti 2006: 114.

6. I discuss the pressures of finance and the downsizing of journalistic labor throughout the case studies and especially in chapter 4.

7. There is an excellent tradition of ethnographic studies of news reporting in anthropology and sociology, including notably Bishara 2006, 2008; Bird 2010; Cottle 1998, 2009; Hannerz 2004; Pedelty 1995; Peterson 2001; Schudson 1989, 2003; Sleurs et al. 2003; Ståhlberg 2002; van Hout and Jacobs 2008; Whitaker 2004.

8. See Williams 1974 and my more extensive discussion of this issue in chapter 4.

9. Tom Boellstorff (2008: 18) writes critically of an analytical tendency to regard digitality as something more than a gloss: "'digital' is a conceptual Klein bottle, incorporating every aspect of contemporary human life under its purview. What, nowadays, is not digital in some way?" See Boyer 2007 and Mosco 2005 for discussion of popular and scholarly discourses on digital revolution.

10. See McLuhan 1962, 1964.

11. Appadurai 1990; Bauman 2000; Castells 1996.

12. See Boyer 2005.

13. Wittgenstein 2001: 28.

14. Here I have in mind also Tim Ingold's fascinating Deleuze-inspired analytics of lines, knots, and meshworks (Ingold 2011: 145–155).

15. In George Marcus's sense, my studies are both "strategically situated" and following not one, but a great many stories (1998: 93, 95).

16. Boyer 2008: 44–45.

17. See, e.g., Harcourt 2006; Harrison and Woods 2007.

18. See, e.g., EIAA 2010.

19. Czepek and Klinger 2010: 824; EIAA 2010.

20. AGOF "Internet facts 2011-05" report (in German) (http://www.agof.de/index.583.html).

21. See also Lemann 2006.

1. The Craft of Slotting

1. Beginning in 2005, I visited the AP-DD headquarters in Frankfurt on average twice per year to interview journalists and to arrange research access for an observational study. In May and June 2008, I spent approximately sixty hours over a period of several weeks observing slotters at work at AP-DD. AP-DD was founded in 1931 and organized as an independent for-profit daughter corporation (GmbH) of the Associated Press in New York. By December 2009, AP-DD had become AP's second-largest European news service with approximately 110 full- and part-time employees and was widely viewed as the second most important news agency in Germany after market leader, dpa. AP-Frankfurt was the main office of AP-DD and employed thirty *Redakteure* (editors/journalists) on site. I audio-recorded my observational sessions and kept close written and photographic records of the slotters' activities. In addition, I conducted lengthy post facto interviews with eight of the slotters whom I observed at work.

2. I occasionally use the past tense in this article to reflect the Associated Press's sale of AP-DD to German news agency competitor ddp in December 2009. The two news agencies were later incorporated as a new agency, dapd (http://www.dapd.de). Although the former

AP-Frankfurt office still exists and likely operates in a similar manner to my portrait here, I have not been able to visit the Frankfurt office since October 2009 and thus have little information about postsale continuities and transformations of organizational routines. A cluster of former AP-DD *Redakteure*, including Paul and Friedrich, now work for dpa in Berlin.

3. http://www.newsaktuell.de/

4. Knorr-Cetina 2005, 2009.

5. For further theoretical discussion of the relationship between "immediation" and "mediation," see Mazzarella 2006; Boyer 2007; Eisenlohr 2009; and Keane 2009.

6. Zaloom 2006: 153.

7. Knorr-Cetina 2005: 41.

8. On the transformation of information practices and technologies of news journalism elsewhere in world, cf. especially Boczkowski 2009; Klinenberg 2005; and Paterson and Domingo 2008.

9. The normal German term for this set of responsibilities is *Chef vom Dienst* (CvD), a job roughly equivalent to "assistant managing editor" in American news journalism. Although the CvD position has a relatively fixed job description at some German news organizations, at AP-DD the position and its responsibilities rotated among several senior members of the editorial collective.

10. Zschunke 2000: 250–251.

11. See Associated Press 2007; Read 1999.

12. Literally, "*auteur*-papers." The connotation is that these newspapers are styling themselves as enterprises where all the news bylines are generated in-house.

13. Wilke 2007: 337.

14. These trends are similar in Europe and North America but bleakest in the United States. A Pew Trust report analyzing the American newspaper market in 2010 concluded:

> Newspapers, contrary to what is frequently alleged, are not dying in droves. . . . But far too many American papers are at risk of becoming insubstantial. . . . Advertising losses, averaging 26% in 2009 (on the heels of a cumulative 23% loss the previous two years) left newspapers downsizing everything – the physical dimensions of the paper, the space devoted to news and, most painfully, their roster of news professionals. By our calculation advertising revenues fell 43% over the three years. Roughly 13,500 jobs for full-time, newsroom professionals disappeared during that period, the total falling from 55,000 to 41,500, a count which includes some 284 new jobs at some online-only newspapers now included in the industry's tallies. That means that newsrooms have shrunk by 25% in three years, and just under 27% since the beginning of the decade. To put it another way, newspapers headed into 2010, devoting $1.6 billion less annually to news than they did three years earlier. (http://stateofthemedia.org/2010/newspapers-summary-essay/)

For a comparative analysis of the challenges facing the American news industry see also the fine 2007 *Frontline* report, "News War" (http://www.pbs.org/wgbh/pages/frontline/newswar/); Bollinger 2010; Cortell 2010; Fuller 2010; and posts at http://www.savethenews.org.

15. The parallels to the situation of the music recording industry in the digital era are striking, as is the dominant discourse on industry "crisis" (see, e.g., Knopper 2009; cf. Kot 2009).

16. Freie Demokratische Partei, a liberal and increasingly neoliberal German political party.

17. http://www.arb.ca.gov/homepage.htm

18. Depending on size and staffing, some AP bureaus operate around the clock and some do not. Smaller, yet regionally important bureaus like Paris and Nairobi send a message out in the morning, called an "opener," when a managing editor is on-site and available for correspondence, and a "closer" at the end of the day when they shut down.

19. The occasion was a national election widely criticized for corruption and voter intimidation by forces loyal to Zimbabwe's President Robert Mugabe.

20. In 1996, AP-DD began offering weekly *Themenpakete* (topical packets) on Cinema, Computers, and Health in addition to their regular coverage. These packets included several longer pieces involving more background research and more detailed coverage. In the 2000s, AP-DD's *Paket* production modestly expanded and diversified as part of the aforementioned transition of news agencies to more elaborate forms of news coverage.

21. A prestigious German literary prize.

22. Since the first decades of the twentieth century, German chimney sweeps have enjoyed a legally recognized craft monopoly on the practice of chimney cleaning. As part of its free trade mission, the European Commission viewed this as an unfair restriction of a labor market and threatened to charge the German government with violating the EU treaty if it did not reform its "chimney sweep law." This dispute came to a head in the summer and fall of 2008.

23. The joke also has another form of cathartic value linked to the increasingly uncomfortable relationship between AP-DD and AP-NY and fears that AP-NY would seek to sell AP-DD to a competitor, which is precisely what happened in the end.

24. http://www.dpa.de/dpa-Text.164.0.html

25. The international practice of celebrating a major football event by driving around in cars, honking horns, and waving national or club flags from the window.

26. See Noveck 2007.

27. See, e.g., Fishman 1980; Gans 1979; Tuchman 1978; and Tunstall 1971.

28. By "praxiological" and "mediological" I mean to highlight the complementarity and tension between (praxiological) discourses and understandings of professional life that emphasize the active, creative, effective powers of human agents and (mediological) discourses and understandings that emphasize the power of mediation, circulation, and flow both within and over human agents.

29. Merleau-Ponty 1962: 121.

30. I have in mind particularly the so-called poststructuralists such as Michel Foucault and Gilles Deleuze. I discuss them and the rise of academic mediology at greater length in the epilogue.

2. Click and Spin

1. http://www.bea.aero/docspa/2009/f-cp090601e3/pdf/f-cp090601e3.pdf; see also Clark 2011.

2. A more detailed account of the reconstructed final minutes of AF 447 would run something like this: shortly after AF 447 flew into the thunderstorm configuration, the airplane's three pitot tubes (which measure airspeed) iced over. This was simply a matter of equipment failure and there had been a few isolated incidents of this brand (Thales Avionics) of pitot malfunctioning on other aircraft. The icing of the pitots caused the plane's autopilot to automatically disengage, an event that investigators surmise caught the pilots off guard. A stall warning briefly sounded due to turbulence although the plane had not, at that point, actually

stalled. For reasons that remain unclear, the pilots' immediate response appears to have been to reduce airspeed and to push the nose of the plane up. This was strange since in stall scenarios pilots are trained to push the plane's nose down to increase speed and lift and to thus recover control. At cruising altitude, a stall is not judged to be a fatal event since there is ample time for recovery. No one knows whether the pilots panicked or whether they were receiving erroneous data in the cockpit that led them to misunderstand the plane's situation. In any event, after briefly reaching 38,000 feet, AF 447 slowed to the point that it did in fact stall and descended, still nose up, for three and a half minutes, striking the surface of the Atlantic at 10,912 feet per minute. The stall warning sounded again continuously for almost a minute, yet the pilots, all three of them experienced, did not correctly apply "the unreliable airspeed procedure," according to BEA. Air France has rejected the implication that its pilots were insufficiently trained in stall procedures and suggested instead that the initial brief sounding of the stall warning due to turbulence may have confused them as to the validity of the second (accurate) stall warning. Given that no more data appears to be forthcoming, investigators agree that the ultimate cause of the pilots' reactions will remain a mystery.

3. http://www.nytimes.com/2009/06/02/world/europe/02plane.html?ref=air_france_flight_447

4. This phase lasted a month.

5. However *Themen* frequently enjoyed a longer subterranean existence on the subpages of their originating desks before eventually being archived in a searchable database.

6. I also confess that by organizing this chapter around a spectacular news event I am deliberately borrowing a technique from news journalism and merging it with anthropological ethnography's own tradition of leveraging spectacle to hold an audience's attention.

7. Of course, it is worth noting that in the specific case of AF 447 there was no direct spot news originating from the crash site itself and all news organizations relied upon the public statements of military and airline officials and other experts to a great extent.

8. Dated January 13, 2009.

9. Informationsgemeinschaft zur Feststellung der Verbreitung von Werbeträgern e. V (http://www.ivw.de).

10. t-online.de's web analytics data was also, as I discuss below, the one area of information that the *Redaktion* of T-Online insisted be off limits to publication in my analysis. I thus offer no specific data on CTRs or page views for any of the stories I discuss in this chapter.

11. In other words, T-Online's *Redaktion* knew that AF 447 was compiling very high CTRs and page views as compared with their own past performance, but they could not compare that performance with their competitors on a fast-time basis nor could they evaluate what aspects of their AF 447 coverage were particularly informative or appealing. More than one journalist described the evaluation of clicks as a "black box" in this respect.

12. Rupert Murdoch, the CEO of News Corporation, has famously and repeatedly accused online news aggregators of "theft." For a review of the complaints and legal issues surrounding aggregation and text copyrights, see Lyons 2009; Isbell 2010. For an insightful normative appraisal of how journalists view aggregators see Carlson 2007.

13. With the partial exception of the t-online.de sports desk (see below).

14. The loci classici of this theoretical tradition lie in eighteenth-century political economy (especially Smith 1976 [1776]) and in its critics (especially Marx 1844).

15. In this, T-Online journalists are not atypical of online news journalists more generally in terms of their struggle to articulate specialized modes of journalistic expertise associated

with the online medium (see Boyer 2010a on "digital expertise"; Boczkowski 2009; Paterson and Domingo 2008).

16. See http://www.innotel.de/nl4/nl4i.htm.

17. In this respect, it is a fine example of what Eitan Wilf (2012: 40) terms the "coconstitution of imitation and creativity" in the era of digital reproduction.

18. Rolf Eden, a colorful German club-owner and lothario, best known internationally perhaps for his 2007 lawsuit against a nineteen-year-old woman for ageism (for failing to agree to have sex with him—he was seventy-seven at the time), suffered an injury in 2009 that received national media attention.

19. *Gleichschaltung* (coordination, synchronization) refers to the Third Reich's policy of bringing all institutions in German society, including media and information services, into alignment with the authority and orientation of the Nazi leadership.

20. Although online news organizations across the world use this "read and release" mechanism to filter offensive commentary and spam, German news organizations have a legal responsibility for any opinions they circulate and could be, in theory, charged with *Volksverhetzung* (sedition) under article 130 of the German criminal code if they permitted the circulation of malicious speech towards minorities or pro-Nazi opinions. German online news organizations thus have little choice but to carefully monitor their user comments.

21. Cookies are stored data packets that were developed in the mid-1990s for web browsers to help streamline e-commerce experience by holding on to certain forms of client data between sessions. They have been controversial for their data privacy implications and most web browsers now offer users the choice as to whether they wish to accept cookies or not.

22. The original German teasers were: "Rolf Eden am Kopf operiert: Er sturzt auf der Kellertreppe" and "Not-OP: Grosse Sorgen um Rolf Eden: Alt-Playboy ist schwer gestürzt."

23. Zaloom 2005.

24. Boczkowski 2009: 48.

25. The procedure invokes for me Derridean *différance* (Derrida 1982).

26. *Frankfurter Allgemeine Zeitung* is one of the most distinguished German national newspapers and certainly the most distinguished representing conservative politics.

27. Germany's largest tabloid paper and a powerful news organization in its own right.

28. On the character of Internet-based publicity see, for example, Kelty 2005, 2008; Sunstein 2009; Warner 2002a: 69.

29. See Boyer 2005.

30. Jay Rosen (2006) makes this argument forcefully.

31. I am adapting Povinelli's concept of "autological subject" here which she defines as "the discourses, practices, and fantasies about self-making, self-sovereignty, and the value of individual freedom associated with the Enlightenment project of contractual, constitutional democracy and capitalism" (2006: 4). I discuss the problem of autology in contemporary news media at greater length in chapter 4.

32. Jackson 2008: 16; Laing 1965.

33. "What does the user want?" I invoke Freud's questioning of femininity and female desire here deliberately (see Freud 1965).

34. Stewart 2007: 59.

35. In addition to the main stories (*Hauptthemen*) on the homepage, whose teaser would usually include an image (*Bildbox*), the homepage offered a box for eight *Schlagzeilen* (headlines) of

three to six words each which linked to full stories on desk subpages. *Schlagzeilen* had lower CTR targets than *Hauptthemen* but were still monitored carefully for performance. Another important criterion was visuality. A story for which there was no relevant image might be chosen as a *Schlagzeile* rather than for a *Bildbox*.

36. This story concerned a heated controversy surrounding a Swiss Canton's plan to develop a so-called "Special Zone for the Wealthy" (see, e.g., http://www.oe24.at/welt/weltchronik/Schweiz-plant-Sonderzone-fuer-Reiche/529773).

37. The *Stammtisch* (regulars' table) is a pub-based social institution that is typically viewed in Germany as a more conservative and working-class intellectual space (see Boyer 2006a).

38. Habermas 1989: 209.

39. Boyer 2005, 2006b, 2010.

40. One of the anonymous reviewers of this manuscript offered the following, very perceptive comment on origination and citationality that is worth copy/pasting here:

> in an age of cut-and-paste journalism, the line between origination and citation appears to be blurrier than ever. But perhaps this blurring also has the retroactive effect of making it seem as if origination and citation were once cleanly separable, as if in the age of intrepid foreign reporters in isolated locations, speech was not also always already citational, only less obviously so. In other words, it might be possible to argue that it is only at the point of exceptional speed and density of circulation that we have reached today that the citationality that is built into all language becomes an obvious problem and idiom of routine professional critique.

Indeed, conditions of digital mediation have helped constitute "citationality" as an epistemic object and challenge in news journalism. Just so, we might consider how digital information has elicited parallel concerns of origination and citation in academic practice (particularly, in terms of the instrumentalization of citationality by audit regimes and anxieties about the spread of plagiarism; see, e.g., Brenneis 2009).

41. Boyer 2005.

42. Roughly the German equivalent of *American Idol* in the United States.

3. Countdown

1. For further information on Agenda 2010, see http://www.dw-world.de/dw/article/0,,988374,00.html.

2. Stagnation measured, of course, in terms of the neoliberal priority of stimulating the growth of private sector wealth.

3. The source is Schröder's March 14, 2003, state of the nation address to the German parliament. See http://archiv.bundesregierung.de/bpaexport/regierungserklaerung/79/472179/multi.htm.

4. Schröder-era labor market reforms are typically known in Germany as the Hartz reforms, named for Peter Hartz, the personnel director of Volkswagen, who Schröder appointed to head a commission to modernize the German labor market in 2002. The first three Hartz reforms came into effect in 2003 and 2004 and focused on developing a network of job centers to retrain the unemployed and on a new grants scheme for entrepreneurs. The Hartz IV reform, which came into effect on January 1, 2005, was by far the most controversial reform in that it fused together unemployment benefits for the long-term unemployed and welfare benefits

(*Sozialhilfe*) and significantly reduced overall unemployment benefits after a year in order to incentivize the unemployed to reenter the labor market, often through new low-wage work-fare programs. The Hartz IV reform provoked demonstrations and political resistance across Germany in 2004.

5. And, most recently, the Pirate Party (http://www.piratenpartei.de/).

6. It is worth noting that the political fortunes of the SPD eventually rebounded in 2011 and 2012, although this turnaround was driven less by the party's own new ideas then by pop-ular dissatisfaction with the CDU/CSU/FDP coalition's management of the Euro crisis.

7. The onsite research phase for this book lasted three weeks, but built upon ongoing con-tacts with the mdr info *Redaktion* since 1996.

8. See, e.g., Habermas 1984, 1987.

9. "MDR hat in seinen Sendungen einen objektiven und umfassenden Überblick über das internationale, nationale und länderbezogene Geschehen in allen wesentlichen Lebensbe-reichen zu geben. Sein Programm soll der Information und Bildung sowie der Beratung und Unterhaltung dienen und hat dem kulturellen Auftrag des Rundfunks zu entsprechen. Er dient der freien individuellen und öffentlichen Meinungsbildung."

10. Lila Abu-Lughod has explored the participation of public broadcasting in what she terms the "hegemony of developmentalism" (2004: 191). This hegemony is internal to the mis-sion of public broadcasting in Europe and the United States as well. It is perhaps especially salient in Germany given postwar anxieties about the fragility of liberal democracy. *Öffentlich-keit* is considered a primary index of liberal-democratic vitality and its defense a matter of vocational duty for public broadcasters.

11. Arbeitsgemeinschaft der öffentlich-rechtlichen Rundfunkanstalten der Bundesrepublik Deutschland.

12. In 1963, a second public television channel, ZDF, was founded which, although more autonomously national in its production basis, was subject to rotating supervision by a different federal state every two years.

13. The fifth new eastern German state, Mecklenburg-Vorpommern, was meanwhile in-corporated into the western German Norddeutscher Rundfunk based in Hamburg.

14. The tax is currently, €17.98 per month for radio and TV usage combined.

15. The ARD also exceeds the BBC in terms of broadcast productivity (approximately 1,400 hours of radio and 240 hours of television daily), although it does not operate an independent news-gathering service on the scale, for example, of BBC News. ARD does however maintain one hundred correspondents across thirty international bureaus, figures roughly equivalent to the international correspondent networks of newspapers like the *New York Times* and the *Wall Street Journal* and far larger than those of any commercial or public television broadcaster in the United States (see Kumar 2011). The BBC developed a web of international reportage to a degree that the ARD never did in large part because of the global reach of the British empire during the twentieth century.

16. With its generous funding base, MDR employs 2,000 full-time staff, contracts 5,500 part-time staff, produces a television channel, eight radio channels (including mdr info), and offers an online service complete with livestream content and podcasts. In 2009, when I began field research, mdr info employed twenty-five full-time *Redakteure* and approximately fifty part-time employees.

17. My data source is ZDF. See http://www.zdf.com/index.php?id=181. For more recent statistics see http://www.quotenmeter.de/cms/?p1=c&p2=28&p3=. It should be noted that the

ZDF figures represent all viewers over the age of three. ARD fares somewhat worse in the desirable 14–49 age demographic and long-term trends seem to be favoring the *Privaten*.

18. "Shovelware" is a semiderogatory term for software that automatically moves content online (see Paterson and Domingo 2008 for the use of shovelware and its impact in several different contexts).

19. See, e.g., Harcourt 2006.

20. Calculated in terms of estimated potential audience.

21. Indeed, the "round the clock" news radio model is quintessentially electronic, with its first experiments dating back to the early 1960s as a means of luring audiences back from another threatening new medium, television, by creating unique niche programming models. See Schwiesau and Heerdegen 1995.

22. The first was Bayerischer Rundfunk's B5 aktuell in 1990.

23. The Abitur is a secondary school degree that entitles a student to attend university.

24. I am thinking particularly of Michael Warner's work on publics and counterpublics (2002a, b).

25. Another reason for the high level of political interest is the influence, usually unspoken, of party politics throughout German public broadcasting. As it was explained to me, broadcasters' administrations are often aligned with the dominant electoral sympathies of the region. MDR, for example, had a reputation as a "black" (Christian conservative) broadcaster because of the relative strength of the CDU in its broadcast region. This is not to suggest that journalists were hired for party affiliation or loyalty. But some felt that party affiliation was taken into account in determining promotions to more senior positions at the *Sender*. I never witnessed a situation in which I could confirm such influence having taken place. But I certainly can confirm that party-political intrigue always hung in the air and reinforced the political attentions of the *Redaktion*.

26. Angela Merkel, chairwoman of the CDU since 2000 and chancellor of Germany since 2005, and Guido Westerwelle, chairman of the FDP party, 2001–2011, and the foreign minister of Germany since 2009.

27. Andrea Nahles and Sigmar Gabriel emerged as the new leaders of the SPD after the 2009 election debacle. Gabriel became chair of the party and Nahles the new secretary general in November 2009.

28. Frank-Walter Steinmeier served as chief of staff and as foreign minister under Schröder. He then headed the SPD ticket in the disastrous 2009 election campaign. Klaus Wowereit, the popular and charismatic mayor of Berlin since 2001, is considered by some observers to be the third-most powerful figure in the SPD today after Gabriel and Nahles and it is suspected that he will be a strong contender to become the next chancellor candidate of the SPD.

29. This work was shared between correspondents and the *Redaktion*. Although mdr info lacked its own correspondents, it maintained an office in Berlin and could additionally draw upon the broader ARD correspondent network for national and international coverage and upon reporters based in the ARD broadcasting centers in Saxony, Saxony-Anhalt, and Thuringia for regional coverage. Depending on the assignment and the day, correspondents might produce anywhere between one and eight features, recording and editing their *Beiträge* themselves and sending them as MP3 files to the CvD for review and occasional reediting. Other features, for example interviews, were often taped and edited in-house in Halle.

30. The co-location of sputnik news within the mdr info group was a relatively recent organizational initiative and one that the *Redakteure* felt had enriched the discursive environment of the department.

31. Christoph Matschie, head of the Thuringian SPD party since 1999 and currently also the deputy minister president of Thuringia.

32. Bodo Ramelow, head of the Thuringian Left Party.

33. For comparison, here are the headlines in the original German: Griechenland verkauft Staatsbesitz, um seinen Schuldenberg einzudämmen (7:30 a.m., 8:30 a.m.) Wegen seines Schuldenbergs trennt sich Griechenland von weiteren Teilen des Staatsbesitzes (8:00 a.m., 9:00 a.m.) Die griechische Regierung hat im Kampf gegen die drohende Staatspleite ein neues Sparprogramm beschlossen (9:30 a.m., 10:30 a.m.) Mit Ausgabenkürzungen und Privatisierungen will sich Griechenland weitere internationale Finanzhilfen sichern (10:00 a.m.) Mit neuen Sparmaßnahmen und dem Verkauf dem Staatsbesitz will Griechenland die drohende Staatspleite abwenden (11:00 a.m.).

34. Schwiesau and Heerdegen 1995: 7.

35. State financial assistance for families raising children.

36. See, e.g., Boyer 2005, 2006a, b.

37. See Todorova and Gille 2010.

38. I would note that many eastern German citizens have rewarded such media characterizations of their alleged antiliberal, antinational differences with partial disinvestment in both national political and public culture. The broadcast area of MDR, for example, included the lowest voter turnout of any of the ARD broadcasters in the 2009 election.

39. *Wende* (literally, "turn" or "change") is a widely used colloquial term for the events of 1989–1990 in eastern Germany.

40. Sarrazin published an immensely controversial book in August 2010, *Deutschland schafft sich ab* (Germany is doing away with itself), which quickly became one of the best-selling German-language political texts of the postwar period for its much debated theses concerning the failure of German immigration policy and multiculturalism. The book led to Sarrazin's dismissal from the Executive Board of the German Bundesbank and very nearly to his ouster from the SPD.

41. ARD's evening news program, often considered the gold standard of both public broadcasting and broadcast news.

4. The News Informatic

1. Williams 1974: 17, 120–128.

2. See Boyer 2007 and the following examples of the recent turn toward exploring causality and mediation in anthropological media theory: Engelke 2010; Eisenlohr 2006, 2011; Ginsburg 2008).

3. See McLuhan 1962, 1964, and Williams's (1974: 120–122) critique of McLuhan.

4. By "multiattentional method" I posit an ethics of social analysis that seeks to harness the beneficial theoretical insights of specialized analytical attentions (for example, into principles of causality) without becoming dogmatically invested in any particular configuration of specialized attention as the ultimate explanation of the others. The key to multiattentional method, in my view, is to sustain a multiplicity of specialized modes and languages of theoretical inquiry

without allowing any of them to be trivialized relative to the others. See Boyer 2010b for a more extensive discussion.

5. Williams 1974: 14.

6. Ibid., 20.

7. See Yurchak 2006: 256–259.

8. Williams 1974: 145.

9. I use the terms "northern" and "western" in this chapter to refer to a similar set of elite nations in North America, Europe, Australia and Asia at different times. "Western" indexes the Cold War geopolitics of East/West whereas "northern" refers to the more recent, neoliberal polarization of Global North and Global South.

10. Quandt 2008: 87, and also Quandt 2005.

11. I think it is important to recognize that the consolidation of screenwork as the dominant norm of journalistic activity is more common in countries of the Global North than elsewhere (cf. Bishara 2006; Hannerz 2004; Hasty 2005; Ståhlberg 2002; Wahl-Jorgensen and Cole 2008), where out-of-office reporting and nonscreen-based office work remain stronger staples of professional activity.

12. On the computerization of newsrooms in the 1970s and 1980s, see Carter and Cullen 1983; Chang 1998; Garrison 1982, 1983; Smith 1980.

13. Baisnee and Marchetti 2006: 114.

14. These are too many to recount in any acceptable level of detail. However, the two lines of liberal thinking most relevant to my discussion of digital liberalism below are, firstly, the more strongly autologistic theories of economic and political freedom running from Adam Smith (1976) and John Stuart Mill (1999) through Ludwig von Mises (1952) and Friedrich Hayek (1994) to Milton Friedman (1962) and latter-day "neoliberals" and conservative libertarians. The second line is the pragmatist liberalism running from William James (1995) and John Dewey (1958) to antirepresentationalists like Ludwig Wittgenstein (2001) and Richard Rorty (1979) and to a variety of contemporary ecological liberalisms (Latour 2004 being an excellent example). Both lines share a common ancestry with nineteenth-century liberalism, but the latter has generally evolved a deeper appreciation for communitarianism and pluralism, an appreciation that found its most efficacious geopolitical expression in the welfarist liberalism of John Maynard Keynes (1936).

15. Povinelli 2006.

16. David Graeber offers an interesting discussion of the roots of liberalism, especially its conception of selfhood as form of property, in Roman contract law (see Graeber 2011: 198–207).

17. There is, of course, a third sibling in the family of European social philosophy, conservatism, which opposes the modernizing impulses of both liberalism and socialism. Although I do not regard conservatism as simply residual traditionalism—it has an epistemic vitality of its own—I do not think that it is as invested in how to direct future forms of human life as the twins liberalism and socialism since, ideally, a conservative future would repeat past forms rather than generating new ones. Thus conservatism also seems more foreign to journalism as a distinctly modernist enterprise.

18. Durkheim 1995: 15.

19. See Mitchell 2009 for a magnificent narration of this history.

20. For discussions of neoliberalism as a response to declining western imperial power see, e.g., Duménil and Levy 2011; Harvey 2007.

21. See n. 18 above and also Klein 2007.

22. See Saad-Filho and Johnston 2005. As with "liberalism," I do not assume that "neoliberalism" is a homogeneous or systemic entity either epistemically or institutionally. Not unlike Hannah Arendt's diagnosis of totalitarianism, neoliberalism appears to me as much a movement as a fixed ideology. It seems anyway much more concerned with a direction of transformation than with the attainment of any particular set of goals or final forms. Thus, its heterogeneity proves no obstacle to its further development.

23. Ethnography has rediscovered this point wherever neoliberalism is at work (see, e.g., Dunn 2004; Elyachar 2005; Graeber 2002).

24. Notable among them Arjun Appadurai (1990), Manuel Castells (1996), Edward LiPuma and Ben Lee (2004), and Saskia Sassen (2001).

25. Chakravarty and Schiller (2010: 673) write, "The liberalization and commercialization of national film, television and print media industries established highly visible sites for the celebration of a global consumer culture promising liberation from statist tyranny. Less visible but equally important was the rush to restructure and expand telecommunications industries to integrate transnational markets from manufacturing to financial services." Schiller (2011:930) also writes, "As it took shape, digital capitalism gave a fresh impulse to accumulation, and—especially during the 1990s—encouraged a fetishistic belief in information as a growth zone and detoxifying agent." Cf. Graham 2000; Dyer-Wetherford 1999.

26. Duménil and Levy 2011: 175–176.

27. Herman and Chomsky 1988; McChesney 2004.

28. Of the more skeptical accounts, see McChesney 2004: 10.

29. Schüll 2005: 74.

30. See, e.g., Suchman 1987. Indeed, the field of HCI (human-computer interaction) studies models a cybernetic communicational partnership between human users and machinic systems that brings computers as well into models of liberal publicity (Warner 2002).

31. Alexander Galloway, for example, argues that new gaming interfaces like *World of Warcraft*, "awash with information" as they are, involve with us new stories about contemporary life: "At root, the game is not simply a fantasy landscape of dragons and epic weapons but a factory floor, an information-age sweat shop, custom tailored in every detail for cooperative ludic labor" (2009: 947). Rather than the idea of "interface" as a window on to another world, Galloway prefers the idea of "intraface" that allegorizes the existing world as aesthetic event.

32. See, e.g., Klinenberg 2012.

33. Boczkowski 2010: 6.

34. How precisely one should define consumer loyalty is debatable, of course. But German news organizations typically report that their audiences are especially *treu* (loyal).

35. See the excellent 2007 *Frontline* series "News War" for an unusually balanced investigation of the different aspects of the challenges facing contemporary newsmakers (http://www.pbs.org/wgbh/pages/frontline/newswar/).

36. There is a publishing industry unto itself documenting the trials and tribulations of newspapers. Some worthwhile analyses include Almiron 2010; Fuller 2010; Kindred 2010.

37. An AP press release from June 4, 2009, reads: "AP Board announces initiative to protect industry's content; Further rate reductions and new 'Limited' service respond to member needs"; see also Farhi 2009.

38. Cases of news hoaxes seem to be proliferating globally (see Boyer and Yurchak 2010). In Germany, in June 2010, the German satire magazine *Titanic* successfully hoaxed the German news media by setting up a fake Twitter feed allegedly from a Green Party parliamentarian

(actress Martina Gedeck, one of the stars of the film *The Lives of Others*) tweeting comments from within the closed-door parliamentary vote to name the next German president. Gedeck's alleged tweets were reported widely in German online media before the hoax was discovered.

39. See Boyer 2005.

40. Cf. Boellstorff's fascinating discussion of virtuality and screen interfaces in online gaming (2008).

41. See Peterson 2001 for a perceptive analysis of the professional practices and semiotic operations involved in how news journalists constitute their sense of objectivity.

42. See Abu-Lughod 2004: 109–110.

43. See Lemann 2006; Rosen 2006.

44. In October 2011, the fifteen most visited online news sources were (in order): Yahoo News, CNN, MSNBC, Google News, *New York Times*, *Huffington Post*, Fox News, Digg, *Washington Post*, *LA Times*, *Mail Online*, Reuters, ABC News, *USA Today* and BBC News. Although the list shows the remarkable presence of news aggregators today, of the aggregators only the *Huffington Post* offers significant original news content that does not derive ultimately from an offline print, broadcast, or news agency source.

45. McLuhan 1969.

46. McLuhan 1964, 1969; see also Boyer 2007.

47. Negroponte 1995: 71.

48. I do not mean to suggest that further enclosure is inevitable—only very likely. Concerted acts of resistance may help retain some commons but privatization and commercialization certainly seem to be dominant trends at the moment. On open access and the Internet commons see Coombe and Herman 2004; Kelty 2008; Lessig 2004.

49. Peters 2011.

50. Schudson 1984: 218; Abu-Lughod 2004: 81.

51. See, e.g., Harrison and Woods 2007.

52. See Bagdikian 1983.

53. Czepek and Klinger 2010: 822–823.

54. Particularly in the left-wing German press, it's not unusual for "solidarity appeals" to be made to readers and users. The premise of audience solidarity allows news organizations other revenue streams as well. For example, many German news organizations advertise travel packages on the assumption that shared informational interests could easily transition into other modes of conviviality as well.

55. See Carr 2008; Glaser 2005.

56. Baran 1967.

57. Baran's theorization of "distributed communications" and his contributions to the development of packet-switched data networks were particularly instrumental for both ARPANET and later for the Internet.

Epilogue

1. Gere 2008: 15.

2. See, e.g., Appadurai 1990; Boellstorff 2008; Gershon 2010; Miller 2011.

3. In the anthropology of digital media, see, among others, Boyer 2010; Budka and Kremser 2004; Coleman 2010; Coleman and Golub 2008; Escobar 1994; Golub 2010; Helmreich 2000; Kelty 2005; Mazzarella 2006; Miller and Slater 2000.

4. Lydia Liu (2010) has also written perceptively, with different conceptual emphases than my own, of the intimate entanglement of psychoanalysis and cybernetics, indeed of a "cybernetic unconscious" that connects information theory to the Freudian model of the mind.

5. Nye 1990: 156.

6. This text is usually glossed in English as the "Project for a scientific psychology" and was not published in Freud's lifetime. For an English transition see Freud 1966[1895].

7. Translated into English as *The Interpretation of Dreams* (see Freud 1913).

8. See especially Pribram and Gill 1976 but also Pribram 1962 and the papers collected in Bilder 1998.

9. Nye 1990; Winther 2008.

10. Pribram 1962: 445.

11. Germine 1998: 82; also, Holt 1989: 318.

12. Mosco 2005.

13. In other words, not within Babbage's lifetime. However, when a prototype was finally completed in 1991 by the London Science Museum on the basis of Babbage's plans and Lovelace's program, it was found to function perfectly.

14. On the early history of the data-processing industry in the United States, see Cortada 1993.

15. See Bush 1931; also, Zachary 1999.

16. Mike Hally (2005) and David Ritchie (1986) offer engaging, detailed histories of electromechanical computation in the period.

17. A U.S. Navy educational film, *Basic Mechanisms in Fire Control Computers*, explains the operation of military analog computers with great detail and clarity (see, e.g., http://www.youtube.com/watch?v=_8aH-M3PzM0). Such analog computers remained standard equipment in the U.S. Navy until the late 1960s.

18. The transcript of a quite fascinating 1982 interview with Shannon concerning the steps that led him to his information theory can be found at http://www.ieeeghn.org/wiki/index.php/Oral-History:Claude_E._Shannon. See also Gleick 2011.

19. Shannon 1945, 1948.

20. In the aforementioned interview (see n. 18 above), Shannon dates his first serious efforts at information theory to 1941, predating his engagement in cryptography. But Shannon saw cryptography as a way of "legitimatizing" his interest in information theory during wartime ("To make it sound like I'm working on decent things [*laughs*]"). Shannon linked his breakthroughs to earlier works in communications engineering by figures like Harry Nyquist (1924) and Ralph Hartley (1928) who sought to work through signal and feedback issues in electric media like telegraphy, telephony, and radio. Nyquist developed a concept of "intelligence" that was not unlike Shannon's concept of "information" as relevant signal. Hartley wrote meanwhile that the problem of transmitting "information" can and should be kept separate from that of meaning, "Hence in estimating the capacity of the physical system to transmit information we should ignore the question of interpretation, make each selection perfectly arbitrary, and base our results on the possibility of the receiver's distinguishing the result of selecting any one signal from that of selecting any other. By this means the psychological factors and their variations are eliminated and it becomes possible to set up a definite quantitative measure of information based on physical considerations alone" (1928: 536). Both Nyquist and Hartley overlapped with Shannon at Bell Labs and were on the internal circulation list for Shannon's watershed classified 1945 cryptography memo (Shannon 1945).

21. See Aspray 1985 for a more complete review.

22. Shannon 1948: 379.

23. See, e.g., Shurkin 1996.

24. See http://www.time.com/time/magazine/article/0,9171,852728,00.html and also a few years later, http://www.time.com/time/magazine/article/0,9171,858601,00.html.

25. See http://www.time.com/time/magazine/article/0,9171,817175-5,00.html.

26. I borrow the term "epistemic ecology" from my friend and brilliant colleague, James Faubion (2008a).

27. Transcripts of the Macy Foundation proceedings (papers and discussions) exist for the final five (of ten total) meetings (see Pias 2003). On the history and impact of Macy across the sciences and social sciences, see also Dupuy 2000; Hagen 1992; Haraway 1981/82; Heims 1993; Lafontaine 2007; Pickering 2011.

28. See Wiener 1948, 1950.

29. McCulloch explained the thematic progression at Macy as follows: "Our meetings began chiefly because Norbert Wiener and his friends in mathematics, communication engineering, and physiology, had shown the applicability of the notions of inverse feedback to all problems of regulation, homeostasis, and goal-directed activity from steam engines to human societies. . . . At the end of the first five sessions . . . we had already discovered that what was crucial in all problems of negative feedback in any servo system was not the energy returned but the information about the outcome of the action to date. Our theme shifted slowly and inevitably to a field where Norbert Wiener and his friends still were the presiding genii. It became clear that every signal had two aspects: one physical, the other mental, formal or logical. This turned our attention to computing machinery, to the storage of information as negative entropy. Here belong questions of coding, of languages and their structures, of how they are learned and how they are understood" (in Pias 2003: 719–720).

30. Bateson 2002: 103. Bateson was likely thinking of the Seventh Macy Conference, held in March 1950, at which Ralph Gerard's paper, "Some of the Problems Concerning Digital Notions in the Central Nervous System" produced a lengthy debate over the "digital and analogical mechanisms in the brain" (Pias 2003: 171f.) During this debate, the participants sought the historical origin of the digital/analogical distinction, which Wiener periodized around 1940 and linked to research on differential analyzers, saying "I doubt if you'll find any clear distinction older than that" (Pias 2003: 192). I take this to confirm my previous argument that the digital/analog distinction was ultimately rooted in computational design work on signal processing.

31. Unlike many analysts of cybernetics (e.g., Galison 1994), Andrew Pickering (2011: 4–5, 55–56) emphasizes the roots of cybernetics in psychiatry and brain research. This is an excellent observation that connects well to the discussion of Freudian psychology and neurology above and invites parallel recognition of the impact of research on organismic systems theory dating back to the 1930s (e.g., Bertalanffy 1949). I suspect that a more thorough historical analysis could also trace links of earlier iterations of systems theory to electric, computational, and thermodynamic sources. Regardless, it is factual that cybernetics incorporated a wide range of influences and accelerants. However, it seems clear to me that it was the militarization of electronic computation that most directly influenced and accelerated those strands of cybernetic and informationalist thinking that most directly contributed to later institutionalizations of digital computation, communication, and media.

32. McCulloch and Pitts 1943. This paper was co-authored with another Macy attendee, Walter Pitts, who had already published another influential protocybernetic paper that likened the operation of neural networks to electric circuits (see Pitts 1942).

33. The proposal was rejected principally because of Bush's conviction that analog computation was sufficient for military defense purposes; he saw no purpose in dividing energy and resources between digital and analog computation.

34. See Price 1998.

35. This characterization is supported by McCulloch's characterization of the origins of the conferences (see n. 29 above) and by Shannon's recollection that Wiener's conceptualization of cybernetics always exceeded the work that Shannon and others had been doing on information and computation theory. Somewhat exasperated by his interviewer's efforts to link his work on data-smoothing back to Wiener, Shannon commented that "When I talked to Norbert, like in the 1950s and so on, I never got the feeling that he understood what I was talking about" (see .n. 18 above).

36. This would be, more or less, Bruno Latour's (1987) interpretation of things and is probably a more accurate characterization of Wiener's investment than of his colleagues. Wiener very clearly sought to use the Macy Conferences to extrapolate, refine, and publicly amplify his thinking on feedback, control, and information.

37. Apparently, neither Bateson nor Mead had a strong background in mathematics, which left them somewhat marginal to several central lines of discussion at Macy. However, Mead exerted considerable authority in the conferences given her fame (see Conway and Siegelman 2004: 168). From the transcripts that exist, it is clear that when the Macy conversations turned to problems in psychology and language, Bateson and Mead were quite active participants. They also presented papers of their own. Mead's paper was titled, "Experience in Learning Primitive Languages through the Use of Learning High Level Linguistic Abstractions" (Pias 2003: 273f.) and Bateson presented "The Position of Humor in Human Communication" (Pias 2003: 541f.).

38. See, e.g., Bertalanffy 1968; Luhmann 1984; Odum and Odum 1953; Parsons 1951.

39. One of Wiener's more significant conceptual breakthroughs during the course of the conferences was how to apply the thermodynamic principle of entropy (here, noise) to the problem of information (relevant signal) (see Conway and Siegelman 2004: 166–167). Shannon was to elaborate the idea at greater length in his communication theory (Shannon 1948).

40. Wiener 1950: 33–34.

41. The alloying of computational thinking with thermodynamic ontology was doubtless very central to this process of conversion.

42. Of course, computational systematicity had its own roots, both conceptual and practical, in electrical and thermodynamic systems.

43. A connection not lost on Jacques Lacan who devoted his 1954–1955 seminar to the study of cybernetics and new calculation machines (Lafontaine 2007: 35). The impact of cybernetics upon Lacanian psychoanalysis was, by many accounts, very significant. André Cornelis Nusselder (2009: 68) writes that Lacan's encounter with cybernetics was a crucial opportunity to "redefine the Freudian unconscious away from what he saw as its biological aberration: 'Don't you know that the energetic is nothing else, whatever the naïve hearts of engineers believe, than the appliance of a network of signifiers on to the world?' [Lacan 1991: 54] . . . Lacan conceives the unconscious as an autonomous cybernetic circuit." See also Johnston 2010: 106; Liu 2010: 196.

44. Cf. Helmreich 2001: 616–617. My analysis here generally confirms Helmreich's characterization that "cybernetics was incorporated into American anthropology as early as the 1950s," although the incorporation was relatively marginal at first.

45. Also salient is the fact that Bateson and Mead separated and divorced during the course of the Macy Conferences. Bateson pursued his cybernetic investigations into psychiatry, developing among other things his theory of the "double bind" (Pickering 2011: 174–175). Mead, meanwhile, showed no immediate interest in championing cybernetics in anthropology either.

46. See, e.g., Oppler 1936 and Eggan 1937. Similar conceptualizations of kinship systematicity date (at least) to Lewis Henry Morgan's (1871) landmark work, *Systems of Consanguinity and Affinity of the Human Family* and thus it would be difficult to label them even as instances of electric reason.

47. Geertz 1957: 34.

48. See, e.g., Feibleman 1954; Oberg 1943; Salisbury 1956.

49. Driver and Kroeber 1932; see also Klimek and Milke 1935; Kluckhohn 1939; Driver 1953.

50. This project later became the Human Relations Area Files (http://www.yale.edu/hraf/).

51. Kluckhohn 1939.

52. Goldenweiser 1941.

53. Meggers 1946.

54. White 1943: 346.

55. For a broader discussion of the relationship between structuralism and cybernetics, see Hayles 1999: 91–98. On the spread of cybernetics beyond the United States, see Gerovitch 2002; Mindell et al. 2003.

56. Lévi-Strauss 1951: 158.

57. Ibid., 155.

58. Ibid., 156.

59. Lévi-Strauss's friendship with Roman Jakobson in the 1940s and their collaboration in the context of the Linguistic Circle of New York was clearly pivotal in terms of Lévi-Strauss's receptivity to information theory (Dosse 1997: 52; Lafontaine 2007: 33). Not unlike the operational work of 1920s communications engineers like Nyquist and Hartley, the structural phonology of the Prague Circle sought to rationalize the analysis of communication. In conjunction with the work of Nicolai Trubetzkoy (1939), Jakobson helped to radicalize Saussure's binary and systemic visions of language, coming to the conclusion that "the phonematic code was binary, like formal, mathematical language" (Dosse 1997: 57). Still, Jürgen van de Walle (2008: 87) notes that "before moving to the US in 1941, Roman Jakobson only occasionally used concepts from natural science and mathematics in his study of language, literature and art."

60. Lévi-Strauss 1951: 157.

61. Jakobson's contact with information theory in New York has been reconstructed in detail by Bernard Geoghegan who argues that "Jakobson's stay in New York enabled him to elaborate a fully technicist approach to language concretized and corroborated by the instruments of communications engineering. This amounted to both an extension and revision of structural linguistics, as it had developed in Europe" (2011: 105). In particular Geoghegan describes a crucial series of meetings in 1944 where members of the Linguistic Circle came into contact with Bell Labs engineers and their speech synthesizer, the Voder (from **V**oice **O**peration **De**monstrator), which had been publicly displayed in Bell System's exhibits at the 1939 World's Fairs in New York and San Francisco. Jakobson and Lévi-Strauss both recognized that making speech an engineering problem had the potential to validate the scientific project of phonology (and therefore structural linguistics and anthropology). Lévi-Strauss wrote later that the Voder proved that in "the intellectual methods governing the work of communication specialists certain main principles of in-

terpretation can be seen in action, which are exactly the same as those at which linguistic theory had arrived" (1954: 582). Jakobson's commitment to information theory was doubtless deepened by his invitation, as a special guest, to the attend the Fifth Macy Foundation Conference in 1948 (which focused on language). Here, Jakobson would have encountered cybernetics and information theory in full bloom and the experience seems to have focused his resolve. Two years later he received a $50,000 grant from the Rockefeller Foundation to apply "to living languages . . . the mathematical theory of communication worked out by Mr. Claude E. Shannon" (in Geoghegan 2011: 111). Jakobson (1971: 224) later reflected on his rationale for turning structural linguistics toward mathematics: "There is a direct help that linguistics is in line to receive from mathematics at this moment, especially from the so-called 'information theory' or theory of communication. The fundamental dichotomous notions of linguistics, particularly singled out by F. de Saussure, A. Gardiner, and E. Sapir and called *langue* and *parole* in France, 'linguistic pattern' and 'speech' in America, now receive a much clearer, simpler, logically less ambiguous, and operationally more productive formulation when matched with the corresponding concepts of communication theory, namely with 'code' and 'message.'" However, Jakobson did also distinguish the practice of the linguist from that of the communications engineer: "The attitude of the communication engineer toward this dichotomy differs essentially from the attitude of the inquirer into an unknown language, who essays, through the messages of native informants, to break their code and develops for this purpose a special cryptanalytic technique. . . . A linguist assimilating an unknown language is compelled to begin as a cryptanalyst but aims to become a regular decoder, and the decoding methodology of descriptive linguistics is to be clearly distinguished from the cryptanalytic approach of the reconnoitering field worker" (ibid.).

62. The earliest statement being a direct result of his collaboration with Jakobson in New York (Lévi-Strauss 1945).

63. Mindell et al. 2003; Lévi-Strauss 1949. The English language edition is titled *The Elementary Structures of Kinship*, Lévi-Strauss 1969 [1949].

64. Geoghagen (2011: 117) dates Lévi-Strauss's full embrace of "the cybernetic apparatus" to 1950 and a meeting with Jakobson in Paris: "Privately he and Lacan began consulting with a French mathematician interested in cybernetics. Publicly he touted cybernetics's capacity to overcome the corrosive effects of historical delay, disciplinary difference, and political antinomy." Lévi-Strauss thereafter sought, without success, to gain support from UNESCO and the Rockefeller Foundation to establish a cybernetically oriented research center in Paris. With Jakobson's support, he was successful in securing a grant from MIT to establish an (unbeknownst to Lévi-Strauss, CIA-funded) interdisciplinary research seminar on cybernetics in 1953. The seminar apparently included Lacan, Jean Piaget, and Emile Benveniste, among others (Geoghagen 2011: 119).

65. Moore and Olmsted 1953: 117.

66. Ibid., 119.

67. Mead 1961: 479.

68. Ibid.

69. Kluckhohn 1961.

70. Hockett had participated in the Linguistic Circle of New York with Jakobson and Lévi-Strauss.

71. See, e.g., Bernstein 1964; Hymes 1964; Scholte 1966; Spiro 1966; Barkow 1967; Hackenberg 1967; Press 1969; Rappaport 1971. Unsurprisingly, cybernetically attentive research began to appear in other English-language anthropological journals as well during this period (see,

e.g., Hall and Whyte 1960; Kroeber 1962; Coult 1967; Hall 1968; Holloway 1969; Sarles 1969; Ardener 1971). And, cybernetics and systems theory likewise began to exercise influence in American archaeology during the same period, especially via the interventions of Lewis Binford (Binford and Binford 1968) and Kent Flannery (1968).

72. See, e.g., Gere 2008: 60–62.

73. Lévi-Strauss 1966: 150–152.

74. Ibid., 17–20.

75. Ibid., 130–131.

76. Ibid., 269.

77. Geoghegan (2011: 123) writes, "In this regard, the status of *The Savage Mind* as a masterpiece rests largely on its infidelity—that is, on a brilliant misreading of information theories to suggest a new interpretation of cultures as dynamic systems of communication in which language, women, plants, hunting procedures, and economic practices circulated among one another to configure immanent possibilities of intelligibility and reasoning." It is also notable that Lévi-Strauss's 1966 essay, "The Scope of Anthropology" (1966b) provides no reference to cybernetics, communication theory, or information theory.

78. Geertz 1967; see also Rossi 1973.

79. Although Marshall Sahlins's *Culture and Practical Reason* (1976) would be another strong contender. Sahlins, a student and later critic of White's, falls somewhere between the structural and interpretive poles of 1970s anthropological culture theory, but his approach is certainly typified by a quasi-cybernetic sense of "culture" as an adaptive system of categories engaging a world that "is under no obligation to conform to the logic by which some people conceive it" (1985: 138).

80. Geertz 1973: 30.

81. Talcott Parsons (1951) was an early convert to cybernetics in sociology. He attended two of the Macy Foundation Conferences and likewise participated in an ongoing conference on systems theory at the University of Chicago from 1952 to 1957. Geertz studied with Parsons at Harvard during this period.

82. Geertz 1973: 60–61.

83. Ibid., 79.

84. Ibid., 216–217.

85. Ibid., 44.

86. See n. 65 above.

87. See, especially, Kelty 2009 and Miller 2011.

88. Appadurai 1990.

89. Deleuze 2004: 270.

90. Faubion, for example, discusses Foucault's fraught relationship to the systematicity of structuralism with great care. Despite working in an intellectual ecology deeply marked by cybernetics, information theory, and game theory, Faubion concludes that, in view of his investment in genealogical method and turn toward ethics, "Foucault is no cybernetician" (2008b: 96; see also Parisi and Terranova 2000).

91. Parisi and Terranova 2000.

92. McLuhan 1964; Deleuze and Guattari 1983: 241.

93. Deleuze 1992.

94. "Power is everywhere, not because it embraces everything, but because it comes from everywhere" (Foucault 1998: 93). My point is that Foucault's theory of *pouvoir* is an experiment, knowingly or not, in postcybernetic digital reason. Although Foucault is interpreted by

some as conceptualizing an absolute systematicity of power when he writes that there is no "outside" to power (e.g., Foucault 1980: 141), his digital thinking seems to me to be straining instead toward the informatic network imagination of the Internet or even toward the informatic clouds of Wi-Fi, rather than toward the closed electric circuits or cybernetic control systems of old. That he does not quite reach the point of crystallizing such a postcybernetic theory is, of course, to be expected given Foucault's time and place. But his efforts, like Deleuze's along similar lines, have rendered his works endlessly fascinating points of departure for the contemporary human sciences as they seek to come to terms with a digital informational environment that can no longer be easily circumscribed or ignored.

95. Indeed, in another context, Alexander Galloway (2009: 952) writes perceptively of how the work of Deleuze and Guattari is "politically 'open source.'"

96. My sense of these ethics is, I would note, somewhat different than Pierre Bourdieu's (1988). Bourdieu clearly believes that "by allowing us to objectify objectification" (ibid.: 7) reflexive sociology offers a higher order of scientific truth than the forms of knowledge it analyzes. I make no such claim. Indeed, Bourdieu's conception of reflexivity is distinctly cybernetic in its faith that operations of critical feedback can distill clearer truth signals. The trouble with this position, from my point of view, is that it allows reflexivity to escape having an ideological-phenomenological basis of its own.

97. Cf. Lukács (1971) on "reification" and Bourdieu (1990) on "doxa."

98. Marx 1857.

99. e.g., "Indifference toward specific labors corresponds to a form of society in which individuals can with ease transfer from one labor to another, and where the specific kind is a matter of chance for them, hence of indifference. Not only the category, labor, but labor in reality has here become the means of creating wealth in general, and has ceased to be organically linked with particular individuals in any specific form" (Marx 1857).

100. Slavoj Žižek (1989: 16–32) makes essentially the same point in his retrieval of the phenomenon of "ideological fantasy" from Marx's sociology of knowledge.

101. I am thinking particularly of simmering public debates over "distance learning" and the necessity of campus-based higher education. Digital liberalism's leveraging of technology over labor is a familiar trend from news journalism as well.

102. See Boyer 2010b.

103. Tim Ingold's work is another good example of ecological phenomenology and one that is, perhaps unsurprisingly, deeply influenced by Deleuze (see Ingold 2011).

BIBLIOGRAPHY

Abu-Lughod, Lila. 2004. *Dramas of Nationhood*. Chicago: University of Chicago Press.

Almiron, Nuria. 2010. *Journalism in Crisis: Corporate Media and Financialization*. New York: Hampton Press.

Appadurai, Arjun. 1990. "Disjuncture and Difference in the Global Cultural Economy." *Public Culture* 2(2): 1–24.

Applegate, Celia. 1990. *A Nation of Provincials: The German Idea of Heimat*. Berkeley: University of California Press.

Ardener, Edwin. 1971. "The New Anthropology and Its Critics." *Man* 6(3): 449–467.

Asad, Talal, ed. 1973. *Anthropology and the Colonial Encounter*. New York: Humanities Press.

Aspray, William. 1985. "The Scientific Conceptualization of Information: A Survey." *IEEE Annals of the History of Computing* 7(2): 117–140.

Associated Press. 2007. *Breaking News*. New York: Princeton Architectural Press.

Bagdikian, Ben. 1983. *The Media Monopoly*. Boston: Beacon.

Baisnée, Olivier, and Dominique Marchetti. 2006. "The Economy of Just-In-Time Television Newscasting: Journalistic Production and Professional Excellence at Euronews." *Ethnography* 7(1): 99–123.

Baran, Paul. 1967. *Some Remarks on Digital Distributed Communications Networks*. Santa Monica, CA: RAND Corporation.

Barkow, Jerome H. 1967. "The Causal Interpretation of Correlation in Cross-Cultural Studies." *American Anthropologist* 69(5): 506–510.

Barnes, Barry, David Bloor, and John Henry. 1996. *Scientific Knowledge: A Sociological Analysis*. Chicago: University of Chicago Press.

Bauman, Zygmunt. 2000. *Liquid Modernity*. Malden, MA: Polity.

Behar, Ruth, and Deborah A. Gordon, eds. 1996. *Women Writing Culture*. Berkeley: University of California Press.

Bernstein, Basil. 1964. "Elaborated and Restricted Codes: Their Social Origins and Some Consequences." *American Anthropologist* 66(2): 55–69.

Bertalanffy, Ludwig von. 1949. "Zu einer allgemeinen Systemlehre." *Biologia Generalis* 195:114–129.

———. 1968. *General System Theory. Foundations, Development, Applications*. New York: George Brazillier.

Bilder, Robert M., and F. Frank LeFever, eds. 1998. *Neuroscience of the Mind on the Centennial of Freud's Project for a Scientific Psychology.* New York: Annals of the New York Academy of Sciences.

Binford, Sally R., and Lewis Binford, eds. 1968. *New Perspectives in Archaeology.* Chicago: Aldine.

Bird, S. Elizabeth, ed. 2010. *The Anthropology of News and Journalism: Global Perspectives.* Bloomington: Indiana University Press.

Bishara, Amahl. 2006. "Local Hands, International News: Palestinian Journalists and the International Media." *Ethnography* 7(2): 19–46.

———. 2008. "Watching U.S. Television from the Palestinian Street: Representational Contests of the Palestinian Authority, the U.S. Media, and the Palestinian Public." *Cultural Anthropology* 23(3): 488–530.

Boczkowski, Pablo J. 2005. *Digitizing the News.* Cambridge, MA: MIT Press.

———. 2009. "Technology, Monitoring, and Imitation in Contemporary News Work." *Communication, Culture & Critique* 2:39–59.

———. 2010. *News at Work.* Chicago: University of Chicago Press.

Boczkowski, Pablo J., and Martin de Santos. 2007. "When More Media Equals Less News: Patterns of Content Homogenization in Argentina's Leading Print and Online Newspapers." *Political Communication* 24(2): 167–180.

Boellstorff, Tom. 2008. *Coming of Age in Second Life: An Anthropologist Explores the Virtually Human.* Princeton: Princeton University Press.

Bohannan, Paul. 1973. "Rethinking Culture: A Project for Current Anthropologists." *Current Anthropology* 14(4): 357–372.

Bollinger, Lee. 2010. "Journalism Needs Government Help." *Wall Street Journal*, July 14.

Bourdieu, Pierre. 1988. *Homo Academicus.* Translated by Peter Collier. Stanford: Stanford University Press.

———. 1990. *The Logic of Practice.* Translated by Richard Nice. Stanford: Stanford University Press.

Boyer, Dominic. 2005. *Spirit and System: Media, Intellectuals and the Dialectic in Modern German Culture.* Chicago: University of Chicago Press.

———. 2006a. "Conspiracy, History, and Therapy at a Berlin *Stammtisch*." *American Ethnologist* 33(3): 327–339.

———. 2006b. "*Ostalgie* and the Politics of the Future in Eastern Germany." *Public Culture* 18(2): 361–381.

———. 2007. *Understanding Media.* Chicago: Prickly Paradigm Press.

———. 2008. "Thinking through the Anthropology of Experts." *Anthropology in Action* 15(2): 38–46.

———. 2010a. "From Algos to Autonomos: Nostalgic Eastern Europe as Postimperial Mania." In *Postcommunist Nostalgia*, edited by Maria Todorova and Zsuzsa Gille, 17–28. New York: Berghahn.

———. 2010b. "On the Ethics and Practice of Contemporary Social Theory: From Crisis Talk to Multiattentional Method." *Dialectical Anthropology* 34(3): 305–324.

Boyer, Dominic, and Alexei Yurchak. 2010. "American Stiob: Or, What Late Socialist Aesthetics of Parody Reveal about Contemporary Political Culture in the West." *Cultural Anthropology* 25(2): 179–221.

Brenneis, Don. 2009. "Anthropology in and of the Academy: Globalization, Assessment and our Field's Future." *Social Anthropology* 17(3): 261–275.

Budka, Philipp, and Manfred Kremser. 2004. "CyberAnthropology—Anthropology of CyberCulture." In *Contemporary Issues in Socio-Cultural Anthropology: Perspectives and Research Activities from Austria*, edited by Stefan Khittel, Barbara Plankensteiner, and Maria Six-Hohenbalken, 213–226. Vienna: Loecker.

Bush, Vannevar. 1931. "The Differential Analyzer. A New Machine for Solving Differential Equations." *Journal of the Franklin Institute* 212(4): 447–488.

Carlson, Matt. 2007. "Order versus Access: News Search Engines and the Challenge to Traditional Journalistic Roles." *Media, Culture and Society* 29(6): 1014–1030.

Carr, David F. 2008. "'One Man Band' Video Journalist Model Proliferates." *Broadcast & Cable*, April 1. (http://www.broadcastingcable.com/article/101401-_One_Man_Band_Video_Journalist_Model_Proliferates.php)

Carter, Nancy M., and John B. Cullen. 1983. *The Computerization of Newspaper Organizations*. Lanham, MD: University Press of America.

Castells, Manuel. 1996. *The Rise of the Network Society, The Information Age: Economy, Society and Culture Vol. I.* Cambridge, MA: Blackwell.

Chakravartty, Paula, and Dan Schiller. 2010. "Neoliberal Newspeak and Digital Capitalism in Crisis." *International Journal of Communication* 4:670–692.

Chang, Li-jing Arthur. "Computerization of Taiwanese Newspapers." Master's thesis, University of Texas-Austin, 1998.

Clark, Nicola. 2011. "Report on Air France Crash Points to Pilot Training." *New York Times*, July 29.

Clifford, James, and George E. Marcus, eds. 1986. *Writing Culture*. Berkeley: University of California Press.

Coleman, E. Gabriella. 2010. "Ethnographic Approaches to Digital Media." *Annual Review of Anthropology* 39:1–16.

Coleman, E. Gabriella, and Alex Golub. 2008. "Hacker Practice: Moral Genres and the Cultural Articulation of Liberalism." *Anthropological Theory* 8(3): 255–277.

Collins, Harry. 1990. *Artificial Experts: Social Knowledge and Intelligent Machines*. Cambridge, MA: MIT Press.

Conway, Flo, and Jim Siegelman. 2004. *Dark Hero of the Information Age: In Search of Norbert Wiener, the Father of Cybernetics*. New York: Basic Books.

Coombe, Rosemary, and Andrew Herman. 2004. "Rhetorical Virtues: Property, Speech, and the Commons on the World-Wide Web." *Anthropological Quarterly* 77(3): 559–574.

Cortada, James W. 1993. *Before the Computer: IBM, NCR, Burroughs, and Remington Rand and the Industry They Created, 1865–1956.* Princeton: Princeton University Press.

Cortell, Neil. 2010. *The Media: Journalism in Crisis*. New York: CreateSpace.

Cottle, Simon. 1998. "Participant Observation: Researching News Production." In *Mass Communication Research Methods*, edited by Anders Hansen, Simon Cottle, R. Negrine, and C. Newbold, 35–65. Basingstoke: Macmillan.

———. 2009. *Global Crisis Reporting: Journalism in the Global Age*. Maidenhead: Open University Press.

Coult, Allan D. 1967. "Lineage Solidarity, Transformational Analysis and the Meaning of Kinship Terminologies." *Man* 2(1): 26–47.

Czepek, Andrea, and Ulrike Klinger. 2010. "Media Pluralism between Market Mechanisms and Control: The German Divide." *International Journal of Communication* 4:820–843.

Deleuze, Gilles. 1992. "Postscript on the Societies of Control." *October* 59(3): 3–7. (http://www
.n5m.org/n5m2/media/texts/deleuze.htm)

———. 2004. *Desert Islands and Other Texts, 1953–1974.* Los Angeles, CA: Semiotext(e).

Deleuze, Gilles, and Felix Guattari. 1983. *Anti-Oedipus: Capitalism and Schizophrenia.* Minneapolis: University of Minnesota Press.

Derrida, Jacques. 1982. *Margins of Philosophy.* Translated by Alan Bass. Chicago: University of Chicago Press.

Deuze, Mark. 2007. *Media Work.* Malden, MA: Polity.

———. 2008. "The Changing Context of News Work: Liquid Journalism and Monitorial Citizenship." *International Journal of Communication* 2: 848–865.

Dewey, John. 1958 [1925]. *Experience and Nature.* Mineola, NY: Dover.

Diener, Paul. 1980. "Ecology and Evolution in Cultural Anthropology." *Man* 15(1): 1–31.

Domingo, David. 2008. "Interactivity in the Daily Routines of Online Newsrooms: Dealing with an Uncomfortable Myth." *Journal of Computer-Mediated Communication* 13(3): 680–704.

Dosse, François. 1997. *History of Structuralism: The Rising Sign, 1945–1966.* Minneapolis: University of Minnesota Press.

Driver, Harold E., and Alfred L. Kroeber. 1932. "Quantitative Expression of Cultural Relationships." *University of California Publications in American Archaeology and Ethnology* 31:211–256.

Duménil, Gérard, and Dominique Lévy. 2011. *The Crisis of Neoliberalism.* Cambridge, MA: Harvard University Press.

Dunn, Elizabeth. 2004. *Privatizing Poland: Baby Food, Big Business, and the Remaking of Labor.* Ithaca: Cornell University Press.

Dupuy, Jean-Pierre. 2000. *The Mechanization of the Mind: On the Origins of Cognitive Science.* Princeton: Princeton University Press.

Dyer-Witheford, Nick. 1999. *Cyber-Marx: Cycles and Circuits of Struggle in High-Technology Capitalism.* Urbana, IL: University of Illinois Press.

Eggan, Fred. 1937. "Historical Changes in the Choctaw Kinship System." *American Anthropologist* 39(1): 34–52.

EIAA (European Interactive Advertising Association). 2010. "EIAA European Media Landscape Report." (www.eiaa.net)

Eisenlohr, Patrick. 2006. "As Makkah is Sweet and Beloved, So Is Madina: Islam, Devotional Genres and Electronic Mediation in Mauritius." *American Ethnologist* 33(2): 230–245.

———. 2009. 'Technologies of the Spirit: Devotional Islam, Sound Reproduction, and the Dialectics of Mediation and Immediacy in Mauritius." *Anthropological Theory* 9:273–296.

———. 2011. "The Anthropology of Media and the Question of Ethnic and Religious Pluralism." *Social Anthropology* 19(1): 40–55.

The Economist. 2011. "Of goats and headaches." May 26. (http://www.economist.com/node /18744177)

Elyachar, Julia. 2005. *Markets of Dispossession: NGOs, Economic Development, and the State in Cairo.* Durham, NC: Duke University Press.

Engelke, Matthew. 2010. "Religion and the Media Turn: A Review Essay." *American Ethnologist* 37(2): 371–379.

Escobar, Arturo. 1994. "Welcome to Cyberia: Notes on the Anthropology of Cyberculture." *Current Anthropology* 35(3): 211–231.

Farhi, Paul. 2009. "A Costly Mistake?" *American Journalism Review*, April/May. (http://www
.ajr.org/article.asp?id=4730)

Faubion, James D. 2008a. "Heterotopia: An Ecology." In *Heterotopia and the City*, edited by
Michael Dehaene and Lieven De Cauter, 31–39. New York: Routledge.

———. 2008b. "Homo absconditus: Lévi-Strauss und Foucault." In *Wirkungen des wilden
Denkens*, edited by Michael Kauppert and Dorett Funcke, 81–97. Frankfurt am Main:
Suhrkamp.

Faubion, James D., and Marcus, George E., eds. 2009. *Fieldwork Is Not What It Used to Be*.
Ithaca: Cornell University Press.

Feibleman, James K. 1954. "Toward an Analysis of the Basic Value System." *American Anthropologist* 56(3): 421–432.

Fishman, Mark. 1980. *Manufacturing the News*. Austin: Texas University Press.

Flannery, Kent V. 1968. "Archaeological Systems Theory and Early Mesoamerica." In *Anthropological Archaeology in the Americas*, edited by Betty J. Meggers, 67–87. Washington, DC:
Anthropological Society of Washington.

Foucault, Michel. 1980. *Power/Knowledge*. Edited by Colin Gordon, translated by Colin Gordon, Leo Marshall, John Mepham, and Kate Soper. New York: Pantheon.

———. 1998. *The History of Sexuality, Vol. 1: The Will to Knowledge*. London: Penguin.

Freud, Sigmund. 1950 [1895]. *Entwurf einer Psychologie*. In *Aus den Anfängen der Psychoanalyse*,
edited by Maria Bonaparte, Anna Freud and Ernst Kris. London: Imago Publishing Company.

———. 1966 [1895]. *Project for a scientific psychology*. In *The Standard Edition of the Complete
Psychological Works of Sigmund Freud*. Vol. 1, edited by Ernest Jones and transalted by James
Strachey. London: Hogarth Press.

———. 1899. *Die Traumdeutung*. Leipzig: Franz Deuticke.

———. 1913. *The Interpretation of Dreams*. Translated by A.A. Brill. New York: Macmillan

———. 1965. *New Introductory Lectures on Psycho-analysis*. Translated and edited by James
Strachey. New York: Norton.

Friedman, Milton. 1962. *Capitalism and Freedom*. Chicago: University of Chicago Press.

Fuller, Jack. 2010. *What Is Happening to News: The Information Explosion and the Crisis in Journalism*. Chicago: University of Chicago Press.

Galison, Peter. 1994. "The Ontology of the Enemy: Norbert Wiener and the Cybernetic Vision."
Critical Inquiry 21:228–265.

Galloway, Alexander. 2009. "The Unworkable Interface." *New Literary History* 39(4): 931–955.

Gans, Herbert J. 1979. *Deciding What's News: A Study of CBS Evening News, NBC Nightly
News, Newsweek, and Time*. New York: Pantheon.

Garrison, Bruce. 1982. "Electronic Editing Systems and Their Impact on News Decision
Making." *Newspaper Research Journal* 3(2): 43–53.

———. 1983. "Computerization of the Newspaper in the 1980s." Paper presented to the Association for Education in Journalism and Mass Communication Annual Convention,
Corvallis, OR, August 6–9.

Geertz, Clifford. 1957. "Ritual and Social Change: A Javanese Example." *American Anthropologist* 59(1): 32–54.

———. 1967. "The Cerebral Savage: The Structural Anthropology of Claude Lévi-Strauss."
Encounter 28(4): 25–32.

———. 1973. *The Interpretation of Cultures*. New York: Basic Books.

Geoghegan, Bernard Dionysius. 2011. "From Information Theory to French Theory: Jakobson, Lévi-Strauss, and the Cybernetic Apparatus." *Critical Inquiry* 38(1): 96–126.

Gere, Charlie. 2008. *Digital Culture*, 2nd ed. London: Reaktion.

Germine, Mark. 1998. "The Concept of Energy in Freud's *Project for a Scientific Psychology*." *Annals of the New York Academy of Sciences* 843(May): 80–90.

Gerovitch, Slava. 2002. *From Newspeak to Cyberspeak: A History of Soviet Cybernetics*. Cambridge, MA: MIT Press.

Gershon, Ilana. 2010. *The Break-Up 2.0*. Ithaca, NY: Cornell University Press.

Ginsburg, Faye. 2008. "Rethinking the Digital Age." In *Global Indigenous Media*, edited by Pam Wilson and Michelle Stewart, 288–305. Durham, NC: Duke University Press.

Glaeser, Andreas. 2000. *Divided in Unity: Identity, Germany, and the Berlin Police*. Chicago: University of Chicago Press.

Glaser, Mark. 2005. "'Video Journalists': Inevitable Revolution or Way to Cut TV Jobs." *OJR: The Online Journalism Review* (http://www.ojr.org/ojr/wiki/video_journalists/).

Gleick, James. 2011. *The Information: A History, a Theory, a Flood*. New York: Pantheon.

Goldenweiser, Alexander A. 1941. "Recent Trends in American Anthropology." *American Anthropologist* 43(2): 151–163.

Golding, P., and P. Elliot. 1979. *Making the News*. London: Longman.

Golub, Alex. 2010. "Being in the World (of Warcraft): Raiding, Realism, and Knowledge Production in Massively Multiplayer Online Games." *Anthropological Quarterly* 83(1): 17–45.

Graeber, David. 2002. "The New Anarchists." *New Left Review* 13: 61–73.

———. 2011. *Debt: The First 5,000 Years*. Brooklyn, NY: Melville House.

Gupta, Akhil, and James Ferguson, eds. 1997. *Anthropological Locations: Boundaries and Grounds of a Field Science*. Berkeley: University of California Press.

Habermas, Jürgen. 1984. *The Theory of Communicative Action I: Reason and the Rationalization of Society*. Translated by Thomas McCarthy. Boston: Beacon Press.

———. 1987. *The Theory of Communicative Action II: Lifeworld and System, a Critique of Functionalist Reason*. Translated by Thomas McCarthy. Boston: Beacon Press.

———. 1989. *The Structural Transformation of the Public Sphere*. Translated by Thomas Burger with Frederick Lawrence. Cambridge: MIT Press.

Hackenberg, Robert A. 1967. "The Parameters of an Ethnic Group: A Method for Studying the Total Tribe." *American Anthropologist* 69(5): 478–492.

Hagen, Joel B. 1992. *An Entangled Bank: The Origins of Ecosystem Ecology*. New Brunswick, NJ: Rutgers University Press.

Hall, Edward T. 1968. "Proxemics." *Current Anthropology* 9(2/3): 83–108.

Hall, Edward T., and William F. Whyte. 1960. "Inter-Cultural Communication." *Human Organization* 19(1): 5–12.

Hally, Mike. 2005. *Electronic Brains: Stories from the Dawn of the Computer Age*. Washington, DC: Joseph Henry.

Hannerz, Ulf. 1998. "Other Transnationals: Perspectives Gained from Studying Sideways." *Paideuma* 44:109–123.

———. 2004. *Foreign News: Exploring the World of Foreign Correspondents*. Chicago: University of Chicago Press.

Haraway, Donna. 1981/82. "The High Cost of Information in Post World War II Evolutionary Biology: Ergonomics, Semiotics, and the Sociobiology of Communications Systems." *Philosophical Forum* XIII(2–3): 244–278.

Harcourt, Alison. 2006. *European Union Institutions and the Regulation of Media Markets*. Manchester: Manchester University Press.

Harrison, Jackie, and Lorna Woods. 2007. *European Broadcasting Law and Policy*. New York: Cambridge University Press.

Hartley, Ralph V.L. 1928. "Transmission of Information." *Bell System Technical Journal* 7(3):535–563.

Harvey, David. 2007. "Neoliberalism as Creative Destruction." *The Annals of the American Academy of Political and Social Science* 610 (March): 22–44.

Hasty, Jennifer. 2005. *The Press and Political Culture in Ghana*. Indianapolis: University of Indiana Press.

Hayek, Friedrich von. 1994 [1944]. *The Road to Serfdom*. Chicago: University of Chicago Press.

Hayles, N. Katherine. 1999. *How We Became Posthuman: Virtual Bodies in Cybernetics, Literature and Informatics*. Chicago: University of Chicago Press.

Heims, Steve J. 1993. *Constructing a Social Science for Postwar America: The Cybernetics Group, 1946–1953*. Cambridge, MA: MIT Press.

Helmreich, Stefan. 2000. *Silicon Second Nature: Culturing Artificial Life in a Digital World*. Berkeley: University of California Press.

———. 2001. "After Culture: Reflections on the Apparition of Anthropology in Artificial Life, a Science of Simulation." *Cultural Anthropology* 16(4): 613–628.

Herman, Edward S., and Noam Chomsky. 1988. *Manufacturing Consent: The Political Economy of the Mass Media*. New York: Pantheon.

Herzfeld, Michael. 1997. *Portrait of a Greek Imagination*. Chicago: University of Chicago Press.

Hine, Christine. 2000. *Virtual Ethnography*. Thousand Oaks, CA: Sage.

Holloway, Ralph Jr. 1969. "Culture: A Human Domain." *Current Anthropology* 10(4): 395–412.

Holmes, Douglas R., and George E. Marcus. 2005. "Cultures of Expertise and the Management of Globalization: Toward the Re-Functioning of Ethnography." In *Global Assemblages*, edited by Aihwa Ong and Steven J. Collier, 235–252. New York: Blackwell.

———. 2008. "Collaboration Today and the Re-Imagination of the Classic Scene of Fieldwork Encounter." *Collaborative Anthropologies* 1:81–101.

Holt, Robert R. 1989. *Freud Reappraised: A Fresh Look at Psychoanalytic Theory*. New York: Guilford.

Hout, Tom van and Geert Jacobs. 2008. "News Production Theory and Practice: Fieldwork Notes on Power, Interaction and Agency." *Pragmatics* 18(1): 59–85.

Hymes, Dell. 1964. "Introduction: Toward the Ethnography of Communication." *American Anthropologist* 66(2): 1–34.

———, ed. 1969. *Reinventing Anthropology*. New York: Vintage.

Ingold, Tim. 2011. *Being Alive: Essays on Movement, Knowledge and Description*. New York: Routledge.

Isbell, Kimberly. 2010. "The Rise of the News Aggregator: Legal Implications and Best Practices." Berkman Center for Internet & Society Research Publication No. 2010-10 (http://cyber.law.harvard.edu/publications).

Jackson, Jason Baird. 2011. "How Enclosed by Large For-Profit Publishers Is the Anthropology Journal Literature?" (http://jasonbairdjackson.com/2011/09/05/how-enclosed-by-large-for-profit-publishers-is-the-anthropology-journal-literature/).

Jackson, Michael. 1978. "Ecology and Evolution in Cultural Anthropology." *Man* 13(3): 341–361.

———. 1998. *Minima Ethnographica*. Chicago: University of Chicago Press.

Jakobson, Roman. 1971. *Selected Writings: Word and Language*, Vol. 2. The Hague: Mouton de Gruyter.

James, William. 1995 [1907]. *Pragmatism*. New York: Dover.

Jamieson, Kathleen Hall, and Joseph N. Cappella. 2008. *Echo Chamber: Rush Limbaugh and the Conservative Media Establishment*. New York: Oxford University Press.

Johns, Adrian. 1998. *The Nature of the Book: Print and Knowledge in the Making*. Chicago: University of Chicago Press.

Johnston, John. 2010. *The Allure of Machinic Life: Cybernetics, Artificial Life and the New AI*. Cambridge, MA: MIT Press.

Jones, Alex. 2009. *Losing the News: The Future of the News That Feeds Democracy*. New York: Oxford University Press.

Keane, Webb. 2009. "Freedom and Blasphemy: On Indonesian Press Bans and Danish Cartoons." *Public Culture* 21:47–76.

Kelty, Christopher M. 2005. "Geeks, Social Imaginaries, and Recursive Publics." *Cultural Anthropology* 20(2): 185–214.

———. 2008. *Two Bits: The Cultural Significance of Free Software and the Internet*. Durham, NC: Duke University Press.

———. 2009. "Collaboration, Coordination, and Composition: Fieldwork after the Internet." In *Fieldwork Is Not What It Used to Be*, edited by James D. Faubion and George E. Marcus, 184–206. Ithaca, NY: Cornell University Press.

Kelty, Christopher M., Michael M.J. Fischer, Alex Golub, Jason Baird Jackson, Kimberly Christen, Michael F Brown, and Tom Boellstorff. 2008. "Anthropology of/in Circulation: The Future of Open Access and Scholarly Societies." *Cultural Anthropology* 23(3): 559–588.

Keynes, John Maynard. 1936. *The General Theory of Employment, Interest and Money*. London: Palgrave MacMillan.

Kindred, David. 2010. *Morning Miracle: Inside* The Washington Post: *A Great Newspaper Fights for Its Life*. New York: Doubleday.

Klein, Naomi. 2007. *The Shock Doctrine: The Rise of Disaster Capitalism*. New York: Picador.

Klimek, Stanislaw, and Wilhelm Milke. 1935. "An Analysis of the Material Culture of Tupi Peoples." *American Anthropologist* 37:71–91.

Klinenberg, Eric. 2005. "Convergence: News Production in a Digital Age." *Annals of the American Academy of Political and Social Science* 597:48–64.

———. 2012. *Going Solo: The Extraordinary Rise and Surprising Appeal of Living Alone*. New York: Penguin.

Kluckhohn, Clyde. 1936. "Some Reflections on the Method and Theory of the Kulturkreislehre." *American Anthropologist* 38(2): 157–196.

———. 1939. "On Certain Recent Applications of Association Coefficients to Ethnological Data." *American Anthropologist* 41(3): 345–377.

———. 1961. "Notes on Some Anthropological Aspects of Communication." *American Anthropologist* 63(5): 895–910.

Knopper, Steve. 2009. *Appetite for Self-Destruction: The Spectacular Crash of the Record Industry in the Digital Age*. New York: Free Press.

Knorr-Cetina, Karin. 1991. "Epistemic Cultures: Forms of Reason in Science." *History of Political Economy* 23:105–122.

———. 2005. "How Are Global Markets Global? The Architecture of a Flow World." In *The Sociology of Financial Markets*, edited by Karin Knorr-Cetina and Alex Preda, 38–61. New York: Oxford University Press.

———. 2009. "The Synthetic Situation: Interactionism for a Global World." *Symbolic Interaction* 32(1): 61–87.

Kot, Greg. 2009. *Ripped: How the Wired Generation Revolutionized Music.* New York: Scribner.

Kozinets, Robert V. 2010. *Netnography: Doing Ethnographic Research Online.* Thousand Oaks, CA: Sage.

Kroeber, Alfred L. 1962. "Anthropological Horizons: A Symposium." *Current Anthropology* 3(1): 79–97.

Kulick, Don, and Margaret Wilson, eds. 1995. *Taboo: Sex, Identity and Erotic Subjectivity in Anthropological Fieldwork.* New York: Routledge.

Kumar, Priya. 2011. "Foreign Correspondents: Who Covers What." *American Journalism Review*, December/January. (http://www.ajr.org/article.asp?id=4997)

Lacan, Jacques. 1991. *Le séminaire de Jacques Lacan, livre 17: L'envers de la psychanalyse.* Paris: Seuil.

Lafontaine, Céline. 2007. "The Cybernetic Matrix of 'French Theory.'" *Theory, Culture and Society* 24(5): 27–46.

Laing, R.D. 1965. *The Divided Self: An Existential Study in Sanity and Madness.* Harmondsworth, Middlesex; Baltimore: Penguin Books.

Larsson, Stieg. 2005. *Män som hatar kvinnor.* Stockholm: Nordstedts.

———. 2006. *Flickan som lekte med elden.* Stockholm: Nordstedts.

———. 2007. *Luftslottet som sprängdes.* Stockholm: Nordstedts.

Latour, Bruno. 1987. *Science in Action: How to Follow Scientists and Engineers through Society.* Cambridge, MA: Harvard University Press.

———. 2004. *Politics of Nature: How to Bring the Sciences into Democracy.* Cambridge, MA: Harvard University Press.

———. 2005. *Reassembling the Social: An Introduction to Actor Network Theory.* New York: Oxford University Press.

Law, John. 2002. *Aircraft Stories: Decentering the Object in Technoscience.* Durham, NC: Duke University Press.

Lemann, Nicholas. 2006. "Amateur Hour: Journalism without Journalists." *The New Yorker*, August 7.

Lessig, Lawrence. 2004. *Free Culture.* New York: Penguin. (http://www.free-culture.cc/free-culture.pdf)

Lévi-Strauss, Claude. 1945. "L'analyse structurale en linguistique et anthropologie." *Word* 1:33–53.

———. 1949. *Les Structures Élémentaires de la Parenté.* Paris: Presses Universitaires de France.

———. 1969 [1949]. *The Elementary Structures of Kinship.* Translated by James Harle Bell. London: Eyre & Spottiswoode.

———. 1951. "Language and the Analysis of Social Laws." *American Anthropologist* 53(2): 155–163.

———. 1954. "Introduction: The Mathematics of Man." *International Social Science Bulletin* 6(4):581–590.

———. 1966a. *The Savage Mind.* Chicago: University of Chicago Press.

———. 1966b. "The Scope of Anthropology." *Current Anthropology* 7(2): 112–123.

LiPuma, Edward, and Benjamin Lee. 2004. *Financial Derivatives and the Globalization of Risk.* Durham, NC: Duke University Press.

Liu, Lydia H. 2010. *The Freudian Robot: Digital Media and the Future of the Unconscious.* Chicago: University of Chicago Press.

Luhmann, Niklas. 1984. *Sozial Systeme: Grundriß einer allgemeinen Theorie.* Frankfurt am Main: Suhrkamp.

Lukács, Georg. 1971. *History and Class Consciousness: Studies in Marxist Dialectics.* Cambridge, MA: MIT Press.

Lyons, Daniel. 2009. "Exterminate the Parasites." *Newsweek*, September 3. (http://www.the-dailybeast.com/newsweek/2009/09/03/exterminate-the-parasites.html)

MacKenzie, Donald. 2006. *An Engine, not a Camera: How Financial Models Shape the Markets.* Cambridge, MA: MIT Press.

Marcus, George E. 1998. *Ethnography through Thick and Thin.* Princeton: Princeton University Press.

Marcus, George E., and Fischer, Michael. 1986. *Anthropology as Cultural Critique: An Experimental Moment in the Human Sciences.* Chicago: University of Chicago Press.

Maruyama, Magoroh. 1980. "Mindscapes and Science Theories." *Current Anthropology* 21(5): 589–608.

Marx, Karl. 1844. "Die entfremdete Arbeit." (http://www.mlwerke.de/me/me40/me40_510.htm)

———. 1857. "The Method of Political Economy." (http://www.marxists.org/archive/marx/works/1857/grundrisse/ch01.htm#3)

Mazzarella, William. 2006. "Internet X-ray: E-Governance, Transparency, and the Politics of Immediation in India." *Public Culture* 18: 473–505.

McChesney, Robert W. 2004. *The Problem of the Media: U.S. Communication Politics in the 21st Century.* New York: Monthly Review Press.

McChesney, Robert W., and John Nichols. 2010. *The Death and Life of American Journalism.* Philadelphia: Nation Books.

McChesney, Robert W., and Victor Pickard, eds. 2011. *Will the Last Reporter Please Turn out the Lights: The Collapse of Journalism and What Can Be Done To Fix It.* New York: New Press.

McCulloch, Warren Sturgis, and Walter Pitts. 1943. "A Logical Calculus of the Ideas Immanent in Nervous Activity." *Bulletin of Mathematical Biophysics* 5:115–133.

McGuigan, Glenn S., and Robert D. Russell. 2008. "The Business of Academic Publishing." *Electronic Journal of Academic and Special Librarianship* 9(3). (http://southernlibrarianship.icaap.org/content/v09n03/mcguigan_g01.html)

McLuhan, Marshall. 1962. *The Gutenberg Galaxy.* Toronto: University of Toronto Press.

———. 1964. *Understanding Media: The Extensions of Man.* New York: McGraw Hill.

———. 1969. "The Playboy Interview: Marshall McLuhan." *Playboy*, March. (http://www.nextnature.net/2009/12/the-playboy-interview-marshall-mcluhan/)

Mead, Margaret. 1961. "Anthropology among the Sciences." *American Anthropologist* 63(3): 475–482.

Meggers, Betty J. 1946. "Recent Trends in American Ethnology." *American Anthropologist* 48(2): 176–214.

Merleau-Ponty, Maurice. 1962. *Phenomenology of Perception.* Translated by Colin Smith. New York: Routledge.

Merton, Robert K. 1957. *Social Theory and Social Structure*. New York: The Free Press.

Mill, John Stuart. 1999 [1859]. *On Liberty*. Peterborough, ON: Broadview.

Miller, Daniel. 2011. *Tales from Facebook*. Malden, MA: Polity.

Miller, Daniel, and Don Slater. 2000. *The Internet: An Ethnographic Approach*. Oxford: Berg.

Mindell, David, Jérôme Ségal, and Slava Gerovitch. 2003. "From Communications Engineering to Communications Science: Cybernetics and Information Theory in the United States, France, and the Soviet Union." In *Science and Ideology: A Comparative History*, edited by Mark Walker, 66–95. London: Routledge.

Mises, Ludwig von. 1952. *Planning for Freedom*. South Holland, IL: Libertarian Press.

Mitchell, Timothy. 2009. "Carbon Democracy." *Economy and Society* 38(3): 399–432.

Monbiot, George. 2011. "The Lairds of Learning." (http://www.monbiot.com/2011/08/29/the-lairds-of-learning/)

Moore, Omar Khayyam, and David L. Olmsted. 1953. "Language and Professor Lévi-Strauss." *American Anthropologist* 54(1): 116–119.

Mosco, Vincent. 2005. *The Digital Sublime: Myth, Power, and Cyberspace*. Cambridge, MA: MIT Press.

Negroponte, Nicholas. 1995. *Being Digital*. New York: Vintage Books.

Noveck, Jocelyn. 2007. "Even Ignoring Paris Hilton Makes News." (http://www.usatoday.com/life/television/2007-03-01-919715477_x.htm)

Nusselder, André. 2009. *Interface Fantasy: A Lacanian Cyborg Ontology*. Cambridge, MA: MIT Press.

Nye, David E. 1990. *Electrifying America: Social Meanings of a New Technology, 1880–1940*. Cambridge, MA: MIT Press.

Nyquist, Harry. 1924. "Certain Factors Affecting Telegraph Speed." *Bell System Technical Journal* 3:324–346.

Oberg, Kalervo A. 1943. "Comparison of Three Systems of Primitive Economic Organization." *American Anthropologist* 45(4): 572–587.

Odum, Eugene P., and Howard T. Odum. 1953. *Fundamentals of Ecology*. Philadelphia: W.B. Saunders.

Opler, Morris E. 1936. "The Kinship Systems of the Southern Athabaskan-Speaking Tribes." *American Anthropologist* 38(4): 620–633.

O'Shea, James. 2011. *The Deal from Hell: How Moguls and Wall Street Plundered Great American Newspapers*. New York: PublicAffairs.

Parisi, Luciana, and Tiziana Terranova. 2000. "Heat Death: Emergence and Control in Genetic Engineering and Artificial Life." *ctheory.net* (http://www.ctheory.net/articles.aspx?id=127).

Parsons, Talcott. 1951. *The Social System*. London: Routledge & Kegan Paul.

Paterson, Chris, and David Domingo, eds. 2008. *Making Online News*. New York: Peter Lang.

Pedelty, Mark. 1995. *War Stories: The Culture of Foreign Correspondents*. New York: Routledge.

Peters, Jeremy W. 2011. "Times's Online Pay Model Was Years in the Making." *New York Times*, March 20. (http://www.nytimes.com/2011/03/21/business/media/21times.html?pagewanted=all)

Peterson, Mark Allen. 2001. "Getting to the Story: Unwriteable Discourse and Interpretive Practice in American Journalism." *Anthropological Quarterly* 74(4): 201–211.

———. 2003. *Anthropology and Mass Communication: Media and Myth in the New Millennium*. Oxford: Berghahn Books.

————. 2011. *Connected in Cairo: Growing up Cosmopolitan in the Modern Middle East*. Bloomington: Indiana University Press.

Pew Trust. 2010. "The State of the News Media 2010." (http://stateofthemedia.org/2010/)

Pias, Claus, ed. 2003. *Cybernetics-Kybernetik: The Macy Conferences, 1946–1953*. Zürich: Diaphanes.

Pickering, Andrew. 2011. *The Cybernetic Brain: Sketches of Another Future*. Chicago: University of Chicago Press.

Pinch, Trevor J., and Frank Trocco. 2002. *Analog Days: The Invention and Impact of the Moog Synthesizer*. Cambridge, MA: Harvard University Press.

Pitts, Walter. 1942. "Some Observations on the Simple Neuron Circuit." *Bulletin of Mathematical Biology* 4(3): 121–129.

Povinelli, Elizabeth. 2006. *The Empire of Love: Toward a Theory of Intimacy, Genealogy, and Carnality*. Durham, NC: Duke University Press.

Powell, Michael G., and Tara Schwegler. 2008. "Unruly Experts: Methods and Forms of Collaboration in the Anthropology of Policy." *Anthropology in Action* 15(2): 1–9.

Press, Irwin. 1969. "Ambiguity and Innovation: Implications for the Genesis of the Culture Broker." *American Anthropologist* 71(2): 205–217.

Pribram, Karl. 1962. "The Neuropsychology of Sigmund Freud." In *Experimental Foundations of Clinical Psychology*, edited by Arthur J. Bachrach, 442–468. New York: Basic Books.

Pribram, Karl, and Morton M. Gill. 1976. *Freud's "Project" Re-Assessed: Preface to Contemporary Cognitive Theory and Neuropsychology*. New York: Basic Books.

Price, David H. 1998. "Gregory Bateson and the OSS: World War II and Bateson's Assessment of Applied Anthropology." *Human Organization* 57(4): 379–384.

Quandt, Thorsten. 2005. *Journalisten im Netz*. Opladen: VS Verlag.

————. 2008. "News Tuning and Content Management: An Observation Study of Old and New Routines in German Online Newsrooms." In *Making Online News*, edited by Chris Paterson and David Domingo, 77–97. New York: Peter Lang.

Rabin, Nathan. 2006. "Interview: Stephen Colbert." January 25. (http://www.avclub.com/articles/stephen-colbert,13970/)

Rabinow, Paul. 2003. *Anthropos Today*. Princeton: Princeton University Press.

Rappaport, Roy A. 1971. "Ritual, Sanctity and Cybernetics." *American Anthropologist* 73(1): 59–76.

Read, Donald. 1999. *The Power of News*. New York: Oxford University Press.

Rheinberger, Hans-Jörg. 1997. *Toward a History of Epistemic Things: Synthesizing Proteins in the Test Tube*. Stanford: Stanford University Press.

Ritchie, David. 1986. *The Computer Pioneers*. New York: Simon & Schuster.

Rodin, Miriam. 1978. "Systems Theory in Anthropology." *Current Anthropology* 19(4): 747–762.

Rorty, Richard. 1979. *Philosophy and the Mirror of Nature*. Princeton: Princeton University Press.

Rosen, Jay. 2006. "The People Formerly Known as the Audience." (http://journalism.nyu.edu/pubzone/weblogs/pressthink/2006/06/27/ppl_frmr.html)

Rossi, Ino. 1973. "The Unconscious in the Anthropology of Claude Lévi-Strauss." *American Anthropologist* 75(1): 20–48.

Rubinstein, Robert A. 1977. "Bridging Levels of Systemic Organization." *Current Anthropology* 18(3):459–481.

Saad-Filho, Alfredo, and Deborah Johnston, eds. 2005. *Neoliberalism: A Critical Reader*. London: Pluto.

Sade-Beck, Liav. 2004. "Internet Ethnography: Online and Offline." *International Journal of Qualitative Methods* 3(2): 1–14.

Sahlins, Marshall. 1976. *Culture and Practical Reason.* Chicago: University of Chicago Press.

———. 1985. *Islands of History.* Chicago: University of Chicago Press.

Salisbury, Richard F. 1956. "Asymmetrical Marriage Systems." *American Anthropologist* 56(4): 639–655.

Sanjek, Roger. 1990. *Fieldnotes: The Makings of Anthropology.* Ithaca, NY: Cornell University Press.

Sarles, Harvey B. 1969. "The Study of Language and Communication Across Species." *Current Anthropology* 7(2): 112–123.

Sassen, Saskia. 2001. *The Global City: New York, London, Tokyo.* Princeton: Princeton University Press.

Schiller, Dan. 2011. "Power under Pressure: Digital Capitalism in Crisis." *International Journal of Communication* 5:924–941.

Scholte, Bob. 1966. "Epistemic Paradigms: Some Problems in Cross-Cultural Research on Social Anthropological History and Theory." *American Anthropologist* 68(5): 1192–1201.

Schudson, Michael. 1984. *Advertising, the Uneasy Persuasion.* New York: Basic Books.

———. 1989. "The Sociology of News Production." *Media, Culture and Society* 11:263–282.

———. 2003. *The Sociology of News.* New York: W.W. Norton.

Schüll, Natasha Dow. 2005. "Digital Gambling: The Coincidence of Desire and Design." *ANNALS of the American Academy of Political and Social Science* 597:65–81.

Schwiesau, Dietz, and Mike Heerdegen. 1995. "Chronik der laufenden Ereignisse: Die Geschichte der Nachrichtenradios." *epd-medien*, 9/20:3–10.

Shannon, Claude E. 1945. "A Mathematical Theory of Cryptography." September 1. (Classified internal memorandum reprinted in 1949 as: "Communication Theory of Secrecy Systems." *Bell System Technical Journal* 28:656–715.)

———. 1948. "A Mathematical Theory of Communication." *Bell System Technical Journal* 27(3): 379–423.

Shapin, Steven. 1994. *A Social History of Truth: Civility and Science in Seventeenth-Century England.* Chicago: University of Chicago Press.

Shurkin, Joel. 1996. *Engines of the Mind: The Evolution of the Computer from Mainframes to Microprocessors.* New York: W.W. Norton.

Slayden, David, and Rita Kirk Whillock, eds. 1999. *Soundbite Culture.* London: Sage.

Sleurs, Kim, Geert Jacobs, and Luuk Van Waes. 2003. "Constructing Press Releases, Constructing Quotations: A Case Study." *Journal of Sociolinguistics* 7:192–212.

Smith, Adam. 1976 [1776]. *An Inquiry into the Nature and Causes of the Wealth of Nations.* Oxford: Clarendon.

Smith, Anthony. 1980. *Goodbye Gutenberg: The Newspaper Revolution of the 1980s.* New York: Oxford University Press.

Spiro, Melford E. 1966. "Buddhism and Economic Action in Burma." *American Anthropologist* 68(5): 1163–1173.

Ståhlberg, Per. 2002. Lucknow Daily: *How a Hindi Newspaper Constructs Society.* Stockholm: Stockholm Studies in Social Anthropology.

Steinbuch, Karl. 1957. *Informatik: Automatische Informationsverarbeitung.* Berlin: SEG-Nachrichten.

Stewart, Kathleen. 2007. *Ordinary Affects.* Durham, NC: Duke University Press.

Suchman, Lucy. 1987. *Plans and Situated Actions: The Problem of Human-Machine Communication*. New York: Cambridge University Press.

Sunstein, Cass R. 2009. *Republic.com 2.0*. Princeton: Princeton University Press.

Todorova, Maria, and Zsuzsa Gille, eds. 2010. *Post-Communist Nostalgia*. New York: Berghahn Books.

Trubetzkoy, Nicolai. 1939. *Principles of Phonology*. Paris: Klincksieck.

Tuchman, Gaye. 1972. "Objectivity as Strategic Ritual: An Examination of Newsmen's Notions of Objectivity." *American Journal of Sociology* 77:660–679.

———. 1978. *Making News: A Study in the Construction of Reality*. New York: MacMillan.

———. 2003. "The Production of News." In *A Handbook of Media and Communication Research: Qualitative and Quantitative Methodologies*, edited by Klaus Bruhn Jensen, 78–90. London: Routledge.

Tunstall, Jeremy. 1971. *Journalists at Work*. London: Constable.

Van de Walle, Jürgen. 2008. "Roman Jakobson, Cybernetics and Information Theory: A Critical Assessment." *Folia Linguistica Historica* 29(1): 87–123.

Wahl-Jorgensen, Karen, and Bernardette Cole. 2008. "Newspapers in Sierra Leone: A Case Study of Conditions for Print Journalism in a Post-Conflict Society. *Ecquid Novi* 29(1): 1–20.

Warner, Michael. 2002a. "Public and Counterpublics." *Public Culture* 14(1): 49–90.

———. 2002b. *Public and Counterpublics*. Cambridge: Zone Books.

Waters, Lindsay. 2004. *Enemies of Promise: Publishing, Perishing and the Eclipse of Scholarship*. Chicago: Prickly Paradigm Press.

Whitaker, Mark P. 2004. "Tamilnet.com: Some Reflections on Popular Anthropology, Nationalism, and the Internet." *Anthropological Quarterly* 77(3): 469–498.

White, Leslie A. 1943. "Energy and the Evolution of Culture." *American Anthropologist* 45(3): 335–356.

Wiener, Norbert. 1948. *Cybernetics, or Control and Communication in the Animal and the Machine*. Cambridge, MA: MIT Press.

———. 1950. *The Human Use of Human Beings: Cybernetics and Society*. New York: Avon Books.

Wilf, Eitan. 2012. "Rituals of Creativity: Tradition, Modernity and the 'Acoustic Unconscious' in a U.S. Collegiate Jazz Music Program." *American Anthropologist* 114(1): 32–44.

Wilke, Jürgen. 2007. "Das Nachrichtenangebot der Nachrichtenagenturen im Vergleich." *Publizistik* 52:329–354.

Williams, Matthew. 2007. "Avatar Watching: Participant Observation in Online Environments." *Qualitative Research* 7(1): 5–24.

Williams, Raymond. 1974. *Television*. Hanover, NH: Wesleyan University Press.

Wilson, Samuel M., and Leighton C. Peterson. 2002. "The Anthropology of Online Communities." *Annual Review of Anthropology* 31:449–467.

Winther, Tanja. 2008. *The Impact of Electricity: Development, Desires and Dilemmas*. New York: Berghahn.

Wittgenstein, Ludwig. 2001 [1953]. *Philosophical Investigations*. Translated by G.E.M. Anscombe. Malden, MA: Blackwell.

Wulff, Helena, Don Handelman, Marion Berghahn, Virginia R. Dominguez, and Brian Moeran. 2009. "What is Happening to the Anthropological Monograph? Live Debate at the EASA Conference in Ljubljana 2008." *Social Anthropology* 17:217–234.

Yurchak, Alexei. 2006. *Everything Was Forever until It Was No More: The Last Soviet Generation*. Princeton: Princeton University Press.

Zachary, G. Pascal. 1999. *Endless Frontier: Vannevar Bush, Engineer of the American Century*. Cambridge, MA: MIT Press.

Zaloom, Caitlin. 2005. "The Discipline of Speculators." In *Global Assemblages: Technology, Politics, and Ethics as Anthropological Problems*, edited by Aihwa Ong and Stephen J. Collier, 253–269. New York: Blackwell.

———. 2006. *Out of the Pits: Traders and Technology from Chicago to London*. Chicago: University of Chicago Press.

Zelizer, Barbie. 2004. *Taking Journalism Seriously*. Thousand Oaks, CA: Sage.

———, ed. 2009 *The Changing Faces of Journalism: Tabloidization, Technology and Truthiness*. New York: Routledge.

Žižek, Slavoj. 1989. *The Sublime Object of Ideology*. London: Verso.

Zschunke, Peter. 2000. *Agenturjournalismus*. Konstanz: Uvk Verlag.